The Four Seasons

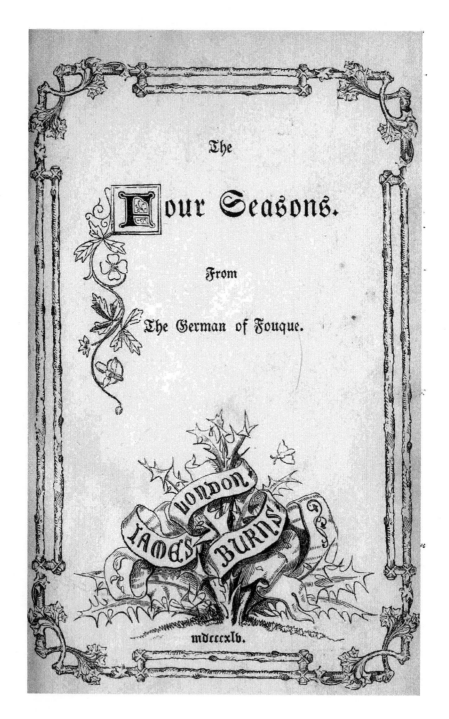

The Four Seasons.

From

The German of Fouque.

London
James Burns

mdcccxlv.

To the Reader.

IN sending forth this volume, which, with some new matter, comprises also new, and it is hoped improved, editions of romances already known to the English reader, it has been thought desirable to prefix the following explanatory remarks by the Author, extracted from the Postscript to the last edition of his Selected Works.[1]

An edition of the last hand! It is a serious, weighty word for an author who, not accustomed to trifle with time and eternity, earnestly weighs and considers what needs to be weighed and considered.

And—God be praised!—this has been the manner of him who now addresses the reading world, for many years. It is, indeed, not exactly a parting salutation to the reading world that he hereby contemplates. There are still many arrows in his quiver, some ready forged, some in process of forging, some only thought of, but all without poison, which he purposes to send forth when the fit time shall come, or, perhaps, his survivors may do this when his own last hour shall have passed, and all time for him have vanished. However this may be, the present task assumes

[1] In 12 vols. 16mo. Halle, 1841.

the character of a bequest, in relation to that which he has already sent into the world,—and bequests are matters of a sufficiently serious nature.

These fictions belonged, at one time, to my very self—yea, as I may well say, they were myself—and now I resign them once more to the world, and, after this last review, for ever. I have made scarcely any alteration in them, for, even as they are, they have gained the approbation of the reading world; and, therefore, I repelled that critical fury which sometimes assailed me in my labours, remembering how thereby many a gifted master has injured rather than improved his compositions, while the reader searches with painful anxiety after the earlier features of the much-loved work, and, alas, too often in vain! What I deemed indispensably to need reforming were chiefly errors arising from former ignorance either in respect of the old northern manners or names, or similar matters, of which one previously unversed in such studies could scarcely be aware. So that now I venture, with full confidence, to say to the reader, "Receive, renewed, what has delighted you;—what has already been dear to you for many years." Conscious, however, of the obligation to render some account of the origin and foundation of these various works, I offer to the reading world, and especially to fellow-artists, the following communications:—

UNDINE.

How this darling gift of my muse first arose (1807), from the mystical laboratory of the aged, whimsical Theophrastus Paracelsus [Treatise of Elemental Spirits], has already been alluded to:[1] here, however, the particulars shall be given more at length. It was not so easy, out of the deeply mysterious natural philosopher, sometimes seized with ostentation, and even charlatanery, as also contentious pride, but at the same time penetrated and enlightened by ever valid presentiments, and rich in an undeniably genuine experience, in any degree to make any thing, as the saying is. All the less easy was it, inasmuch as his oracles are delivered in a mixture of kitchen, or at best monkish, Latin and indolent provincial dialect, similar to the present Tyrolese, so that the like in literature can scarcely any where else be found. Very few treatises, and not

[1] The reference is to the author's autobiography, which appeared the previous year.

exactly the most interesting, are composed throughout in Latin; and yet, perhaps, there is no one quite free from the occurrence, as it were by accident, of German phrases. It resembles the communication of an adventurer, far-travelled in foreign lands, who yet could never quite forget his mother-tongue, and now throws all together in confused variety, as it may chance to fall. Something of this sort, I have been told of a French sailor, and numberless times has the old Theophrastus Paracelsus Bombastus ab Hohenheim (for thus stands his full title) reminded me of it. I, notwithstanding, ceased not to study an old edition of my speech-monger, which fell to me at an auction;—and that carefully. Even his receipts I read through in their order, just as they had been showered into the text, still continuing in the firm expectation, that from every line something wonderfully magical might float up to me and strike the understanding. Single sparks, here and there darting up, confirmed my hopes, and drew me still deeper into the mines beneath. Somewhat thereto might have been contributed by the symbolic figures, very skilfully impressed upon the leathern covers of the ten or twelve quarto volumes, as also by the, to me unintelligible, gold letters here and there dispersed among them, and the wood-cut (inserted as a title-page) of the wonderful master, representing him in an antiquated jacket; his features strongly marked, almost inclined to wrath, yet bearing a true-hearted mildness; his head already grey and bald, but with one lock, almost Apollonian, over the forehead; both his nerved hands folded together and resting on a knight's two-handed sword.

> "Now, ancient master, thanks to thee,
> A valiant course thou leddest me,"—

for, as a pearl of soft radiance, that may be compared to a mild tear of melancholy, there at last sparkled towards me, from out its rough-edged shell-work—"UNDINE!"

My reflection of the image succeeded all the better, and more naturally, as the hoary magician treated with the most unshaken conviction, one is almost induced to say faith, of the indisputable reality of his elemental spirits; not only of the undines or undenes, as he expresses it, but also of sylphs, or spirits of the air; salamanders, or spirits of the fire; gnomes, or spirits of the earth. Founded upon such ideas, the author, at a later period, called some other tales into light, and, as he may well say, not without success. But the words of his old master, A. W. Schlegel, spoken for a very different occasion, will yet here apply: "Undine remains the first love, and this is felt only once!"

In those times of gloomy events for the poet's fatherland, wherein it sprang from out his spirit, not untinged, as it well might be, with many of his own peculiar sufferings, it assumed a hue of deep melancholy, which yet its subject might have also called forth amid the sunshine of brighter days. The eyes of a water-maiden must, according to her nature, beam bright with tears, although sometimes the wanton sports of aquatic nymphs, like luxuriant loop-plants on the banks of a rivulet, may juggle around the lovely child. Thus might the bleeding heart of the poet, with the pelican's faculty, have poured somewhat into his fiction, and so gained for it that abundant sympathy which it so heartily met with, both in and out of the German land.

And now, my darling child, go forth on thy renewed appearance, accompanied by the gracious salutation of our exalted master Goethe, on sending thee back to a noble lady, after having replaced the worn-out binding of a library-copy by a new one:—

"Here one may see how men are fabricated
Of passion only—conscience have they none;
How ill have they the beauteous child entreated—
Its dress almost from off its body gone!
In later time, howe'er, this luck befell me—
The pious youth will envy me, I trow;
You gave me, friend, the opportunity
To clothe the lovely prize from top to toe."

[The author then goes on to mention the various languages into which "Undine" had been translated—French, Italian, English,[1] Russian, Polish.]

[1] "Let me not part with England (the author adds) without quoting the following judgment of Sir Walter Scott, the greatest master of the romantic, properly so called, which Britain has ever produced:—'Fouqué's Undine or Naiade,' he says, after a hasty glance at the author's other romances, 'is *ravishing*. The suffering of the heroine is a real one, though it be the suffering of a fantastic being.'"

To this Coleridge's judgment may be added:—"'Undine' is a most exquisite work. The character of the heroine, before she receives a soul, is marvellously beautiful."—*Table-Talk*, p. 83. To which is subjoined, in a note by the Editor:—"Mr. C.'s admiration of this romance was unbounded. He said there was something here even beyond Scott—that his characters and conceptions were *composed*, by which I understood him to mean, that Baillie Nicol Jarvie, for instance, was made up of old particulars, and received its individuality from the author's power of fusion;

THE MAGIC RING.[1]

It happened to the poet one evening, while in familiar converse with his beloved and now deceased spouse, Caroline Baroness de la Motte Fouqué, that he informed her, with respect to an ancient French novel on which she was then engaged, many particulars as to the customs of that chivalric period. For although his lady was greatly more familiar and conversant with the modern French than himself, yet, on the other hand, he was much more at home with those days of departed heroes and their language; partly on account of his ancestry, partly also through his studies, and, above all, by the general tendency of his inward life.

The conversation was attended with much fervency; at last she said, "How unaccountable that thou never yet hast attempted a fiction on those times wherein thy French ancestors fought and vanquished!"

The thought kindled, and soon there gradually rose before the author the lights of the "Magic Ring." He determined to construct a romance of ancient French chivalry; and a glance into his own recesses sufficed to shew him the necessity of an original German hero, as the radical stem for the French knighthood, as also for the related European, and even the Arabian, therewith united. Thus arose in its primitive features the variegated texture which has here again unfolded itself. There might further, amid the numerous sympathies of which this work can boast, have been many a minuter feature welcome, as it occurred to the poet, and determined him during its composition. Next to the propitious appearance of Bertha (in the reality), and Gabrielle, there hovered before the eyes of the bard the image of a female friend, then long since beatified as Blanchefleur. At all events, this form at a later period arose upon his consciousness in immeasurably brighter splendour. He is certainly not the first poet to whom the like

being in the result an admirable product, as Corinthian brass was said to be the conflux of the spoils of a city. But 'Undine,' he said, was one and single in projection; and had presented to his imagination—what Scott had never done—an absolutely new idea."

[1] It has been thought well to include these remarks on the "Magic Ring," both because of its connexion with "Sintram," and because it is probably known (through the English translation above alluded to) to many of the readers of this volume.

has happened, nor, in this respect, will he be the last. Quite otherwise did the poet forebode by an impending exploit of arms, when describing the victory of the Swedes over the Finns, where Otho of Trautwangen, rushing on the enemy's infantry, shouts exultingly to his squadron of horsemen, " Strike ye, my Swedes! strike ye!" As he wrote these words, and whenever he afterwards read them, he was seized by a deeply powerful, and, as one might say, melancholy inspiration. In the battle of Lützen, where at the head of his Jagers he rushed on a French battalion, he felt the fulfilment of it; and thinking on Otho of Trautwangen, mingled in the huzza-cry of his squadron his own jubilant call, " Strike, my Jágers! strike!" And manifold tones besides, from out the magic ring sounding and re-echoing in the souls of my brethren in arms, accompanied me joyfully all through the great and eventful year of " thirteen;" at the same time, often meeting me from cities and castles, through which and to which the marches of the army or crusades, as in more senses than one they might be called, conducted us.

A gallant young prince,—I had just been sent out upon command, and still bore the trace of a slight wound between the eyebrows,—once asked, when riding in front of the Jager squadron, a volunteer, known to him through my acquaintance, " Where is Heerdegen of Lichtenried?"

" Whom does your royal highness mean?"

" I mean him with the scar upon his brow—Fouqué."

So now, again, unlock thyself once more, my dear " Magic Ring," and that just as thou wert first unlocked; only now be decked with more adornment than at that time, which indeed has not despoiled thee of thy propriety, since already for twenty years thy second edition has brought it to thee, and thereto thy name (of " ring," I mean) well belongs.

From numerous quarters it was ardently desired; and many a real ring for noble hands has since then been fashioned after it. Some have gone so far as to desire of me a fourth part to the three which already have existence. My answer has been, that as for the *ring* there remained no additions; let it as a ring be recognised and for such be taken. What, in other respects, may have contributed to impart to the book a peculiar vigour is, the author's familiarity with its *matériel*,—as weapons, horses, castles, and other like characteristics of the period; vivified still more through his own warlike and knightly experience. A sure foundation for his intuitions into the world of knighthood had been already laid even in boyhood, and especially by the fictions of Veit Weber (Leonhard Wächter), under the title of "Tales of former Ages." In these pictures all is undoubtedly true, whatever is brought before us of the manners and customs of our forefathers, whether as to battles, festivities, or aught else of the manifold relationships of life. In the year 1815 it was permitted to the poet of the "Magic Ring" personally to express his thanks to the author of "Tales of former Ages." Wherever, in this respect, a similar rich spring had opened itself, the bard was ever at hand with fresh gladness to draw from it; more by contemplating ancient buildings, armour, and pictures, than from books, which during his youthful years were, for the most part, sufficiently superficial in this kind of information. His somewhat later investigations, namely, those of the armoury at Dresden, he yet well knew all the more powerfully how to apply and elaborate. In many ways also, since a perhaps very intentional hostility was raised against him and his fictions, has the exactness of his armorial descriptions been a subject of censure, as also his predilection for noble horses; indeed, many a report concerning these has, at once, been consigned to the region of the fabulous. There is, however, no knight without weapons; and they in a manner form together a unity, so that an *Orlando* who should divest himself of these, would, of all things, only degenerate into an *Orlando Furioso*. And as concerning the wonderful properties of horses, many such might be related of indisputable reality, besides those in the "Magic Ring," as the author could abundantly prove, as well from his own experience, as from incontestable tradition; not to mention the well-authenticated noble qualities, mentioned by travellers, of the Arabian and Persian horses. Besides, to skilful horsemen those pictures in the "Magic Ring" have never given scandal; but only to those who, conscious of their own weakness and timidity, approach their horses, when necessary, only with trembling, scolding, and murmuring.

With respect, now, to the more important criticisms on the "Magic Ring," I willingly allude to one which has never appeared in print, but which was communicated to me by a worthy hand, without the name of its author. I at first took it for the work of an evangelical ecclesiastic, but afterwards perceived this was not the case. It is clear, however, that it proceeded from the pen of an earnest religious person. The author has erred in his view, that the poet was self-conscious of laying as its *foundation* a designed allegory. Ingeniously, however, and from his standing-point, as if inspired, has the critic interpreted the imagery; and the poet cheerfully acknowledges, that such also might in part lie within his vision, although till then in no wise, even to himself, had it arisen through the medium of the understanding. Similar phenomena often present themselves in poetic works, on account of the mysterious richness of the gift, whereby the gifted one has much more imparted than he can evolve with his own intellectual power, if not excited thereto by some bright hint from another quarter.

After this serious relation, shall another *naïve* judgment be mentioned? It may be, if only for the sake of contrast. Not long since, a friend brought me a library-copy of the "Magic Ring," with which he had accidentally become acquainted, on the cover of which were written these words, "By a boy or a girl? It looks very like it. It is, however, very bad *that Arinbiorn gets nothing!*"

I readily confess, that scarcely ever has unlimited applause afforded me such hearty joy as this censure, proceeding from inmost sympathy with my dear sea-king. The more so, as even my own mind, on arriving at the final chord, felt almost melancholy, as I saw in spirit the hero of the sea floating on so lonesomely to future scenes of war.

In regard to translations into foreign languages of the "Magic Ring," I have heard of a French one, which I have never seen, but which has probably had an essential share in the far-spread celebrity of the fiction. The French language, now as ever, still holds its established office of interpreter amongst the European tongues. Whether, however, this "Anneau Magique" has efficiently rendered the spirit and essence of the German work, may, in the mean time, especially from the then condition of modern French literature, be well doubted. What especially befell the ballads which lie scattered through the work, I know not! On the contrary, a brave Englishman has successfully solved the problem in a translation, to which is prefixed a friendly notice of the author, who once met his translator at a noble, hospitable mansion, not anticipating at that time a future nigher relationship. As regards the ballads, the English author, not deeming himself qualified to render them metrically into his own language, has been content to present the first lines in a corresponding measure, and the remainder briefly and well in an unconfined prose version. Truly and with perfect reason is it here said "briefly and well," for the sense is most ably apprehended; and thus, in every case, a far more accurate picture is brought to the mind of reader and hearer than if an abortive, because constrained, imitation had entered the lists, or even a so-called free translation. The prose is every where penetrated with the spirit of the original writing. It is reported that there are also versions of the "Magic Ring," at least of parts, in the Sclavonic languages. Respecting these, however, the poet, alas! through his entire ignorance of those tongues, is unable to give any further information; as little also concerning an Arabic translation of the episode of the "Emir Nureddin," resolved upon many years ago at Berlin by a then youthful Orientalist, now of high celebrity, in order to gratify an Ottoman grandee at Tunis. May this imagery please anew those readers to whom already it has long been dear, both lovely women and noble men; —and first of all in our beloved German fatherland!

SINTRAM AND HIS COMPANIONS.

If the foregoing remarks on the "Magic Ring" contained a justly serious censure against those who presume that one may at pleasure, and at whatever request, add to the three parts of a work of fiction already complete in itself, yet a fourth,—(and why not, with equal reason, a fifth, sixth, and so forth? for if the present generation become extinct to us, possibly their children and children's children may still live on), such disapproval could nevertheless in no way affect the after-vibrations which assuredly will pervade and reverberate in every truly poetic soul on accomplishing an extensive poetic work. As the plastic or picturesque artist ever feels impelled to add still a grace, an ornament, an inscription, or the like, to his already finished performance, in order not quite to part from his beloved work, so happens it likewise with the poet. Work and worker are so identified, have so, as it were, become *one self*, that they cannot easily part from one another again. Nevertheless, it is with full reason that we shun the use of the over-valued file, which has undoubtedly rubbed off and smoothed away much of the beauty and vigour of many a noble image.

What else, then, remains to us, but, with illustrations of tones and imagery, to temper the parting, and to hover with adornment around the shape that we have called forth? In this spirit, I ween, our Schiller composed his echoes from "The Robbers," as also, by so many victor-steps still more exalted, "Thekla's Voice of Spirits," as sequel to his "Wallenstein." The like is also met with in other poets; and from a similar point of view the fiction now under notice may be regarded.

Folko of Montfauçon was and is peculiarly endeared to my heart as a true type of that old French chivalric glory which now only emerges in individual appearances; for instance, beautifully, in the Vendéan wars, which, though failing in victory, were rich in honours. With these feelings, the poet could not forbear from arraying him in the colours of his own escutcheon, and assigning to him the emblems of the same, and even in some measure denoting him by his own ancestral name; for Foulqué we were called in old times, which was probably derived, according to our Norman descent, from the Northlandish name Folko, or Fulko; and a castle "Montfauçon" was among our ancient possessions. But here that only properly concerns the noble pair, Folko and Gabrielle, as interwoven in the tale of "Sintram." The tale itself is the offspring of my own fantasy, immediately suggested by Albrecht Durer's admirable woodcut of "The Knight, Death, and Satan," the birthday-gift of a former friend, with the happy proposal that I should frame from it a romance or a ballad. It became more than this; and the present tale shews it to be so, being supported by divers traditions, in part derived to me orally, of the Germanic northern customs in war and festivity, and in many other relationships beside. The legend indicated at the conclusion of the information respecting Sintram, of the terrific stories of the north, transformed into southern splendour and mirthful dreams, would really then have been executed, and arose still more clearly from the fantastic tones of a congenial harpsichord-player, who accidentally met the poet. Partly, however, other avocations, partly interruptions from without, have hitherto driven the project into the background. But it still lives within me; and now again, from the powerful and yet childlike harmonies of the Northman Ole Bull, seems to stir more vigorously and brightly than before. Who knows what yet may happen? Meanwhile here gushes from me a song of salutation to one who, honoured by me as master, is not less dear to me as a man:—

Profoundly dreamt a youth on Northland waste;
But no—it is not waste where fairy rings
Reflect the past as well as future things,
Where love and woe in boding tones are drest.

They greeted him, they kissed him, and retreated;
They left for him an instrument of sound,
Whose forceful strings with highest deeds could bound,
And yet with childish frolics be entreated.

He wakes—the gift he seizes, comprehending
Its sweet mysterious pleasure how to prove,
And pours it forth in pure harmonious blending.

O mayst thou, ever victor, joyful move,
Thou Northland sailor, on life's voyage wending,
Conscious of God within thee and above.

It may not be uninteresting to append in this place an extract from the introduction to "Guy Mannering," as it appeared in the collected edition of the works of the author of "Waverley," in 1830:

"The novel or romance of Waverley made its way to the public slowly, of course, at first, but afterwards with such accumulating popularity as so encourage the author to a second attempt. He looked about for a name and a subject; and the manner in which the novels were composed cannot be better illustrated than by reciting the simple narrative on which 'Guy Mannering' was originally founded; but to which, in the progress of the work, the production ceased to bear any, even the most distant resemblance. . . . . A grave and elderly person, according to old John MacKinlay's account, while travelling in the wilder parts of Galloway, was benighted. With difficulty he found his way to a country-seat, where, with the hospitality of the time and country, he was readily admitted. The owner of the house, a gentleman of good fortune, was much struck by the reverend appearance of his guest, and apologised to him for a certain degree of confusion which must unavoidably attend his reception, and could not escape his eye. The lady of the house was, he said, confined to her apartment, and on the point of making her husband a father for the first time, though they had been ten years married. At such an emergency, the laird said he feared his guest might meet with some apparent neglect.

"'Not so, sir,' said the stranger; 'my wants are few, and

easily supplied; and I trust the present circumstances may even afford an opportunity of shewing my gratitude for your hospitality. Let me only request that I may be informed of the exact minute of the birth; and I hope to be able to put you in possession of some particulars, which may influence, in an important manner, the future prospects of the child now about to come into this busy and changeful world. I will not conceal from you that I am skilful in understanding and interpreting the movements of those planetary bodies which exert their influences on the destiny of mortals. It is a science which I do not practise, like others who call themselves astrologers, for hire or reward; for I have a competent estate, and only use the knowledge I possess for the benefit of those in whom I feel an interest.' The laird bowed in respect and gratitude; and the stranger was accommodated with an apartment which commanded an ample view of the astral regions.

"The guest spent a part of the night in ascertaining the position of the heavenly bodies, and calculating their probable influence; until at length the result of his observations induced him to send for the father, and conjure him, in the most solemn manner, to cause the assistants to retard the birth, if practicable, were it but for five minutes. The answer declared this to be impossible; and almost at the instant the message was returned, the father and his guest were made acquainted with the birth of a boy.

"The astrologer on the morrow met the party who gathered around the breakfast-table, with looks so grave and ominous, as to alarm the fears of the father, who had hitherto exulted in the prospects held out by the birth of an heir to his ancient property, failing which event, it must have passed to a distant branch of the family. He hastened to draw the stranger into a private room.

"'I fear from your looks,' said the father, 'that you have bad tidings to tell me of my young stranger; perhaps God will resume the blessing He has bestowed ere he attains the age of manhood; or perhaps he is destined to be unworthy of the affection which we are naturally disposed to devote to our offspring.'

"'Neither the one nor the other,' answered the stranger; 'unless my judgment greatly err, the infant will survive the years of minority, and in temper and disposition will prove all that his parents can wish. But with much in his horoscope which promises many blessings, there is one evil influence strongly predominant, which threatens to subject him to an unhallowed and unhappy temptation about the time when he shall attain the age of twenty-one, which period the constellations intimate will be the crisis of his fate. In what shape, or with what peculiar urgency, this temptation may beset him, my art cannot discover.'

"'Your knowledge, then, can afford us no defence,' said the anxious father, 'against the threatened evil!'

"'Pardon me,' answered the stranger, 'it can. The influence

of the constellations is powerful; but He who made the heavens is more powerful than all, if His aid be invoked in sincerity and truth. You ought to dedicate this boy to the immediate service of his Maker, with as much sincerity as Samuel was devoted to the worship in the temple by his parents. You must regard him as a being separated from the rest of the world. In childhood, in boyhood, you must surround him with the pious and virtuous, and protect him, to the utmost of your power, from the sight or hearing of any crime, in word or action. He must be educated in religious and moral principles of the strictest description. Let him not enter the world, lest he learn to partake of its follies, or perhaps of its vices. In short, preserve him as far as possible from all sin, save that of which too great a portion belongs to all the fallen race of Adam. With the approach of his twenty-first birthday comes the crisis of his fate. If he survive it, he will be happy and prosperous on earth, and a chosen vessel among those elected for heaven. But if it be otherwise'—the astrologer stopped, and sighed deeply.

"'Sir,' replied the parent, still more alarmed than before, 'your words are so kind, your advice so serious, that I will pay the deepest attention to your behests. But can you not aid me farther in this most important concern? Believe me, I will not be ungrateful.'

"'I require and deserve no gratitude for doing a good action,' said the stranger, 'in especial for contributing all that lies in my power to save from an abhorred fate the harmless infant to whom, under a singular conjunction of planets, last night gave life. There is my address; you may write to me from time to time concerning the progress of the boy in religious knowledge. If he be bred up as I advise, I think it will be best that he come to my house at the time when the fatal and decisive period approaches, that is, before he has attained his twenty-first year complete. If you send him such as I desire, I humbly trust that God will protect His own, through whatever strong temptation his fate may subject him to.' He then gave his host his address, which was a country-seat near a post-town in the south of England, and bid him an affectionate farewell.

"The mysterious stranger departed; but his words remained impressed upon the mind of the anxious parent. He lost his lady while his boy was still in infancy. This calamity, I think, had been predicted by the astrologer; and thus his confidence, which, like most people of the period, he had freely given to the science, was riveted and confirmed. The utmost care, therefore, was taken to carry into effect the severe and almost ascetic plan of education which the sage had enjoined. A tutor of the strictest principles was employed to superintend the youth's education; he was surrounded by domestics of the most established character, and closely watched and looked after by the anxious father himself.

"The years of infancy, childhood, and boyhood, passed as the father could have wished. A young Nazarene could not have been bred up with more rigour. All that was evil was withheld from his observation—he only heard what was pure in precept—he only witnessed what was worthy in practice.

"But when the boy began to be lost in the youth, the attentive father saw cause for alarm. Shades of sadness, which gradually assumed a darker character, began to overcloud the young man's temper. Tears, which seemed involuntary, broken sleep, moonlight wanderings, and a melancholy for which he could assign no reason, seemed to threaten at once his bodily health, and the stability of his mind. The astrologer was consulted by letter, and returned for answer, that this fitful state of mind was but the commencement of his trial, and that the poor youth must undergo more and more desperate struggles with the evil that assailed him. There was no hope of remedy, save that he shewed steadiness of mind in the study of the Scriptures. 'He suffers,' continued the letter of the sage, 'from the awakening of those harpies, the passions, which have slept with him, as with others, till the period of life which he has now attained. Better, far better, that they torment him by ungrateful cravings than that he should have to repent having satiated them by criminal indulgence.'

"The dispositions of the young man were so excellent, that he combated, by reason and religion, the fits of gloom which at times overcast his mind; and it was not till he attained the commencement of his twenty-first year that they assumed a character which made his father tremble for the consequences. It seemed as if the gloomiest and most hideous of mental maladies was taking the form of religious despair. Still the youth was gentle, courteous, affectionate, and submissive to his father's will, and resisted with all his power the dark suggestions which were breathed into his mind, as it seemed, by some emanation of the Evil Principle, exhorting him, like the wicked wife of Job, to curse God and die.

"The time at length arrived when he was to perform what was then thought a long and somewhat perilous journey, to the mansion of the early friend who had calculated his nativity. His road lay through several places of interest, and he enjoyed the amusement of travelling, more than he himself thought would have been possible. Thus he did not reach the place of his destination till noon, on the day preceding his birthday. It seemed as if he had been carried away with an unwonted tide of pleasurable sensation, so as to forget, in some degree, what his father had communicated concerning the purpose of his journey. He halted at length before a respectable but solitary old mansion, to which he was directed as the abode of his father's friend.

"The servants who came to take his horse told him he had been expected for two days. He was led into a study, where the stranger, now a venerable old man, who had been his father's guest, met him with a shade of displeasure, as well as gravity, on his brow. 'Young man,' he said, 'wherefore so slow on a journey of such importance?'—'I thought,' replied the guest, blushing and looking downward, 'that there was no harm in travelling slowly, and satisfying my curiosity, providing I could reach your residence by this day; for such was my father's charge.'—'You were to blame,' replied the sage, 'in lingering, considering that the avenger of blood was pressing on your footsteps. But you are come at last, and we will hope for the best, though the conflict in which you are to be engaged will be found more dreadful, the longer it is postponed. But first, accept of such refreshments as nature requires, to satisfy, but not to pamper, the appetite.'

"The old man led the way into a summer parlour, where a frugal meal was placed on the table. As they sat down to the board, they were joined by a young lady about eighteen years of age, and so lovely that the sight of her carried off the feelings of the young stranger from the peculiarity and mystery of his own lot, and riveted his attention to every thing she did or said. She spoke little, and it was on the most serious subjects. She played on the harpsichord at her father's command, but it was hymns with which she accompanied the instrument. At length, on a sign from the sage, she left the room, turning on the young stranger, as she departed, a look of inexpressible anxiety and interest.

"The old man then conducted the youth to his study, and conversed with him upon the most important points of religion, to satisfy himself that he could render a reason for the faith that was in him. During the examination, the youth, in spite of himself, felt his mind occasionally wander, and his recollections go in quest of the beautiful vision who had shared their meal at noon. On such occasions the astrologer looked grave, and shook his head at this relaxation of attention; yet, on the whole, he was pleased with the youth's replies.

"At sunset the young man was made to take the bath; and, having done so, he was directed to attire himself in a robe, somewhat like that worn by Armenians, having his long hair combed down on his shoulders, and his neck, hands, and feet bare. In this guise, he was conducted into a remote chamber totally devoid of furniture, excepting a lamp, a chair, and a table, on which lay a Bible. 'Here,' said the astrologer, 'I must leave you alone, to pass the most critical period of your life. If you can, by recollection of the great truths of which we have spoken, repel the attacks which will be made on your courage and your principles, you have nothing to apprehend. But the trial will be severe and arduous.' His features then assumed a pathetic solemnity, the tears stood in his eyes, and his voice faltered with emotion as he said, 'Dear child, at whose coming into the world I foresaw this fatal trial, may God give thee grace to support it with firmness!'

"The young man was left alone; and hardly did he find himself so, when like a swarm of demons, the recollection of all his sins of omission and commission, rendered even more terrible by the scrupulousness with which he had been educated, rushed on his mind, and, like furies armed with fiery scourges, seemed determined to drive him to despair. As he combated these horrible recollections with distracted feelings, but with a resolved mind, he became aware that his arguments were answered by the sophistry of another, and that the dispute was no longer confined to his own thoughts. The author of evil was present in the room with him in bodily shape, and, potent with spirits of a melancholy cast, was impressing upon him the desperation of his state, and urging suicide as the readiest mode to put an end to his sinful career. Amid his errors, the pleasure he had taken in prolonging his journey unnecessarily, and the attention which he had bestowed on the beauty of the fair female, when his thoughts ought to have been dedicated to the religious discourse of her father, were set before him in the darkest colours; and he was treated as one who, having sinned against light, was therefore deservedly left a prey to the prince of darkness.

"As the fated and influential hour rolled on, the terrors of the hateful presence grew more confounding to the mortal senses of the victim, and the knot of the accursed sophistry became more inextricable in appearance, at least to the prey whom its meshes surrounded. He had not power to explain the assurance of pardon which he continued to assert, or to name the victorious name in which he trusted. But his faith did not abandon him, though he lacked for a time the power of expressing it. 'Say what you will,' was his answer to the tempter; 'I know there is as much betwixt the two boards of this book as can insure me forgiveness for my transgressions, and safety for my soul.' As he spoke, the clock, which announced the lapse of the fatal hour, was heard to strike. The speech and intellectual powers of the youth were instantly and fully restored; he burst forth into prayer, and expressed, in the most glowing terms, his reliance on the truth, and on the author, of the gospel. The demon retired, yelling and discomfited; and the old man, entering the apartment with tears, congratulated his guest on his victory in the fated struggle.

"The young man was afterwards married to the beautiful maiden, the first sight of whom had made such an impression on him, and they were consigned over, at the close of the story, to domestic happiness. So ended John MacKinlay's legend.

"The author of Waverley had imagined a possibility of framing an interesting, and perhaps not an unedifying, tale, out of the incidents of the life of a doomed individual, whose efforts at good and virtuous conduct were to be for ever disappointed by the intervention, as it were, of some malevolent being, and who was at last to come off victorious from the fearful struggle. In short, something was meditated upon a plan resembling the imaginative tale of 'Sintram and his Companions,' by Mons. Le Baron de la Motte Fouqué, although, if it then existed, the author had not seen it.

"The scheme projected may be traced in the first three or four chapters of the work; but farther consideration induced the author to lay his purpose aside. It appeared, on mature consideration, that astrology, though its influence was once received and admitted by Bacon himself, does not now retain influence over the general mind sufficient even to constitute the mainspring of a romance. Besides, it occurred, that to do justice to such a subject would have required not only more talent than the author could be conscious of possessing, but also involved doctrines and discussions of a nature too serious for his purpose, and for the character of the narrative. In changing his plan, however, which was done in the course of printing, the early sheets retained the vestiges of the original tenour of the story, although they now hang upon it as an unnecessary and unnatural encumbrance."

It will probably be admitted, even by the greatest admirers of Scott's genius, that it was well he did *not* attempt the prosecution of his tale as at first projected. The truth is, the mind of this great writer was scarcely fitted for the successful handling of a subject which should bring before his readers in serious reality the mysteries of the invisible world. However much he may appear at times to write under such a feeling, one is constantly disappointed in finding that it has been only assumed, as it would seem, for the sake of temporary effect: wherever a character or event is made for a time to wear a supernatural aspect, due care is taken to let the reader see, that the author neither believes any such thing himself, nor wishes *him* to do so, more than is needful to keep up his curiosity to the proper pitch until the evolution of the plot. He often lets us know,—and at times, one would think, gratuitously,—that the mystery which he is describing so beautifully, is, after all, but an apparent one,—some form of natural magic, some ingenious trick, or some fantasy of a diseased imagination. The above instance furnishes no bad specimen of the way in which his taste would naturally lead him to construct a romance on the basis of an old legend. (See the astrological allusions in the first few chapters of "Guy Mannering.") Enough would be taken to keep up that kind of awe and suspense we have alluded to as needful to an effective romance; but the general impression is not very dissimilar to that left on the mind of the thoughtful reader after laying down the "Mysteries of Udolpho," or the "Castle of Otranto," and finding that all the mystery has vanished, with nothing left for us to admire but the stage-machinery which has been so ingeniously employed to mimic the supernatural, and excite our temporary awe.

It will be evident how dissimilar (among various points, however, of resemblance[1]) was the line pursued by De la Motte Fouqué. He writes throughout as if he believed what he is relating; and if the reader is to enter into the charm of the piece, and to derive full enjoyment from its perusal, he must throw himself into the same posture of mind. In his romances the supernatural is carried through consistently to the end, and is there *left*, in all its mystery; and one need hardly remark how much of their solemnising and indescribably beautiful effect upon the mind is due to this characteristic of these tales.[2]

Indeed, as far as the mere interest of the story, and its pleasing effect on the imagination, is concerned, one would rather prefer that there should be no unravelling of its hidden things. Which of us, when in our childish years we drank in the charms of a simple fairy tale, could endure to have the consistency of its struc-

[1] The reader who consults the Preface to "Waverley," in which the author gives an account of his youthful studies, his love of antiquarian lore, of chivalry, &c., and refers back to the foregoing Preface, will see how, in a great measure, the same kind of materials must necessarily have entered into the compositions of both these authors. It may be added, that the early *religious* associations of Scott were not of a kind which were likely to lead to his treating supernatural subjects in a very high tone.

[2] In estimating the impressive effect produced by the writings of our author, it should not be forgotten that many of them partake to some extent of the character of the spiritual allegory, though the meaning is often but indistinctly marked on the surface. This has been overlooked by many, who nevertheless admire his tales as the offspring of high poetical genius. There is somewhere a criticism upon one of them by a very able writer of the present day, who had evidently entered fully into its literary merit, and who expressed a high admiration for the sentiments and tone of the author, but who had, nevertheless, completely missed the beautiful allegory which it embodies, the dim, impressive obscurity of which lends so wondrous a charm to its scenes.

ture tampered with, or any thing hinted which should prevent us fairly throwing ourselves into its scenes, and viewing them in all the truth and reality of the picture? Or who would care, again, to revel in the gorgeous scenery of an Arabian tale, if at every turn we must be dogged by some officious attendant, ready to put in some matter-of-fact remark which should bring us back to common life, and dash in a thousand pieces the enchanted mirror in which we were gazing with our whole souls? The difference (we may here remark) between the two writers alluded to, appears sometimes even in those subordinate parts of their romances, where one might fairly expect it to be otherwise. Both, for instance, occasionally work in old legends as episodes, by putting them in the mouths of some of the characters in the tale. These, at least, as remains of still more ancient days, might well be given in all their unexplained marvel,—just, in fact, as they were believed in at the time supposed. Fouqué does so. Compare, for instance, the sincere way in which his little tale of the "Magician of Finland"[1] is told, in the first volume of the "Magic Ring," with the legends which Scott incidentally introduces, but which are usually accompanied by some hint as to the credulousness of the age in which they were current, or some suggested explanation in accordance with what are called the laws of nature.

But, besides the mere interest and consistency of the story, it must be admitted that to reverential minds there is something cold and unsatisfactory in this habit of clearing away,—always, and as a matter of course,—whatever is mysterious and beyond the range of our senses and present experience. If we believe *at all* in the powers of the invisible world, we do not see why many things which men usually look upon as incredible, though beautiful imaginations, should not, after all, be deemed possible, and even probable. We are not here pleading for a belief in any particular portions of works usually deemed fictitious; nor are we concerned at present to find such instances. We are only suggesting whether we are not too apt, under the name of romance and fiction, to treat as incredible many things which, if we are believers in Holy Writ, we have at least no *à priori* reason for rejecting as fabulous. There is such a thing as superstition; but there is also an opposite and

[1] This beautiful little story will be found in "Popular Tales and Legends." Burns, 1843.

most dangerous extreme. "I had a dream, which was not *all* a dream," says one of our poets; and so too may it be with much that we are apt indiscriminately to call "fictitious or imaginary."

The *tone* of mind which such writings as that of our author tend to foster, is one of faith in the invisible; while, on the other hand, those of most other novelists rather tend to the opposite habit of scepticism.[1] There is, therefore, *one* special charm about the tales of Fouqué, which those of Scott never can possess; though there is doubtless much in the latter which in other ways tends to good.

This, of course, is not the place to point out the merits of the author of "Waverley" as a romance-writer; and the attempt might well be deemed absurd at this time of day. In many respects he is far before Fouqué. One particular may be cited: we think the readers of the latter must often have desiderated that wonderful talent of Scott by which all the parts of his tale are made to hang together—each event and character fitting into its place with graceful order, and yet without stiffness or formality—and at last forming, what is so gratifying to the mind of the reader at the time, and so pleasing in recollection, one symmetrical whole. Fouqué, with all his glowing descriptions and true poetical touches, does certainly sometimes provoke us by his wild confusion and almost contempt of plan.[2] For this we must, of course, account by the cast of his genius. He was unquestionably a true poet—calling up, as he went on, the most beautiful pictures, and presenting them before us, as they arose to his own mind, in all their primitive freshness and simplicity, but lacking that *talent* which would bring them into due order and method, and which, though a lower gift than poetical *genius*, is yet very needful for one who would not only make a series of beautiful sketches, but who would also form a well-compacted tale. It seems probable that this defect has operated against the general popularity of these works

1 Such books as Scott's "Demonology," Brewster's "Natural Magic," &c., are dangerous in this way. They attempt to prove too much; and by their off-hand way of treating every thing which savours of miraculous agency, they—unconsciously it may be, but really—play into the hands of the rationalist, and furnish weapons with which a worse class of persons will go on to demolish altogether a belief in invisible influences.

2 It must be admitted, however, that many of his shorter pieces are very perfect in their structure.

amongst ourselves; though this may also be attributed, in some degree, to the characteristic already alluded to, which, if it recommends them to some minds, may cause them to find less favour in the eyes of others. He writes at times, in fact, under a kind of heavenly inspiration, which, without a congenial disposition on the part of the reader, it is vain to hope will be appreciated.

It ought to be remarked here, however, that in one case the author of "Waverley" did make a bold attempt to grapple with the supernatural. We allude, of course, to the "Monastery;" and it is singular that in this instance he should have taken the idea from the first tale in this collection. In his Introduction, where he speaks of the origin of the story, he says:—

". . . . Machinery remained,—the introduction of the supernatural and marvellous—the resort of distressed authors since the days of Horace, but whose privileges as a sanctuary have been disputed in the present age, and well-nigh exploded. The popular belief no longer allows the possibility of existence to the race of mysterious beings which hovered betwixt this world and that which is invisible. The fairies have abandoned their moonlight turf; the witch no longer holds her black orgies in the hemlock dell; and

'Even the last lingering phantom of the brain,
The churchyard-ghost, is now at rest again.'

"From the discredit attached to the vulgar and more common modes in which the Scottish superstition displays itself, the author was induced to have recourse to the beautiful, though almost forgotten, theory of astral spirits, or creatures of the elements, surpassing human beings in knowledge and power, but inferior to them, as being subject, after a certain space of years, to a death which is to them annihilation, as they have no share in the promise made to the sons of Adam. These spirits are supposed to be of four distinct kinds, as the elements from which they have their origin, and are known to those who have studied the cabalistical philosophy by the names of sylphs, gnomes, salamanders, and naiads, as they belong to the elements of air, earth, fire, or water. The general reader will find an entertaining account of these elementary spirits in the French book entitled 'Entretiens de Compte du Gabalis.' The ingenious Comte de la Motte Fouqué composed, in German, one of the most successful productions of his fertile brain, where a beautiful and even afflicting effect is produced by the introduction of a water-nymph, who consents to become accessible to human feelings, and unites her lot with that of a mortal, who treats her with ingratitude.

"In imitation of an example so successful, the White Lady of Avenel was introduced into the following sheets. . . .

"Either, however, the author executed his purpose indifferently, or the public did not approve of it; for the 'White Lady of Avenel' was far from being popular. He does not now make the present statement in the view of arguing readers into a more favourable opinion on the subject, but merely with the purpose of exculpating himself from the charge of having wantonly intruded into the narrative a being of inconsistent powers and propensities."

The inferior success which this romance met with, (chiefly, it would seem, on account of the introduction of the White Lady,) is probably due to both the causes alluded to by the author in the above extract. The public were not prepared for this kind of machinery in *his* writings. And it is not unlikely, that, if he had treated it differently, and had made some person to act the part of a supernatural being, who should come out at the wind-up as one of flesh and blood, and explain her proceedings, the same objection might not have been taken by some. It is possible too, however, that had the present idea been better executed, the public might have been reconciled to it. There is certainly an awkwardness and want of dignity about this part of the romance; and, much as there is of beauty in some of the details, one does not, after the perusal, dwell with full satisfaction upon the vision of the White Nymph.

As has been said, this was not the line which Scott was fitted to excel in. With respect to his idea, that popular belief no longer allows the possibility of the existence of such mysterious beings, it may be doubted whether this is of itself a good reason why writers of romance should eschew them. Indeed, he himself did not,—as we see in this case: he avoided certainly the more *hackneyed* ground of fairies and witches;—but he chose one equally, or more, removed from popular belief, though recommended to him in this case by the advantage of novelty. Perhaps the most likely way to ensure consistency and success, would be to dismiss the question as to whether people *now-a-days* believe such things or not, and to choose such a period and such characters as will admit of this machinery being naturally made use of; so that whether readers in the present day are found to give credence or not, they may at least look on a picture which was true at the time supposed, and which will be true and consistent to them, too, if they will throw their sympathies into the scenes which are opened before them. The satisfactory effect produced by Fouqué's tales may be in part ascribed to this circumstance. He carries you into far-off scenes, and among ancient days and manners; and you see at once that you must feel as men then felt, and believe as they believed.

It may be doubted, indeed, whether, with our present habits and tone of mind, it would be possible to work up an endurable piece of fiction, of which the scene should be laid in our own country and in our own day, and which yet should embody the machinery of our old tales. Relate a fairy tale to some youthful circle of open-mouthed listeners on a winter's evening, and see if half the enchantment does not depend upon their realising the scene as having existed in times far removed from their own days. Tell the same story, only altering the circumstantials to those among which they themselves live,—as if, for instance, the things had happened in some neighbouring village, and within the last year,—and the magical effect will be gone. They feel that the thing is unnatural; and the quiet, earnest look of wonder and awe with which the little audience hung upon the lips of the narrator will soon, we fear, be changed for one of mingled disappointment and scorn. They will shew not only that they disbelieve, but that they despise, what you are telling them.[1]

To conclude:—these Tales, with their no less pleasing companions,[2] are commended to the attention of all lovers amongst us of what is noble and beautiful in external nature, as well as in the human heart and life. We do so with hearty confidence; nor do we fear that they will suffer, even by oft-repeated perusal. Manly Christian grace, virgin purity, hoary wisdom, happy child-like innocence; the grand, the severe, the tender, the lowly, the affectionate, and whatever else is calculated to touch and elevate

[1] Perhaps the modern "ghost-story" may occur to some as an apparent exception to this remark; and we believe that in some places popular belief would almost admit of such machinery being employed, without fatally destroying the consistency and verisimilitude of a tale. Still, as a general remark, what Sir W. Scott says in a previous page of the church-yard ghost is true; and any of our tale-writers, therefore, who should be adventurous enough to make use of such machinery without due care to clear up the mystery at the end, would run a great risk of making shipwreck of his or her popularity. It *might* do, were the scene laid amongst characters supposed to live under the influence of such forms of belief; there would then be so far a coherence. But we suspect this must be in "Dreamland"—not in England.

[2] See the Tales of Fouqué in the volume entitled "Romantic Fiction."

the heart,—set off at times by the exhibition of the darker and more repulsive traits of human character, (held up, however, only to be avoided,)—find in the writings of our author their happy and appropriate exemplification. The noble, courteous Christian knight—the tender, modest, but high-minded maiden—the affectionate spouse—the aged man, in all the commanding dignity of years and wisdom—the pious peasant—the faithful domestic,—are all mingled in the goodly array of characters which they present to us. And as the fair procession passes before us, and its magic colours float around the imagination and linger in the memory, who does not feel the best sympathies and aspirations of his heart irresistibly drawn forth?—who, too, will refuse his tribute of love and admiration to the gifted—and now, alas! deceased—author, the impress of whose own calm and beautiful mind they so fully bear?

UNDINE.

p. 48.

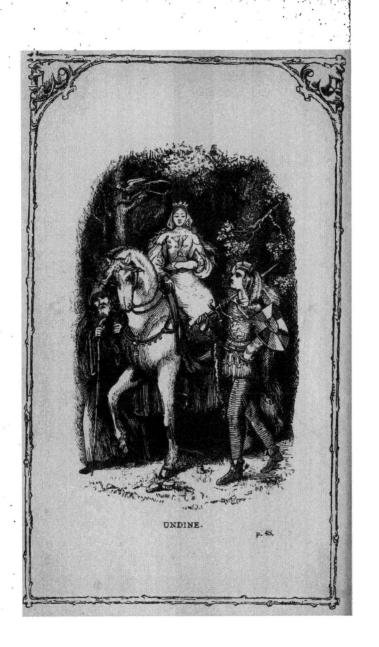

Undine.
London. James Burns.

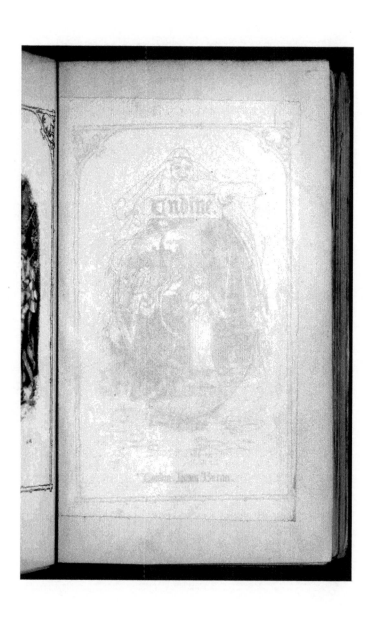

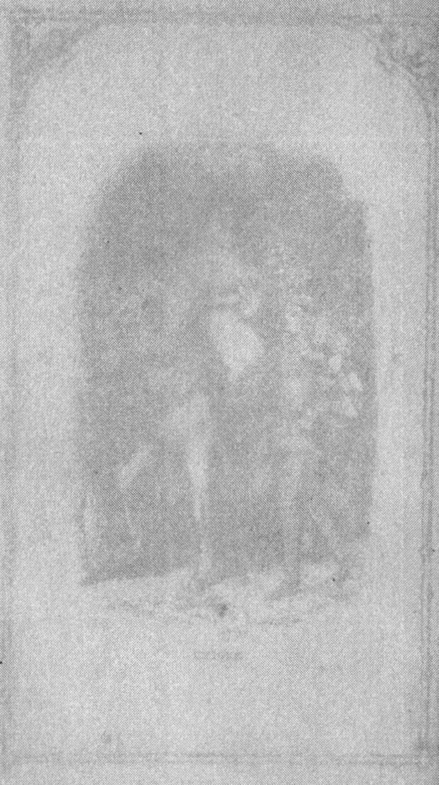

Undine.
London. James. Burns.

To Undine.

UNDINE! thou fair and lovely sprite,
Since first from out an ancient lay
I saw gleam forth thy fitful light,
How hast thou sung my cares away!

How hast thou nestled next my heart,
And gently offered to impart
Thy sorrows to my listening ear,
Like a half-shy, half-trusting child,
The while my lute, in woodnotes wild,
Thine accents echo'd far and near!

Then many a youth I won to muse
With love on thy mysterious ways,
And many a fair one to peruse
The legend of thy wondrous days.

And now both dame and youth would fain
List to my tale yet once again;
Nay, sweet Undine, be not afraid!
Enter their halls with footstep light,
Greet courteously each noble knight,
But fondly every German maid.

And should they ask concerning me,
Oh, say, "He is a cavalier,
Who truly serves and valiantly,
In tournay and festivity,
With lute and sword, each lady fair!"

FOUQUÉ.

CHAPTER I.

On a beautiful evening, many hundred years ago, a worthy old fisherman sat mending his nets. The spot where he dwelt was exceedingly picturesque. The green turf on which he had built his cottage ran far out into a great lake; and this slip of verdure appeared to stretch into it as much through love of its clear waters, as the lake, moved by a like impulse, strove to fold the meadow, with its waving grass and flowers, and the cooling shade of the trees, in its embrace of love. They seemed to be drawn toward each other, and the one to be visiting the other as a guest.

With respect to human beings, indeed, in this pleasant spot, excepting the fisherman and his family, there were few, or rather none, to be met with. For as in the background of the scene, toward the west and north-west, lay a forest of extraordinary wildness, which, owing to its sunless gloom and almost impassable recesses, as well as to fear of the strange creatures and visionary illusions to be encountered in it, most people avoided entering, unless in cases of extreme necessity. The pious old fisherman, however, many times passed through it without harm, when he carried the fine fish, which he caught by his beautiful strip of land, to a great city lying only a short distance beyond the forest.

Now the reason he was able to go through this wood with so much ease may have been chiefly this, because he entertained scarcely any thoughts but such as were of a religious nature; and besides, every time he crossed the evil-reported shades, he used to sing some holy song with a clear voice and from a sincere heart.

Well, while he sat by his nets this evening, neither fearing nor devising evil, a sudden terror seized him, as he heard a rushing in the darkness of the wood, that resembled the trampling of a mounted steed, and the noise continued every instant drawing nearer and nearer to his little territory.

What he had fancied, when abroad in many a stormy night, respecting the mysteries of the forest, now flashed through his mind in a moment; especially the figure of a man of gigantic stature and snow-white appearance, who kept nodding his head in a portentous manner. And when he raised his eyes towards the wood, the form came before him in perfect distinctness, as he saw the nodding man burst forth from the mazy web-work of leaves and branches. But he immediately felt emboldened, when he reflected that nothing to give him alarm had ever befallen him even in the forest; and moreover, that on this open neck of land the evil spirit, it was likely, would be still less daring in the exercise of his power. At the same time, he prayed aloud with the most earnest sincerity of devotion, repeating a passage of the Bible. This inspired him with fresh courage; and soon perceiving the illusion, and the strange mistake into which his imagination had betrayed him, he could with difficulty refrain from laughing. The white nodding figure he had seen, became transformed, in the twinkling of an eye, to what in reality it was, a small brook, long and familiarly known to him, which ran foaming from the forest, and discharged itself into the lake.

But what had caused the startling sound was a knight arrayed in sumptuous apparel, who from under the shadows of the trees came riding toward the cottage. His doublet was violet embroidered with gold, and his scarlet cloak hung gracefully over it; on his cap of burnished gold waved red and violet-coloured plumes; and in his golden shoulder-belt flashed a sword, richly ornamented and extremely beautiful. The white barb that bore the knight was more slenderly built than war-horses usually are; and he touched the turf with a step so light and elastic, that the green and flowery carpet seemed hardly to receive the slightest injury from his tread. The old fisherman, notwithstanding, did not feel perfectly secure in his mind, although he was forced to believe that no evil could be feared from an appearance so pleasing; and therefore, as good manners dictated, he took off his hat on the knight's coming near, and quietly remained by the side of his nets.

When the stranger stopped, and asked whether he, with his horse, could have shelter and entertainment there for the night, the fisherman returned answer: "As to your horse, fair sir, I have no better stable for him than this shady meadow, and no better provender than the grass that is growing here. But with respect to yourself, you shall be welcome to our humble cottage, and to the best supper and lodging we are able to give you."

The knight was well contented with this reception; and alighting from his horse, which his host assisted him to relieve from saddle and bridle, he let him hasten away to the fresh pasture, and thus spoke: "Even had I found you less hospitable and kindly disposed, my worthy old friend, you would still, I suspect, hardly have got rid of me to-day; for here, I perceive, a broad lake lies before us, and as to riding back into that wood of wonders, with the shades of evening deepening around me, may Heaven in its grace preserve me from the thought."

"Pray not a word of the wood, or of returning into it!" said the fisherman, and took his guest into the cottage.

There, beside the hearth, from which a frugal fire was diffusing its light through the clean twilight room, sat the fisherman's aged wife in a great chair. At the entrance of their noble guest, she rose and gave him a courteous welcome, but sat down again in her seat of honour, not making the slightest offer of it to the stranger. Upon this the fisherman said with a smile:

"You must not be offended with her, young gentleman, because she has not given up to you the best chair in the house; it is a custom among poor people to look upon this as the privilege of the aged."

"Why, husband!" cried the old lady with a quiet smile, "where can your wits be wandering? Our guest, to say the least of him, must belong to a Christian country; and how is it possible, then, that so well-bred a young man as he appears to be could dream of driving old people from their chairs? Take a seat, my young master," continued she, turning to the knight; "there is still quite a snug little chair on the other side of the room there, only be careful not to shove it about too roughly, for one of its legs, I fear, is none of the firmest."

The knight brought up the seat as carefully as she could desire, sat down upon it good-humouredly, and it seemed to him almost as if he must be somehow related to this little household, and have just returned home from abroad.

These three worthy people now began to converse in the most friendly and familiar manner. In relation to the forest, indeed, concerning which the knight occasionally made some inquiries, the old man chose to know and say but little; he was of opinion, that slightly touching upon it, at this hour of twilight, was most suitable and safe; but of the cares and comforts of their home, and their business abroad, the aged couple spoke more freely, and listened also with eager curiosity, as the knight recounted to them his travels, and how he had a castle near one of the sources of the Danube, and that his name was Sir Huldbrand of Ringstetten.

Already had the stranger, while they were in the midst of their talk, heard at times a splash against the little low window, as if some one were dashing water against it. The old man, every time he heard the noise, knit his brows with vexation; but at last, when the whole sweep of a shower came pouring like a torrent against the panes, and bubbling through the decayed frame into the room, he started up indignant, rushed to the window, and cried with a threatening voice,—

"Undine! will you never leave off these fooleries? not even to-day, when we have a stranger-knight with us in the cottage?"

All without now became still, only a low laugh was just audible, and the fisherman said, as he came back to his seat: "You will have the goodness, my honoured guest, to pardon this freak, and it may be a multitude more; but she has no thought of evil, or of any harm. This mischievous Undine, to confess the truth, is our adopted daughter, and she stoutly refuses to give over this frolicsome childishness of hers, although she has already entered her eighteenth year. But in spite of this, as I said before, she is at heart one of the very best children in the world."

"*You* may say so," broke in the old lady, shaking her head; "you can give a better account of her than I can. When you return home from fishing, or from selling your fish in the city, you may think her frolics very delightful. But to have her dancing about you the whole day long, and never from morning to night to hear her speak one word of sense; and then, as she grows older, instead of having any help from her in the family, to find her a continual cause of anxiety, lest her wild humours should completely ruin us,—that is quite another thing, and enough at last to weary out the patience even of a saint."

"Well, well," replied the master of the house, with a smile; "you have your trials with Undine, and I have mine with the lake. The lake often beats down my dams, and breaks the meshes of my nets, but for all that I have a strong affection for it; and so have you, in spite of your mighty crosses and vexations, for our graceful little child. Is it not true?"

"One cannot be very angry with her," answered the old lady, as she gave her husband an approving smile.

That instant the door flew open, and a fair girl, of wondrous beauty, sprang laughing in, and said: "You have only been making a mock of me, father; for where now is the guest you mentioned?"

The same moment, however, she perceived the knight also, and continued standing before the young man in fixed astonishment. Huldbrand was charmed with her graceful figure, and viewed her lovely features with the more intense interest, as he imagined it was only her surprise that allowed him the opportunity, and that she would soon turn away from his gaze with increased bashfulness. But the event was the very reverse of what he expected. For, after looking at him for a long while, she became more confident, moved nearer, knelt down before him, and, while she played with a gold medal which he wore attached to a rich chain on his breast, exclaimed,—

"Why, you beautiful, you kind guest! how have you reached our poor cottage at last? Have you been obliged for years and years to wander about the world before you could catch one glimpse of our nook? Do you come out of that wild forest, my beautiful knight?"

The old woman was so prompt in her reproof, as to allow him no time to answer. She commanded the maiden to rise, shew better manners, and go to her work. But Undine, without making any reply, drew a little footstool near Huldbrand's chair, sat down upon it with her netting, and said in a gentle tone:

"I will work here."

The old man did as parents are apt to do with children to whom they have been over-indulgent. He affected to observe nothing of Undine's strange behaviour, and was beginning to talk about something else. But this the maiden did not permit him to do. She broke in upon him: "I have asked our kind guest from whence he has come among us, and he has not yet answered me."

"I come out of the forest, you lovely little vision," Huldbrand returned; and she spoke again:

"You must also tell me how you came to enter that forest, so feared and shunned, and the marvellous adventures you met with in it; for there is no escaping without something of this kind."

Huldbrand felt a slight shudder on remembering what he had witnessed, and looked involuntarily toward the window, for it seemed to him that one of the strange shapes which had come upon him in the forest must be there grinning in through the glass; but he discerned nothing except the deep darkness of night, which had now enveloped the whole prospect. Upon this he became more collected, and was just on the point of beginning his account, when the old man thus interrupted him:

"Not so, sir knight; this is by no means a fit hour for such relations."

But Undine, in a state of high excitement, sprang up from her little stool, and cried, placing herself directly before the fisherman: "He shall *not* tell his story, father? he shall not? But it is my will:—he shall!—stop him who may!"

Thus speaking, she stamped her little foot vehemently on the floor, but all with an air of such comic and good-humoured simplicity, that Huldbrand now found it quite as hard to withdraw his gaze from her wild emotion, as he had before from her gentleness and beauty. The old man, on the contrary, burst out in unrestrained displeasure. He severely reproved Undine for her disobedience and her unbecoming carriage toward the stranger, and his good old wife joined him in harping on the same string.

By these rebukes Undine was only excited the more. "If you want to quarrel with me," she cried, "and will not let me hear what I so much desire, then sleep alone in your smoky old hut!" And swift as an arrow she shot from the door, and vanished amid the darkness of the night.

Huldbrand and the fisherman sprang from their seats, and were rushing to stop the angry girl; but before they could reach the cottage-door, she had disappeared in the stormy darkness without: and no sound, not so much even as that of her light footstep, betrayed the course she had taken. Huldbrand threw a glance of inquiry toward his host: it almost seemed to him as if the whole of the sweet apparition, which had so suddenly plunged again amid the night, were no other than a continuation of the wonderful forms that had just played their mad pranks with him in the forest. But the old man muttered between his teeth:

"This is not the first time she has treated us in this manner. Now must our hearts be filled with anxiety, and our eyes find no sleep the whole night; for who can assure us, in spite of her past escapes, that she will not some time or other come to harm, if she thus continue out in the dark and alone until daylight?"

"Then pray, for God's sake, father, let us follow her," cried Huldbrand anxiously.

"Wherefore should we?" replied the old man. "It would be a sin were I to suffer you, all alone, to search after the foolish girl amid the lonesomeness of night; and my old limbs would fail to carry me to this wild rover, even if I knew to what place she has betaken herself."

"Still we ought at least to call after her, and beg her to return," said Huldbrand; and he began to call, in tones of earnest entreaty, "Undine! Undine! come back, come back!"

The old man shook his head, and said, "All your shouting, however loud and long, will be of no avail; you know not as yet, sir knight, how self-willed the little thing is." But still, even hoping against hope, he could not himself cease calling out every minute, amid the gloom of night, "Undine! ah, dear Undine! I beseech you, pray come back,—only this once."

It turned out, however, exactly as the fisherman had said. No Undine could they hear or see; and as the old man would on no account consent that Huldbrand should go in quest of the fugitive, they were both obliged at last to return into the cottage. There they found the fire on the hearth almost gone out, and the mistress of the house, who took Undine's flight and danger far less to heart than her husband, had already gone to rest. The old man blew up the coals, put on dry wood, and by the firelight hunted for a flask of wine, which he brought and set between himself and his guest.

"You, sir knight, as well as I," said he, "are anxious on the silly girl's account; and it would be better, I think, to spend part of the night in chatting and drinking, than keep turning and turning on our rush-mats, and trying in vain to sleep. What is your opinion?"

Huldbrand was well pleased with the plan; the fisherman pressed him to take the empty seat of honour, its worthy occupant having now left it for her couch; and they relished their beverage and enjoyed their chat, as two such good men and true ever ought to do. To be sure, whenever the slightest thing moved before the windows, or at times when even nothing was moving, one of them would look up and exclaim, "Here she comes!" Then would they continue silent a few moments, and afterward, when nothing appeared, would shake their heads, breathe out a sigh, and go on with their talk.

But as neither could think of any thing but Undine, the best plan they could devise was, that the old fisherman should relate, and the knight should hear, in what manner Undine had come to the cottage. So the fisherman began as follows:

"It is now about fifteen years since I one day crossed the wild forest with fish for the city-market. My wife had remained at home as she was wont to do; and at this time for a reason of more than common interest, for although we were beginning to feel the advances of age, God had bestowed upon us an infant of wonderful beauty. It was a little girl; and we already began to ask ourselves the question, whether we ought not, for the advantage of the new-comer, to quit our solitude, and, the better to bring up this precious gift of Heaven, to remove to some more inhabited place. Poor people, to be sure, cannot in these cases do all you may think they ought, sir knight; but we must all do what we can.

"Well, I went on my way, and this affair would keep running in my head. This slip of land was most dear to me, and I trembled when, amidst the bustle and broils of the city, I thought to myself, 'In a scene of tumult like this, or at least in one not much more quiet, I must soon take up my abode.' But I did not for this murmur against our good God; on the contrary, I praised Him in silence for the new-born babe. I should also speak an untruth, were I to say that any thing befell me, either on my passage through the forest to the city, or on my returning homeward, that gave me more alarm than usual, as at that time I had never seen any appearance there which could terrify or annoy me. The Lord was ever with me in those awful shades."

Thus speaking, he took his cap reverently from his bald head, and continued to sit for a considerable time in devout thought. He then covered himself again, and went on with his relation:

"On this side the forest, alas! it was on this side, that woe burst upon me. My wife came wildly to meet me, clad in mourning apparel, and her eyes streaming with tears. 'Gracious God!' I cried, 'where's our child? Speak!'

"'With Him on whom you have called, dear husband,' she answered; and we now entered the cottage together, weeping in silence. I looked for the little corpse, almost fearing to find what I was seeking; and then it was I first learnt how all had happened.

"My wife had taken the little one in her arms, and walked out to the shore of the lake. She there sat down by its very brink; and while she was playing with the infant, as free from all fear as she was full of delight, it bent forward on a sudden, as if seeing something very beautiful in the water. My wife saw her laugh, the dear angel, and try to catch the image in her tiny hands; but in a moment—with a motion swifter than sight—she sprang from her mother's arms, and sank in the lake, the watery glass into which she had been gazing. I searched for our lost darling again and again; but it was all in vain; I could nowhere find the least trace of her.

"The same evening we childless parents were sitting together by our cottage hearth. We had no desire to talk, even if our tears would have permitted us. As we thus sat in mournful stillness, gazing into the fire, all at once we heard something without,—a slight rustling at the door. The door flew open, and we saw a little girl, three or four years old, and more beautiful than I can say, standing on the threshold, richly dressed, and smiling upon us. We were struck dumb with astonishment, and I knew not for a time whether the tiny form were a real human being, or a mere mockery of enchantment. But I soon perceived water dripping from her golden hair and rich garments, and that the pretty child had been lying in the water, and stood in immediate need of our help.

"'Wife,' said I, 'no one has been able to save our child for us; but let us do for others what would have made us so blessed could any one have done it for us.'

"We undressed the little thing, put her to bed, and gave her something to drink: at all this she spoke not a word, but only turned her eyes upon us—eyes blue and bright as sea or sky—and continued looking at us with a smile.

"Next morning we had no reason to fear that she had received any other harm than her wetting, and I now asked her about her parents, and how she could have come to us. But the account she gave was both confused and incredible. She must surely have been born far from here, not only because I have been unable for these fifteen years to learn any thing of her birth, but because she then said, and at times continues to say, many things of so very singular a nature, that we neither of us know, after all, whether she may not have dropped among us from the moon; for her talk runs upon golden castles, crystal domes, and Heaven knows what extravagances beside. What, however, she related with most distinctness was this: that while she was once taking a sail with her mother on the great lake, she fell out of the boat into the water; and that when she first recovered her senses, she was here under our trees, where the gay scenes of the shore filled her with delight.

"We now had another care weighing upon our minds, and one that caused us no small perplexity and uneasiness. We of course very soon determined to keep and bring up the child we had found, in place of our own darling that had been drowned; but who could tell us whether she had been baptised or not? She herself could give us no light on the subject. When we asked her the question, she commonly made answer, that she well knew she was created for God's praise and glory, and that she was willing to let us do with her all that might promote His glory and praise.

"My wife and I reasoned in this way: 'If she has not been baptised, there can be no use in putting off the ceremony; and if she has been, it still is better to have too much of a good thing than too little.'

"Taking this view of our difficulty, we now endeavoured to hit upon a good name for the child, since, while she remained without one, we were often at a loss, in our familiar talk, to know what to call her. We at length agreed that Dorothea would be most suitable for her, as I had somewhere heard it said that this name signified a *gift of God,* and surely she had been sent to us by Providence as a gift, to comfort us in our misery. She, on the contrary, would not so much as hear Dorothea mentioned; she insisted, that as she had been named Undine by her parents, Undine she ought still to be called. It now occurred to me that this was a heathenish name, to be found in no calendar, and I resolved to ask the advice of a priest in the city. He would not listen to the name of Undine; and yielding to my urgent request, he came with me through the enchanted forest, in order to perform the rite of baptism here in my cottage.

"The little maid stood before us so prettily adorned, and with such an air of gracefulness, that the heart of the priest softened at once in her presence; and she coaxed him so sweetly, and jested with him so merrily, that he at last remembered nothing of his many objections to the name of Undine.

"Thus, then, was she baptised Undine; and, during the holy ceremony, she behaved with great propriety and gentleness, wild and wayward as at other times she invariably was; for in this my wife was quite right, when she mentioned the anxiety the child has occasioned us. If I should relate to you"—

At this moment the knight interrupted the fisherman, to direct his attention to a deep sound as of a rushing flood, which had caught his ear during the talk of the old man. And now the waters came pouring on with redoubled fury before the cottage-windows. Both sprang to the door. There they saw, by the light of the now risen moon, the brook which issued from the wood rushing wildly over its banks, and whirling onward with it both stones and branches of trees in its rapid course. The storm, as if awakened by the uproar, burst forth from the clouds, whose immense masses of vapour coursed over the moon with the swiftness of thought; the lake roared beneath the wind that swept the foam from its waves; while the trees of this narrow peninsula groaned from root to topmost branch as they bowed and swung above the torrent.

"Undine! in God's name, Undine!" cried the two men in an agony. No answer was returned. And now, regardless of every thing else, they hurried from the cottage, one in this direction, the other in that, searching and calling.

CHAPTER II.

The longer Huldbrand sought Undine beneath the shades of night, and failed to find her, the more anxious and confused he became. The impression that she was a mere phantom of the forest gained a new ascendancy over him; indeed, amid the howling of the waves and the tempest, the crashing of the trees, and the entire change of the once so peaceful and beautiful scene, he was tempted to view the whole peninsula, together with the cottage and its inhabitants, as little more than some mockery of his senses. But still he heard afar off the fisherman's anxious and incessant shouting, "Undine!" and also his aged wife, who was praying and singing psalms.

At length, when he drew near to the brook, which had overflowed its banks, he perceived, by the moonlight, that it had taken its wild course directly in front of the haunted forest, so as to change the peninsula into an island.

"Merciful God!" he breathed to himself, "if Undine has ventured a step within that fearful wood, what will become of her? Perhaps it was all owing to her sportive and wayward spirit, because I would give her no account of my adventures there. And now the stream is rolling between us, she may be weeping alone on the other side in the midst of spectral horrors!"

A shuddering groan escaped him; and clambering over some stones and trunks of overthrown pines, in order to step into the impetuous current, he resolved, either by wading or swimming, to seek the wanderer on the further shore. He felt, it is true, all the dread and shrinking awe creeping over him which he had already suffered by daylight among the now tossing and roaring branches of the forest. More than all, a tall man in white, whom he knew but too well, met his view, as he stood grinning and nodding on the grass beyond the water. But even monstrous forms like this only impelled him to cross over toward them, when the thought rushed upon him that Undine might be there alone and in the agony of death.

He had already grasped a strong branch of a pine, and stood supporting himself upon it in the whirling current, against which he could with difficulty keep himself erect; but he advanced deeper in with a courageous spirit. That instant a gentle voice of warning cried near him, "Do not venture, do not venture!—that OLD MAN, the STREAM, is too full of tricks to be trusted!" He knew the soft tones of the voice; and while he stood as it were entranced, beneath the shadows which had now duskily veiled the moon, his head swam with the swell and rolling of the waves as he saw them momentarily rising above his knee. Still he disdained the thought of giving up his purpose.

"If you are not really there, if you are merely gambolling round me like a mist, may I, too, bid farewell to life, and become a shadow like you, dear, dear Undine!" Thus calling aloud, he again moved deeper into the stream. "Look round you—ah, pray look round you, beautiful young stranger! why rush on death so madly?" cried the voice a second time close by him; and looking on one side, he perceived, by the light of the moon, again cloudless, a little island formed by the flood; and crouching upon its flowery turf, beneath the branches of embowering trees, he saw the smiling and lovely Undine.

O how much more gladly than before the young man now plied his sturdy staff! A few steps, and he had crossed the flood that was rushing between himself and the maiden; and he stood near her on the little spot of greensward in security, protected by the old trees. Undine half rose, and she threw her arms around his neck to draw him gently down upon the soft seat by her side.

"Here you shall tell me your story, my beautiful friend," she breathed in a low whisper; "here the cross old people cannot disturb us; and, besides, our roof of leaves here will make quite as good a shelter as their poor cottage."

"It is heaven itself," cried Huldbrand; and folding her in his arms, he kissed the lovely girl with fervour.

The old fisherman, meantime, had come to the margin of the stream, and he shouted across, "Why how is this, sir knight! I received you with the welcome which one true-hearted man gives to another; and now you sit there caressing my foster-child in secret, while you suffer me in my anxiety to wander through the night in quest of her."

"Not till this moment did I find her myself, old father," cried the knight across the water.

"So much the better," said the fisherman; "but now make haste, and bring her over to me upon firm ground."

To this, however, Undine would by no means consent. She declared, that she would rather enter the wild forest itself with the beautiful stranger, than return to the cottage, where she was so thwarted in her wishes, and from which the knight would soon or late go away. Then throwing her arms round Huldbrand, she sung the following verse with the warbling sweetness of a bird:

"A Rill would leave its misty vale,
And fortunes wild explore;
Weary at length it reached the main,
And sought its vale no more."

The old fisherman wept bitterly at her song; but his emotion seemed to awaken little or no sympathy in her. She kissed and caressed her new friend, who at last said to her: "Undine, if the distress of the old man does not touch your heart, it cannot but move mine. We ought to return to him."

She opened her large blue eyes upon him in amazement, and spoke at last with a slow and doubtful accent: "If you think so, it is well; all is right to me which you think right. But the old man over there must first give me his promise that he will allow you, without objection, to relate what you saw in the wood, and——Well, other things will settle themselves."

"Come—only come!" cried the fisherman to her, unable to utter another word. At the same time he stretched his arms wide over the current toward her, and to give her assurance that he would do what she required, nodded his head: this motion caused his white hair to fall strangely over his face, and Huldbrand could not but remember the nodding white man of the forest. Without allowing any thing, however, to produce in him the least confusion, the young knight took the beautiful girl in his arms, and bore her across the narrow channel which the stream had torn away between her little island and the solid shore. The old man fell upon Undine's neck, and found it impossible either to express his joy or to kiss her enough; even the ancient dame came up and embraced the recovered girl most cordially. Every word of censure was carefully avoided; the more so indeed as even Undine, forgetting her waywardness, almost overwhelmed her foster-parents with caresses and the prattle of tenderness.

When at length the excess of their joy at recovering their child had subsided, morning had already dawned, shining upon the waters of the lake; the tempest had become hushed; the small birds sung merrily on the moist branches.

As Undine now insisted upon hearing the recital of the knight's promised adventures, the aged couple readily agreed to her wish. Breakfast was brought out beneath the trees which stood behind the cottage toward the lake on the north, and they sat down to it with contented hearts,—Undine at the knight's feet, on the grass. These arrangements being made, Huldbrand began his story in the following manner:—

"It is now about eight days since I rode into the free imperial city, which lies yonder on the farther side of the forest. Soon after my arrival, a splendid tournament and running at the ring took place there, and I spared neither my horse nor my lance in the encounters.

"Once, while I was pausing at the lists to rest from the brisk exercise, and was handing back my helmet to one of my attendants, a female figure of extraordinary beauty caught my attention, as, most magnificently attired, she stood looking on at one of the balconies. I learned, on making inquiry of a person near me, that the name of the young lady was Bertalda, and that she was a foster-daughter of one of the powerful dukes of this country. She too, I observed, was gazing at me; and the consequences were such as we young knights are wont to experience; whatever success in riding I might have had before, I was now favoured with still better fortune. That evening I was Bertalda's partner in the dance, and I enjoyed the same distinction during the remainder of the festival."

A sharp pain in his left hand, as it hung carelessly beside him, here interrupted Huldbrand's relation, and drew his eye to the part affected. Undine had fastened her pearly teeth, and not without some keenness too, upon one of his fingers, appearing at the same time very gloomy and displeased. On a sudden, however, she looked up in his eyes with an expression of tender melancholy, and whispered almost inaudibly,—

"It is all your own fault."

She then covered her face; and the knight, strangely embarrassed and thoughtful, went on with his story:

"This lady Bertalda of whom I spoke is of a proud and wayward spirit. The second day I saw her she pleased me by no means so much as she had the first, and the third day still less. But I continued about her because she shewed me more favour than she did any other knight: and it so happened that I playfully asked her to give me one of her gloves. 'When you have entered the haunted forest all alone,' said she; 'when you have explored its wonders, and brought me a full account of them, the glove is yours.' As to getting her glove, it was of no importance to me whatever; but the word had been spoken, and no honourable knight would permit himself to be urged to such a proof of valour a second time."

"I thought," said Undine, interrupting him, "that she loved you."

"It did appear so," replied Huldbrand.

"Well!" exclaimed the maiden, laughing, "this is beyond belief; she must be very stupid. To drive from her one who was dear to her! And, worse than all, into that ill-omened wood! The wood and its mysteries, for all I should have cared, might have waited long enough."

"Yesterday morning, then," pursued the knight, smiling kindly upon Undine, "I set out from the city, my enterprise before me. The early light lay rich upon the verdant turf. It shone so rosy on the slender boles of the trees, and there was so merry a whispering among the leaves, that in my heart I could not but laugh at people who feared meeting any thing to terrify them in a spot so delicious. 'I shall soon pass through the forest, and as speedily return,' I said to myself in the overflow of joyous feeling; and ere I was well aware, I had entered deep among the green shades; while of the plain that lay behind me, I was no longer able to catch a glimpse.

"Then the conviction for the first time impressed me, that in a forest of so great extent I might very easily become bewildered, and that this perhaps might be the only danger which was likely to threaten those who explored its recesses. So I made a halt, and turned myself in the direction of the sun, which had meantime risen somewhat higher; and while I was looking up to observe it, I saw something black among the boughs of a lofty oak. My first thought was, 'It is a bear!' and I grasped my weapon: the object then accosted me from above in a human voice, but in a tone most harsh and hideous; 'If I overhead here do not gnaw off these dry branches, Sir Noodle, what shall we have to roast you with, when midnight comes?' And with that it grinned, and made such a rattling with the branches, that my courser became mad with affright, and rushed furiously forward with me, before I had time to see distinctly what sort of a devil's beast it was."

"You must not speak so," said the old fisherman, crossing himself; his wife did the same, without saying a word; and Undine, while her eye sparkled with delight, looked at the knight, and said, "The best of the story is, however, that as yet they have not roasted you! Go on, now, you beautiful knight!"

UNDINE.

p. 24.

The knight then went on with his adventures: "My horse was so wild, that he well nigh rushed with me against limbs and trunks of trees. He was dripping with sweat, through terror, heat, and the violent straining of his muscles. Still he refused to slacken his career. At last, altogether beyond my control, he took his course directly up a stony steep; when suddenly a tall white man flashed before me, and threw himself athwart the way my mad steed was taking. At this apparition he shuddered with new affright, and stopped trembling. I took this chance of recovering my command of him, and now for the first time perceived that my deliverer, so far from being a white *man*, was only a brook of silver brightness, foaming near me in its descent from the hill, while it crossed and arrested my horse's course with its rush of waters."

"Thanks, thanks, dear Brook!" cried Undine, clapping her little hands. But the old man shook his head, and looked down in deep thought.

"Hardly had I well settled myself in my saddle, and got the reins in my grasp again," Huldbrand pursued, "when a wizard-like dwarf of a man was already standing at my side, diminutive and ugly beyond conception, his complexion of a brownish yellow, and his nose scarcely smaller than the rest of him together. The fellow's mouth was slit almost from ear to ear; and he shewed his teeth with a grinning smile of idiot courtesy; while he overwhelmed me with bows and scrapes innumerable. The farce now becoming excessively irksome, I thanked him in the fewest words I could well use, turned about my still trembling charger, and purposed either to seek another adventure, or, should I meet with none, to take my way back to the city; for the sun, during my wild chase, had passed the meridian, and was now hastening toward the west. But this villain of a dwarf sprang at the same instant, and, with a turn as rapid as lightning, stood before my horse again. 'Clear the way there!' I cried fiercely;

'the beast is wild, and will make nothing of running over you.'

"'Ay, ay!' cried the imp with a snarl, and snorting out a laugh still more frightfully idiotic; 'pay me, first pay what you owe me,—I stopped your fine little nag for you; without my help, both you and he would be now sprawling below there in that stony ravine. Hu! from what a horrible plunge I've saved you!'

"'Well, don't make any more faces,' said I, 'but take your money and be off, though every word you say is false. It was the brook there, you miserable thing, and not you, that saved me.'—And at the same time I dropped a piece of gold into his wizard cap, which he had taken from his head while he was begging before me.

"I then trotted off and left him; but he screamed after me; and on a sudden, with inconceivable quickness, he was close by my side. I started my horse into a gallop. He galloped on with me, though it seemed with great difficulty; and with a strange movement, half ludicrous and half horrible, forcing at the same time every limb and feature into distortion, he held up the gold piece, and screamed at every leap, 'Counterfeit! false! false coin! counterfeit!' and such was the strange sound that issued from his hollow breast, you would have supposed that at every scream he must have tumbled upon the ground dead. All this while, his disgusting red tongue hung lolling from his mouth.

"I stopped, bewildered, and asked, 'What do you mean by this screaming? Take another piece of gold,—take two, but leave me!'

"He then began again his hideous salutations of courtesy, and snarled out as before, 'Not gold, it shall not be gold, my young gentleman; I have too much of that trash already, as I will shew you in no time.'

"At that moment, and thought itself could not have been more instantaneous, I seemed to have acquired new powers of sight. I could see through the solid green plain, as if it were green glass, and the smooth surface of the earth were round as a globe; and within it I saw crowds of goblins, who were pursuing their pastime and making themselves merry with silver and gold. They were tumbling and rolling about, heads up and heads down; they pelted one another in sport with the precious metals, and with irritating malice blew gold-dust in one another's eyes. My odious companion ordered the others to reach him up a vast quantity of gold; this he shewed to me with a laugh, and then flung it again ringing and chinking down the measureless abyss.

"After this contemptuous disregard of gold, he held up the piece I had given him, shewing it to his brother goblins below; and they laughed immoderately at a coin so worthless, and hissed me. At last, raising their fingers all smutched with ore, they pointed them at me in scorn; and wilder and wilder, and thicker and thicker, and madder and madder, the crowd were clambering up to where I sat gazing at these wonders. Then terror seized me, as it had before seized my horse. I drove my spurs into his sides; and how far he rushed with me through the forest, during this second of my wild beats, it is impossible to say.

"At last, when I had now come to a dead halt again, the cool of evening was around me. I caught the gleam of a white footpath through the branches of the trees; and presuming it would lead me out of the forest toward the city, I was desirous of working my way into it. But a face perfectly white and indistinct, with features ever changing, kept thrusting itself out and peering at me between the leaves. I tried to avoid it; but, wherever I went, there too appeared the unearthly face. I was maddened with rage at this interruption, and determined to drive my steed at the appearance full tilt; when such a cloud of white foam came rushing upon me and my horse, that we were almost blinded, and glad to turn about and escape. Thus, from step to step, it forced us on, and ever aside from the footpath, leaving us, for the most part, only one direction open. When we advanced in this, it kept following close behind us, yet did not occasion the smallest harm or inconvenience.

"When at times I looked about me at the form, I perceived that the white face, which had splashed upon us its shower of foam, was resting on a body equally white, and of more than gigantic size. Many a time, too, I received the impression that the whole appearance was nothing more than a wandering stream or torrent; but respecting this I could never attain to any certainty. We both of us, horse and rider, became weary, as we shaped our course according to the movements of the white man, who continued nodding his head at us, as if he would say, 'Quite right!' And thus, at length, we came out here, at the edge of the wood, where I saw the fresh turf, the waters of the lake, and your little cottage, and where the tall white man disappeared."

"Well, Heaven be praised that he is gone!" cried the old fisherman; and he now began to talk of how his guest could most conveniently return to his friends in the city. Upon this, Undine began laughing to herself, but so very low, that the sound was hardly perceivable. Huldbrand observing it, said, "I thought you were glad to see me here; why, then, do you now appear so happy, when our talk turns upon my going away?"

"Because you cannot go away," answered Undine. "Pray make a single attempt; try with a boat, with your horse, or alone, as you please, to cross that forest-stream which has burst its bounds. Or rather, make no trial at all; for you would be dashed to pieces by the stones and trunks of trees which you see driven on with such violence. And as to the lake, I know that well; even my father dares not venture out with his boat far enough to help you."

Huldbrand rose, smiling, in order to look about and

observe whether the state of things were such as Undine had represented it to be. The old man accompanied him; and the maiden went merrily dancing beside them. They found all, in fact, just as Undine had said; and that the knight, whether willing or not willing, must submit to remaining on the island, so lately a peninsula, until the flood should subside.

When the three were now returning to the cottage after their ramble, the knight whispered in the ear of the little maiden, "Well, dear Undine, are you angry at my remaining?"

"Ah," she pettishly replied, "do not speak to me! If I had not bitten you, who knows what fine things you would have put into your story about Bertalda?"

CHAPTER III.

It may have happened to thee, my dear reader, after being much driven to and fro in the world, to reach at length a spot where all was well with thee. The love of home and of its peaceful joys, innate to all, again sprang up in thy heart; thou thoughtest that thy home was decked with all the flowers of childhood, and of that purest, deepest love which had grown upon the graves of thy beloved, and that here it was good to live and to build houses. Even if thou didst err, and hast had bitterly to mourn thy error, it is nothing to my purpose, and thou thyself wilt not like to dwell on the sad recollection. But recall those unspeakably sweet feelings, that angelic greeting of peace, and thou wilt be able to understand what was the happiness of the knight Huldbrand during his abode on that narrow slip of land.

He frequently observed, with heartfelt satisfaction, that the forest-stream continued every day to swell and roll on with a more impetuous sweep; and this forced him to prolong his stay on the island. Part of the day he wandered about with an old cross-bow, which he found in a corner of the cottage and had repaired, in order to shoot the water-fowl that flew over; and all that he was lucky enough to hit, he brought home for a good roast in the kitchen. When he came in with his booty, Undine seldom failed to greet him with a scolding, because he had cruelly deprived the happy joyous little creatures of life as they were sporting above in the blue ocean of the air; nay more, she often wept bitterly when she viewed the water-fowl dead in his hand. But at other times, when he returned without having shot any, she gave him a scolding equally serious, since, owing to his carelessness and want of skill, they must now put up with a dinner of fish. Her playful taunts ever touched his heart with delight; the more so, as she generally strove to make up for her pretended ill-humour with endearing caresses.

The old people saw with pleasure this familiarity of Undine and Huldbrand: they looked upon them as betrothed, or even as married, and living with them in their old age on their island, now torn off from the mainland. The loneliness of his situation strongly impressed also the young Huldbrand with the feeling that he was already Undine's bridegroom. It seemed to him as if, beyond those encompassing floods, there were no other world in existence, or at any rate as if he could never cross them, and again associate with the world of other men; and when at times his grazing steed raised his head and neighed to him, seemingly inquiring after his knightly achievements and reminding him of them, or when his coat-of-arms sternly shone upon him from the embroidery of his saddle and the caparisons of his horse, or when his sword happened to fall from the nail on which it was hanging in the cottage, and flashed on his eye as it slipped from the scabbard in its fall,—he quieted the doubts of his mind by saying to himself: "Undine cannot be a fisherman's daughter; she is, in all probability, a native of some remote region, and a member of some illustrious family."

There was one thing, indeed, to which he had a strong aversion: this was, to hear the old dame reproving Undine. The wild girl, it is true, commonly laughed at the reproof, making no attempt to conceal the extravagance of her mirth; but it appeared to him like touching his own honour; and still he found it impossible to blame the aged wife of the fisherman, since Undine always deserved at least ten times as many reproofs as she received: so he continued to feel in his heart an affectionate tenderness for the ancient mistress of the house, and his whole life flowed on in the calm stream of contentment.

There came, however, an interruption at last. The fisherman and the knight had been accustomed at dinner, and also in the evening when the wind roared without, as it rarely failed to do towards night, to enjoy together a flask of wine. But now their whole stock, which the fisherman had from time to time brought with him from the city, was at last exhausted, and they were both quite out of humour at the circumstance. That day Undine laughed at them excessively, but they were not disposed to join in her jests with the same gaiety as usual. Toward evening she went out of the cottage, to escape, as she said, the sight of two such long and tiresome faces.

While it was yet twilight, some appearances of a tempest seemed to be again mustering in the sky, and the waves already heaved and roared around them: the knight and the fisherman sprang to the door in terror, to bring home the maiden, remembering the anguish of that night when Huldbrand had first entered the cottage. But Undine met them at the same moment, clapping her little hands in high glee.

"What will you give me," she cried, "to provide you with wine? or rather, you need not give me any thing," she continued; "for I am already satisfied, if you look more cheerful, and are in better spirits, than throughout this last most wearisome day. Only come with me; the forest-stream has driven ashore a cask; and I will be condemned to sleep through a whole week, if it is not a wine-cask."

The men followed her, and actually found, in a bushy cove of the shore, a cask, which inspired them with as much joy as if they were sure it contained the generous old wine for which they were thirsting. They first of all, and with as much expedition as possible, rolled it toward the cottage; for heavy clouds were again rising in the west, and they could discern the waves of the lake in the fading light lifting their white foaming heads, as if looking out for the rain, which threatened every instant to pour upon them. Undine helped the men as much as she was able; and as the shower, with a roar of wind, came suddenly sweeping on in rapid pursuit, she raised her finger with a merry menace toward the dark mass of clouds, and cried:

"You cloud, you cloud, have a care!—beware how you wet us; we are some way from shelter yet."

The old man reproved her for this sally, as a sinful presumption; but she laughed to herself softly, and no mischief came from her wild behaviour. Nay more, what was beyond their expectation, they reached their comfortable hearth unwet, with their prize secured; but the cask had hardly been broached, and proved to contain wine of a remarkably fine flavour, when the rain first poured unrestrained from the black cloud, the tempest raved through the tops of the trees, and swept far over the billows of the deep.

Having immediately filled several bottles from the cask, which promised them a supply for a long time, they drew round the glowing hearth; and, comfortably secured from the tempest, they sat tasting the flavour of their wine and bandying jests.

But the old fisherman suddenly became extremely grave, and said: "Ah, great God! here we sit, rejoicing over this rich gift, while he to whom it first belonged, and from whom it was wrested by the fury of the stream, must there also, it is more than probable, have lost his life."

"No such thing," said Undine, smiling, as she filled the knight's cup to the brim.

But he exclaimed: "By my unsullied honour, old father, if I knew where to find and rescue him, no fear of exposure to the night, nor any peril, should deter me from making the attempt. At least, I can promise you that if I again reach an inhabited country, I will find out the owner of this wine or his heirs, and make double and triple reimbursement."

The old man was gratified with this assurance; he gave the knight a nod of approbation, and now drained his cup with an easier conscience and more relish.

Undine, however, said to Huldbrand: "As to the repayment and your gold, you may do whatever you like. But what you said about your venturing out, and searching, and exposing yourself to danger, appears to me far from wise. I should cry my very eyes out, should you perish in such a wild attempt; and is it not true that you would prefer staying here with me and the good wine?"

"Most assuredly," answered Huldbrand, smiling.

"Then, you see," replied Undine, "you spoke unwisely. For charity begins at home; and why need we trouble ourselves about our neighbours?"

The mistress of the house turned away from her, sighing and shaking her head; while the fisherman forgot his wonted indulgence toward the graceful maiden, and thus rebuked her:

"That sounds exactly as if you had been brought up by heathens and Turks;" and he finished his reproof by adding, "May God forgive both me and you,—unfeeling child!"

"Well, say what you will, that is what *I* think and feel," replied Undine, "whoever brought me up; and all your talking cannot help it."

"Silence!" exclaimed the fisherman, in a voice of stern rebuke; and she, who with all her wild spirit was extremely alive to fear, shrunk from him, moved close up to Huldbrand, trembling, and said very softly:

"Are you also angry, dear friend?"

The knight pressed her soft hand, and tenderly stroked her locks. He was unable to utter a word, for his vexation, arising from the old man's severity toward Undine, closed his lips; and thus the two couple sat opposite to each other, at once heated with anger and in embarrassed silence.

In the midst of this stillness a low knocking at the door startled them all; for there are times when a slight circumstance, coming unexpectedly upon us, startles us like something supernatural. But there was the further source of alarm, that the enchanted forest lay so near them, and that their place of abode seemed at present inaccessible to any human being. While they were looking upon one another in doubt, the knocking was again heard, accompanied with a deep groan. The knight sprang to seize his sword. But the old man said, in a low whisper:

"If it be what I fear it is, no weapon of yours can protect us."

Undine in the mean while went to the door, and cried with the firm voice of fearless displeasure: "Spirits of the earth! if mischief be your aim, Kühleborn shall teach you better manners."

The terror of the rest was increased by this wild speech; they looked fearfully upon the girl, and Huldbrand was just recovering presence of mind enough to ask what she meant, when a voice reached them from without:

"I am no spirit of the earth, though a spirit still in its earthly body. You that are within the cottage there, if you fear God and would afford me assistance, open your door to me."

By the time these words were spoken, Undine had already opened it; and the lamp throwing a strong light upon the stormy night, they perceived an aged priest without, who stepped back in terror, when his eye fell on the unexpected sight of a little damsel of such exquisite beauty. Well might he think there must be magic in the wind, and witchcraft at work, when a form of such surpassing loveliness appeared at the door of so humble a dwelling. So he lifted up his voice in prayer:

"Let all good spirits praise the Lord God!"

"I am no spectre," said Undine, with a smile. "Do I look so very frightful? And you see that I do not shrink from holy words. I too have knowledge of God, and understand the duty of praising him; every one, to be sure, has his own way of doing this, for so He has created us. Come in, father; you will find none but worthy people here."

The holy man came bowing in, and cast round a glance of scrutiny, wearing at the same time a very placid and venerable air. But water was dropping from every fold of his dark garments, from his long white beard and the white locks of his hair. The fisherman and the knight took him to another apartment, and furnished him with a change of raiment, while they gave his own clothes to the women to dry. The aged stranger thanked them in a manner the most humble and courteous; but on the knight's offering him his splendid cloak to wrap round him, he could not be persuaded to take it, but chose instead an old grey coat that belonged to the fisherman.

They then returned to the common apartment. The mistress of the house immediately offered her great chair to the priest, and continued urging it upon him till she saw him fairly in possession of it. "You are old and exhausted," said she, "and are, moreover, a man of God."

Undine shoved under the stranger's feet her little stool, on which at all other times she used to sit near to Huldbrand, and shewed herself most gentle and amiable towards the old man. Huldbrand whispered some raillery in her ear, but she replied gravely:

"He is a minister of that Being who created us all; and holy things are not to be treated with lightness."

The knight and the fisherman now refreshed the priest with food and wine; and when he had somewhat recovered his strength and spirits, he began to relate how he had the day before set out from his cloister, which was situated far off beyond the great lake, in order to visit the bishop, and acquaint him with the distress into which the cloister and its tributary villages had fallen, owing to the extraordinary floods. After a long and wearisome wandering, on account of the rise of the waters, he had been this day compelled toward evening to procure the aid of a couple of boatmen, and cross over an arm of the lake which had burst its usual boundary.

"But hardly," continued he, "had our small ferry-boat touched the waves, when that furious tempest burst forth which is still raging over our heads. It seemed as if the billows had been waiting our approach only to rush on us with a madness the more wild. The oars were wrested from the grasp of my men in an instant; and shivered by the resistless force, they drove farther and farther out before us upon the waves. Unable to direct our course, we yielded to the blind power of nature, and seemed to fly over the surges toward your distant shore, which we already saw looming through the mist and foam of the deep. Then it was at last that our boat turned short from its course, and rocked with a motion that became more and more wild and dizzy: I know not whether it was overset, or the violence of the motion threw me overboard. In my agony and struggle at the thought of a near and terrible death, the waves bore me onward, till I was cast ashore here beneath the trees of your island."

"Yes, an island!" cried the fisherman; "a short time ago it was only a point of land. But now, since the forest-stream and lake have become all but mad, it appears to be entirely changed."

"I observed something of it," replied the priest, "as I

stole along the shore in the obscurity; and hearing nothing around me but a sort of wild uproar, I perceived at last that the noise came from a point, exactly where a beaten footpath disappeared. I now caught the light in your cottage, and ventured hither, where I cannot sufficiently thank my heavenly Father, that, after preserving me from the waters, He has also conducted me to such pious people as you are; and the more so, as it is difficult to say whether I shall ever behold any other persons in this world except you four."

"What mean you by those words?" asked the fisherman.

"Can you tell me, then, how long this commotion of the elements will last?" replied the priest. "I am old; the stream of my life may easily sink into the ground and vanish, before the overflowing of that forest-stream shall subside. And, indeed, it is not impossible that more and more of the foaming waters may rush in between you and yonder forest, until you are so far removed from the rest of the world, that your small fishing-canoe may be incapable of passing over, and the inhabitants of the continent entirely forget you in your old age amid the dissipation and diversions of life."

At this melancholy foreboding the old lady shrank back with a feeling of alarm, crossed herself, and cried, "God forbid!"

But the fisherman looked upon her with a smile, and said, "What a strange being is man! Suppose the worst to happen: our state would not be different, at any rate your own would not, dear wife, from what it is at present. For have you, these many years, been farther from home than the border of the forest? And have you seen a single human being beside Undine and myself? It is now only a short time since the coming of the knight and the priest. They will remain with us, even if we do become a forgotten island; so, after all, you will be a gainer."

"I know not," replied the ancient dame; "it is a dismal thought, when brought fairly home to the mind, that we are for ever separated from mankind, even though in fact we never do know nor see them."

"Then *you* will remain with us—then you will remain with us!" whispered Undine, in a voice scarcely audible and half-singing, while she nestled closer to Huldbrand's side. But he was immersed in the deep and strange musings of his own mind. The region, on the farther side of the forest-river, seemed, since the last words of the priest, to have been withdrawing farther and farther, in dim perspective, from his view; and the blooming island on which he lived grew green and smiled more freshly in his fancy. His bride glowed like the fairest rose, not of this obscure nook only, but even of the whole wide world; and the priest was now present.

Added to which, the mistress of the family was directing an angry glance at Undine, because, even in the presence of the priest, she leant so fondly on the knight; and it seemed as if she was on the point of breaking out in harsh reproof. Then burst forth from the mouth of Huldbrand, as he turned to the priest, "Father, you here see before you an affianced pair; and if this maiden and these good old people have no objection, you shall unite us this very evening."

The aged couple were both exceedingly surprised. They had often, it is true, thought of this, but as yet they had never mentioned it; and now when the knight spoke, it came upon them like something wholly new and unexpected. Undine became suddenly grave, and looked down thoughtfully, while the priest made inquiries respecting the circumstances of their acquaintance, and asked the old people whether they gave their consent to the union. After a great number of questions and answers, the affair was arranged to the satisfaction of all; and the mistress of the house went to prepare the bridal apartment for the young couple, and also, with a view to grace the nuptial solemnity, to seek for two consecrated tapers, which she had for a long time kept by her, for this occasion.

The knight in the mean while busied himself about his golden chain, for the purpose of disengaging two of its links, that he might make an exchange of rings with his bride. But when she saw his object, she started from her trance of musing, and exclaimed,—

"Not so! my parents by no means sent me into the world so perfectly destitute; on the contrary, they foresaw, even at that early period, that such a night as this would come."

Thus speaking, she went out of the room, and a moment after returned with two costly rings, of which she gave one to her bridegroom, and kept the other for herself. The old fisherman was beyond measure astonished at this; and his wife, who was just re-entering the room, was even more surprised than he, that neither of them had ever seen these jewels in the child's possession.

"My parents," said Undine, "sewed these trinkets to that beautiful raiment which I wore the very day I came to you. They also charged me on no account whatever to mention them to any one before my wedding evening. At the time of my coming, therefore, I took them off in secret, and have kept them concealed to the present hour."

The priest now cut short all further questioning and wondering, while he lighted the consecrated tapers, placed them on a table, and ordered the bridal pair to stand opposite to him. He then pronounced the few solemn words of the ceremony, and made them one. The elder couple gave the younger their blessing; and the bride, gently trembling and thoughtful, leaned upon the knight.

The priest then spoke out: "You are strange people, after all; for why did you tell me that you were the only inhabitants of the island? So far is this from being true, I have seen, the whole time I was performing the ceremony, a tall, stately man, in a white mantle, standing opposite to me, looking in at the window. He must be still waiting before the door, if peradventure you would invite him to come in."

"God forbid!" cried the old lady, shrinking back; the fisherman shook his head, without opening his lips; and Huldbrand sprang to the window. It seemed to *him* that he could still discern a white streak, which soon disappeared in the gloom. He convinced the priest that he must have been mistaken in his impression; and they all sat down together round a bright and comfortable hearth.

CHAPTER IV.

Before the nuptial ceremony, and during its performance, Undine had shewn a modest gentleness and maidenly reserve; but it now seemed as if all the wayward freaks that effervesced within her burst forth with an extravagance only the more bold and unrestrained. She teased her bridegroom, her foster-parents, and even the priest, whom she had just now revered so highly, with all sorts of childish tricks; but when the ancient dame was about to reprove her too frolicsome spirit, the knight, in a few words, imposed silence upon her by speaking of Undine as his wife.

The knight was himself, indeed, just as little pleased with Undine's childish behaviour as the rest; but all his looks and half-reproachful words were to no purpose. It is true, whenever the bride observed the dissatisfaction of her husband,—and this occasionally happened,—she became more quiet, placed herself beside him, stroked his face with caressing fondness, whispered something smilingly in his ear, and in this manner smoothed the wrinkles that were gathering on his brow. But the moment after, some wild whim would make her resume her antic movements; and all went worse than before.

The priest then spoke in a kind although serious tone: "My fair young maiden, surely no one can look on you without pleasure; but remember betimes so to attune your soul, that it may produce a harmony ever in accordance with the soul of your wedded bridegroom."

"SOUL!" cried Undine, with a laugh. "What you say has a remarkably pretty sound; and for most people, too, it may be a very instructive and profitable caution. But when a person has no soul at all, how, I pray you, can such attuning be then possible? And this, in truth, is just my condition."

The priest was much hurt, but continued silent in holy displeasure, and turned away his face from the maiden in sorrow. She, however, went up to him with the most winning sweetness, and said:

"Nay, I entreat you, first listen to me, before you are angry with me; for your anger is painful to me, and you ought not to give pain to a creature that has not hurt you. Only have patience with me, and I will explain to you every word of what I meant."

It was evident that she had come to say something important; when she suddenly faltered, as if seized with an inward shuddering, and burst into a passion of tears. They were none of them able to understand the intenseness of her feelings; and, with mingled emotions of fear and anxiety, they gazed on her in silence. Then wiping away her tears, and looking earnestly at the priest, she at last said:

"There must be something lovely, but at the same time something most awful, about a SOUL. In the name of God, holy man, were it not better that we never shared a gift so mysterious?"

Again she paused, and restrained her tears, as if waiting for an answer. All in the cottage had risen from their seats, and stepped back from her with horror. She, however, seemed to have eyes for no one but the holy man; an awful curiosity was painted on her features, which appeared terrible to the others.

"Heavily must the soul weigh down its possessor," she pursued, when no one returned her any answer—"very heavily!—for already its approaching image overshadows me with anguish and mourning. And, alas, I have till now been so merry and light-hearted!"—And she burst into another flood of tears, and covered her face with her veil.

The priest, going up to her with a solemn look, now addressed himself to her, and conjured her by the name of God most holy, if any spirit of evil possessed her, to remove the light covering from her face. But she sank before him on her knees, and repeated after him every sacred expression he uttered, giving praise to God, and protesting "that she wished well to the whole world."

The priest then spoke to the knight: "Sir bridegroom, I leave you alone with her whom I have united to you in marriage. So far as I can discover, there is nothing of evil in her, but assuredly much that is wonderful. What I recommend to you is—prudence, love, and fidelity."

Thus speaking, he left the apartment; and the fisherman, with his wife, followed him, crossing themselves.

Undine had sunk upon her knees. She uncovered her face, and exclaimed, while she looked fearfully round upon Huldbrand, "Alas! you will now refuse to look upon me as your own; and still I have done nothing evil, poor unhappy child that I am!" She spoke these words with a look so infinitely sweet and touching, that her bridegroom forgot both the confession that had shocked and the mystery that had perplexed him; and hastening to her, he raised her in his arms. She smiled through her tears; and that smile was like the morning light playing upon a small stream. "You cannot desert me!" she whispered, confidingly, and stroked the knight's cheeks with her little soft hands. He turned away from the frightful thoughts that still lurked in the recesses of his soul, and were persuading him that he had been married to a fairy, or some spiteful and mischievous being of the spirit-world. Only this single question, and .that almost unawares, escaped from his lips:

"Dearest Undine, tell me this one thing: what was it you meant by 'spirits of earth' and 'Kühleborn,' when the priest stood knocking at the door?"

"Tales! mere tales of children!" answered Undine, laughing, now quite restored to her wonted gaiety. "I first frightened you with them, and you frightened me. This is the end of the story and of our nuptial evening."

"Nay, not so," replied the enamoured knight, extinguishing the tapers, and a thousand times kissing his beautiful and beloved bride; while, lighted by the moon that shone brightly through the windows, he bore her into their bridal apartment.

The fresh light of morning awoke the young married pair; but Huldbrand lay lost in silent reflection. Whenever during the night he had fallen asleep, strange and horrible dreams of spectres had disturbed him; and these shapes, grinning at him by stealth, strove to disguise themselves as beautiful females; and from beautiful females they all at once assumed the appearance of dragons. And when he started up, aroused by the intrusion of these hideous forms, the moonlight shone pale and cold before the windows without. He looked affrighted at Undine, in whose arms he had fallen asleep; and she was reposing in unaltered beauty and sweetness beside him. Then pressing her rosy lips with a light kiss, he again fell into a slumber, only to be awakened by new terrors.

When fully awake, he had thought over this connexion. He reproached himself for any doubt that could lead him into error in regard to his lovely wife. He also confessed to her his injustice; but she only gave him her fair hand, sighed deeply, and remained silent. Yet a glance of fervent tenderness, an expression of the soul beaming in her eyes, such as he had never witnessed there before, left him in undoubting assurance that Undine bore him no ill-will.

He then rose joyfully, and, leaving her, went to the common apartment, where the inmates of the house had already met. The three were sitting round the hearth with an air of anxiety about them, as if they feared trusting themselves to raise their voice above a low, apprehensive undertone. The priest appeared to be praying in his inmost spirit, with a view to avert some fatal calamity. But when they observed the young husband come forth so cheerful, they dispelled the cloud that remained upon their brows: the old fisherman even began to laugh with the knight, till his aged wife herself could not help smiling with great good-humour.

Undine had in the mean time got ready, and now entered the room; all rose to meet her, but remained fixed in perfect admiration—she was so changed, and yet the same. The priest, with paternal affection beaming from his countenance, first went up to her; and as he raised his hand to pronounce a blessing, the beautiful bride sank on her knees before him with religious awe; she begged his pardon in terms both respectful and submissive for any foolish things she might have uttered the evening before, and entreated him with emotion to pray for the welfare of her soul. She then rose, kissed her foster-parents, and, after thanking them for all the kindness they had shewn her, said:

"O, I now feel in my inmost heart how much, how infinitely much, you have done for me, you dear, dear friends of my childhood!"

At first she was wholly unable to tear herself away from their affectionate caresses; but the moment she saw the good old mother busy in getting breakfast, she went to the hearth, applied herself to cooking the food and putting it on the table, and would not suffer her to take the least share in the work.

She continued in this frame of spirit the whole day: calm, kind, attentive—half matronly and half girlish. The three who had been longest acquainted with her expected every instant to see her capricious spirit break out in some whimsical change or sportive vagary. But their fears were quite unnecessary. Undine continued as mild and gentle as an angel. The priest found it all but impossible to remove his eyes from her; and he often said to the bridegroom:

"The bounty of Heaven, sir, through me its unworthy instrument, entrusted to you yesterday an invaluable treasure; cherish it as you ought, and it will promote your temporal and eternal welfare."

Toward evening Undine was hanging upon the knight's arm with lowly tenderness, while she drew him gently out before the door, where the setting sun shone richly over the fresh grass, and upon the high, slender boles of the trees. Her emotion was visible: the dew of sadness and love swam in her eyes, while a tender and fearful secret seemed to hover upon her lips, but was only made known by hardly breathed sighs. She led her husband farther and farther onward without speaking. When he asked her questions, she replied only with looks, in which, it is true, there appeared to be no immediate answer to his inquiries, but a whole heaven of love and timid devotion. Thus they reached the margin of the swollen forest-stream, and the knight was astonished to see it gliding away with so gentle a murmuring of its waves, that no vestige of its former swell and wildness was now discernible.

"By morning it will be wholly drained off," said the beautiful wife, almost weeping, "and you will then be able to travel, without any thing to hinder you, withersoever you will."

"Not without you, dear Undine," replied the knight, laughing; "think, only, were I disposed to leave you, both the church and the spiritual powers, the emperor and the laws of the realm, would require the fugitive to be seized and restored to you."

"All this depends on you—all depends on you," whispered his little companion, half weeping and half smiling. "But I still feel sure that you will not leave me; I love you too deeply to fear that misery. Now bear me over to that little island which lies before us. There shall the decision be made. I could easily, indeed, glide through that mere rippling of the water without your aid, but it is so sweet to lie in your arms; and should you determine to put me away, I shall have rested in them once more, ... for the last time."

Huldbrand was so full of strange anxiety and emotion, that he knew not what answer to make her. He took her in his arms and carried her over, now first realising the fact, that this was the same little island from which he had borne her back to the old fisherman, the first night of his arrival. On the farther side, he placed her upon the soft grass, and was throwing himself lovingly near his beautiful burden; but she said to him, "Not here, but opposite me. I shall read my doom in your eyes, even before your lips pronounce it: now listen attentively to what I shall relate to you." And she began:

"You must know, my own love, that there are beings in the elements which bear the strongest resemblance to the human race, and which, at the same time, but seldom become visible to you. The wonderful salamanders sparkle and sport amid the flames; deep in the earth the meagre and malicious gnomes pursue their revels; the forest-spirits belong to the air, and wander in the woods; while in the seas, rivers, and streams, live the wide-spread race of water-spirits. These last, beneath resounding domes of crystal, through which the sky can shine with its sun and stars, inhabit a region of light and beauty; lofty coral-trees glow with blue and crimson fruits in their gardens; they walk over the pure sand of the sea, among exquisitely variegated shells, and amid whatever of beauty the old world possessed, such as the present is no more worthy to enjoy—creations which the floods covered with their secret veils of silver; and now these noble monuments sparkle below, stately and solemn, and bedewed by the water, which loves them, and calls forth from their crevices delicate moss-flowers and enwreathing tufts of sedge.

"Now the nation that dwell there are very fair and lovely to behold, for the most part more beautiful than human beings. Many a fisherman has been so fortunate as to catch a view of a delicate maiden of the waters, while she was floating and singing upon the deep. He would then spread far the fame of her beauty; and to such wonderful females men are wont to give the name of Undines. But what need of saying more?—You, my dear husband, now actually behold an Undine before you."

The knight would have persuaded himself that his lovely wife was under the influence of one of her odd whims, and that she was only amusing herself and him with her extravagant inventions. He wished it might be so. But with whatever emphasis he said this to himself, he still could not credit the hope for a moment: a strange shivering shot through his soul; unable to utter a word, he gazed upon the sweet speaker with a fixed eye. She shook her head in distress, sighed from her full heart, and then proceeded in the following manner:

"We should be far superior to you, who are another race of the human family,—for we also call ourselves human beings, as we resemble them in form and features,—had we not one evil peculiar to ourselves. Both we and the beings I have mentioned as inhabiting the other elements, vanish into air at death and go out of existence, spirit and body, so that no vestige of us remains; and when you hereafter awake to a purer state of being, we shall remain where sand, and sparks, and wind, and waves remain. Thus we have no souls; the element moves us, and, again, is obedient to our will, while we live, though it scatters us like dust when we die; and as we have nothing to trouble us, we are as merry as nightingales, little gold-fishes, and other pretty children of nature.

"But all beings aspire to rise in the scale of existence

higher than they are. It was therefore the wish of my father, who is a powerful water-prince in the Mediterranean Sea, that his only daughter should become possessed of a soul, although she should have to endure many of the sufferings of those who share that gift.

"Now the race to which I belong have no other means of obtaining a soul than by forming with an individual of your own the most intimate union of love. I am now possessed of a soul, and my soul thanks you, my best beloved, and never shall cease to thank you, if you do not render my whole future life miserable. For what will become of me, if you avoid and reject me? Still I would not keep you as my own by artifice. And should you decide to cast me off, then do it now, and return alone to the shore. I will plunge into this brook, where my uncle will receive me; my uncle, who here in the forest, far removed from his other friends, passes his strange and solitary existence. But he is powerful, as well as revered and beloved by many great rivers; and as he brought me hither to the fisherman a light-hearted and laughing child, he will take me home to my parents a woman, gifted with a soul, with power to love and to suffer."

She was about to add something more, when Huldbrand, with the most heartfelt tenderness and love, clasped her in his arms, and again bore her back to the shore. There, amid tears and kisses, he first swore never to forsake his affectionate wife, and esteemed himself even more happy than Pygmalion, for whom Venus gave life to his beautiful statue, and thus changed it into a beloved wife. Supported by his arm, and in the confidence of affection, Undine returned to the cottage; and now she first realised with her whole heart how little cause she had for regretting what she had left—the crystal palaces of her mysterious father.

CHAPTER V.

NEXT morning, when Huldbrand awoke from slumber, and perceived that his beautiful wife was not by his side, he began to give way again to his wild imaginations,—that his marriage, and even the lovely Undine herself, were only shadows without substance—only mere illusions of enchantment. But she entered the door at the same moment, kissed him, seated herself on the bed by his side, and said:

"I have been out somewhat early this morning, to see whether my uncle keeps his word. He has already restored the waters of the flood to his own calm channel, and he now flows through the forest a rivulet as before, in a lonely and dreamlike current. His friends, too, both of the water and the air, have resumed their usual peaceful tenour; all will again proceed with order and tranquillity; and you can travel homeward, without fear of the flood, whenever you choose."

It seemed to the mind of Huldbrand that he must be in some waking dream, so little was he able to understand the nature of his wife's strange relative. Notwithstanding this, he made no remark upon what she had told him, and her surpassing loveliness soon lulled every misgiving and discomfort to rest.

Some time afterward, while he was standing with her before the door, and surveying the verdant point of land, with its boundary of bright waters, such a feeling of bliss came over him in this cradle of his love, that he exclaimed:

"Shall we, then, so early as to-day begin our journey? Why should we? It is probable that abroad in the world we shall find no days more delightful than those we have spent in this green isle so secret and so secure. Let us yet see the sun go down here two or three times more."

"Just as my lord wills," replied Undine meekly. "Only we must remember, that my foster-parents will, at all events, see me depart with pain; and should they now, for the first time, discover the true soul in me, and how fervently I can now love and honour them, their feeble eyes would surely become blind with weeping. As yet they consider my present quietness and gentleness as of no better promise than they were formerly,—like the calm of the lake just while the air remains tranquil,—and they will learn soon to cherish a little tree or flower as they have cherished me. Let me not, then, make known to them this newly bestowed, this loving heart, at the very moment they must lose it for this world; and how could I conceal what I have gained, if we continued longer together?"

Huldbrand yielded to her representation, and went to the aged couple to confer with them respecting his journey, on which he proposed to set out that very hour. The priest offered himself as a companion to the young married pair; and, after taking a short farewell, he held the bridle, while the knight lifted his beautiful wife upon his horse; and with rapid step they crossed the dry channel with her toward the forest. Undine wept in silent but intense emotion; the old people, as she moved away, were more clamorous in the expression of their grief. They appeared to feel, at the moment of separation, all that they were losing in their affectionate foster-daughter.

The three travellers had reached the thickest shades of the forest without interchanging a word. It must have been a fair sight, in that hall of leafy verdure, to see this lovely woman's form sitting on the noble and richly ornamented steed, on her right hand the venerable priest in the white garb of his order, on her left the blooming young knight, clad in splendid raiment of scarlet, gold, and violet, girt with a sword that flashed in the sun, and attentively walking beside her. Huldbrand had no eyes but for his wife; Undine, who had dried her tears of tenderness, had no eyes but for him; and they soon entered into the still and voiceless converse of looks and gestures, from which, after some time, they were awakened by the low discourse which the priest was holding with a fourth traveller, who had meanwhile joined them unobserved.

He wore a white gown, resembling in form the dress of the priests' order, except that his hood hung very low over his face, and that the whole drapery floated in such wide folds around him as obliged him every moment to gather it up and throw it over his arm, or by some management of this sort to get it out of his way, and still it did not seem in the least to impede his movements. When the young couple became aware of his presence, he was saying:

"And so, venerable sir, many as have been the years I have dwelt here in this forest, I have never received the name of hermit in your sense of the word. For, as I said before, I know nothing of penance, and I think, too, that I have no particular need of it. Do you ask me why I am so attached to the forest? It is because its scenery is so peculiarly picturesque, and affords me so much pastime when, in my floating white garments, I pass through its world of leaves and dusky shadows;—and when a sweet sunbeam glances down upon me, at times, unexpectedly."

"You are a very singular man," replied the priest, "and I should like to have a more intimate acquaintance with you."

"And who, then, may you be yourself, to pass from one thing to another?" inquired the stranger.

"I am called Father Heilmann," answered the holy man; "and I am from the cloister of Our Lady of the Salutation, beyond the lake."

"Well, well," replied the stranger, "my name is Kühleborn; and were I a stickler for the nice distinctions of rank, I might, with equal propriety, require you to give me the title of noble lord of Kühleborn, or free lord of Kühleborn; for I am as free as the birds in the forest, and, it may be, a trifle more so. For example, I now have something to tell that young lady there." And before they were aware of his purpose, he was on the other side of the priest, close to Undine, and stretching himself high into the air, in order to whisper something in her ear. But she shrunk from him in terror, and exclaimed:

"I have nothing more to do with you."

"Ho, ho," cried the stranger, with a laugh, "you have made a grand marriage indeed, since you no longer know your own relations! Have you no recollection, then, of your uncle Kühleborn, who so faithfully bore you on his back to this region?"

"However that may be," replied Undine, "I entreat you never to appear in my presence again. I am now afraid of you; and will not my husband fear and forsake me, if he sees me associate with such strange company and kindred?"

"You must not forget, my little niece," said Kühleborn, "that I am with you here as a guide; otherwise those madcap spirits of the earth, the gnomes that haunt this forest, would play you some of their mischievous pranks. Let me therefore still accompany you in peace. Even the old priest there had a better recollection of me than you appear to have; for he just now assured me that I seemed to be very familiar to him, and that I must have been with him in the ferry-boat, out of which he tumbled into the waves. He certainly did see me there; for I was no other than the water-spout that tore him out of it, and kept him from sinking, while I safely wafted him ashore to your wedding."

Undine and the knight turned their eyes upon Father Heilmann; but he appeared to be moving forward, just as if he were dreaming or walking in his sleep, and no longer to be conscious of a word that was spoken. Undine then said to Kühleborn: "I already see yonder the end of the forest. We have no further need of your assistance, and nothing now gives us alarm but yourself. I therefore beseech you, by our mutual love and good-will, to vanish, and allow us to proceed in peace."

Kühleborn seemed to become angry at this: he darted a frightful look at Undine, and grinned fiercely upon her. She shrieked aloud, and called her husband to protect her. The knight sprung round the horse as quick as lightning, and, brandishing his sword, struck at Kühleborn's head. But, instead of severing it from his body, the sword merely flashed through a torrent, which rushed foaming near them from a lofty cliff; and with a splash, which much resembled in sound a burst of laughter, the stream all at once poured upon them, and gave them a thorough wetting. The priest, as if suddenly awaking from a trance, coolly observed: "This is what I have been some time expecting, because the brook has descended from the steep so close beside us,—though at first sight, indeed, it appeared to resemble a man, and to possess the power of speech."

As the waterfall came rushing from its crag, it distinctly uttered these words in Huldbrand's ear: "Rash knight! valiant knight! I am not angry with you; I have no quarrel with you; only continue to defend your lovely little wife with the same spirit, you bold knight! you valiant champion!"

After advancing a few steps farther, the travellers came out upon open ground. The imperial city lay bright before them; and the evening sun, which gilded its towers with gold, kindly dried their garments that had been so completely drenched.

The sudden disappearance of the young knight, Huldbrand of Ringstetten, had occasioned much remark in the imperial city, and no small concern amongst those who, as well on account of his expertness in tourney and dance as of his mild and amiable manners, had become attached to him. His attendants were unwilling to quit the place without their master, although not a soul of them had been courageous enough to follow him into the fearful recesses of the forest. They remained, therefore, at the hostelry, idly hoping, as men are wont to do, and keeping the fate of their lost lord fresh in remembrance by their lamentations.

Now when the violent storms and floods had been observed immediately after his departure, the destruction of the handsome stranger became all but certain; even Bertalda had openly discovered her sorrow, and detested herself for having been the cause of his taking that fatal excursion into the forest. Her foster-parents, the duke and duchess, had meanwhile come to take her away; but Bertalda persuaded them to remain with her until some certain news of Huldbrand should be obtained, whether he were living or dead. She endeavoured also to prevail upon several young knights, who were assiduous in courting her favour, to go in quest of the noble adventurer in the forest. But she refused to pledge her hand as the reward of the enterprise, because she still cherished, it might be, a hope of its being claimed by the returning knight; and no one would consent, for a glove, a riband, or even a kiss, to expose his life to bring back so very dangerous a rival.

When Huldbrand now made his sudden and unexpected appearance, his attendants, the inhabitants of the city, and almost every one, rejoiced. This was not the case with Bertalda; for although it might be quite a welcome event to others that he brought with him a wife of such exquisite loveliness, and Father Heilmann as a witness of their marriage, Bertalda could not but view the affair with grief and vexation. She had, in truth, become attached to the young knight with her whole soul; and her mourning for his absence, or supposed death, had shewn this more than she could now have wished.

But notwithstanding all this, she conducted herself like a wise maiden in circumstances of such delicacy, and lived on the most friendly terms with Undine, whom the whole city looked upon as a princess that Huldbrand had rescued in the forest from some evil enchantment. Whenever any one questioned either herself or her husband relative to surmises of this nature, they had wisdom enough to remain silent, or wit enough to evade the inquiries. The lips of Father Heilmann had been sealed in regard to idle gossip of every kind; and besides, on Huldbrand's arrival, he had immediately returned to his cloister: so that people were obliged to rest contented with their own wild conjectures; and even Bertalda herself ascertained nothing more of the truth than others.

For the rest, Undine daily felt more love for the fair maiden. "We must have been before acquainted with each other," she often used to say to her, "or else there must be some mysterious connexion between us; for it is incredible that any one so perfectly without cause—I mean, without some deep and secret cause—should be so fondly attached to another as I have been to you from the first moment of our meeting."

And even Bertalda could not deny that she felt a confiding impulse, an attraction of tenderness, toward Undine, much as she deemed this fortunate rival the cause of her bitterest disappointment. Under the influence of this mutual regard, they found means to persuade, the one her foster-parents, and the other her husband, to defer the day of separation to a period more and more remote; nay more, they had already begun to talk of a plan for Bertalda's accompanying Undine to Castle Ringstetten, near one of the sources of the Danube.

Once on a fine evening they happened to be talking over their scheme just as they passed the high trees that bordered the public walk. The young married pair, though it was somewhat late, had called upon Bertalda to invite her to share their enjoyment; and all three proceeded familiarly up and down beneath the dark blue heaven, not seldom interrupted in their converse by the admiration which they could not but bestow upon the magnificent fountain in the middle of the square, and upon the wonderful rush and shooting upward of its water. All was sweet and soothing to their minds. Among the shadows of the trees stole in glimmerings of light from the adjacent houses. A low murmur as of children at play, and of other persons who were enjoying their walk, floated around them—they were so alone, and yet sharing so much of social happiness in the bright and stirring world, that whatever had appeared rough by day, now became smooth of its own accord. And the three friends could no longer see the slightest cause for hesitation in regard to Bertalda's taking the journey.

At that instant, while they were just fixing the day of their departure, a tall man approached them from the middle of the square, bowed respectfully to the company, and spoke something in the young bride's ear. Though displeased with the interruption and its cause, she walked aside a few steps with the stranger; and both began to whisper, as it seemed, in a foreign tongue. Huldbrand thought he recognised the strange man of the forest; and he gazed upon him so fixedly, that he neither heard nor answered the astonished inquiries of Bertalda. All at once Undine clapped her hands with delight, and turned back from the stranger, laughing: he, frequently shaking his head, retired with a hasty step and discontented air, and descended into the fountain. Huldbrand now felt perfectly certain that his conjecture was correct. But Bertalda asked:

"What, then, dear Undine, did the master of the fountain wish to say to you?"

Undine laughed within herself, and made answer: "The day after to-morrow, my dear child, when the anniversary of your name-day returns, you shall be informed." And this was all she could be prevailed upon to disclose. She merely asked Bertalda to dinner on the appointed day, and requested her to invite her foster-parents; and soon afterward they separated.

"Kühleborn?" said Huldbrand to his lovely wife, with an inward shudder, when they had taken leave of Bertalda, and were now going home through the darkening streets.

"Yes, it was he," answered Undine; "and he would have wearied me with his foolish warnings. But, in the midst, quite contrary to his intentions, he delighted me with a most welcome piece of news. If you, my dear lord and husband, wish me to acquaint you with it now, you need only command me, and I will freely and from my heart tell you all without reserve. But would you confer upon your Undine a very, very great pleasure, wait till the day after to-morrow, and then you too shall have your share of the surprise."

The knight was quite willing to gratify his wife in what she had asked so sweetly. And even as she was falling asleep, she murmured to herself, with a smile: "How she will rejoice and be astonished at what her master of the fountain has told me!—dear, dear Bertalda!"

CHAPTER VI.

The company were sitting at dinner. Bertalda, adorned with jewels and flowers without number, the presents of her foster-parents and friends, and looking like some goddess of spring, sat beside Undine and Huldbrand at the head of the table. When the sumptuous repast was ended, and the dessert was placed before them, permission was given that the doors should be left open: this was in accordance with the good old custom in Germany, that the common people might see and rejoice in the festivity of their superiors. Among these spectators the servants carried round cake and wine.

Huldbrand and Bertalda waited with secret impatience for the promised explanation, and hardly moved their eyes from Undine. But she still continued silent, and merely smiled to herself with secret and heartfelt satisfaction. All who were made acquainted with the promise she had given could perceive that she was every moment on the point of revealing a happy secret; and yet, as children sometimes delay tasting their choicest dainties, she still withheld the communication. Bertalda and Huldbrand shared the same delightful feeling, while in anxious hope they were expecting the unknown disclosure which they were to receive from the lips of their friend.

At this moment several of the company pressed Undine to sing. This she seemed pleased at; and ordering her lute to be brought, she sang the following words:—

"Morning so bright,
Wild flowers so gay,
Where high grass so dewy
Crowns the wavy lake's border.

On the meadow's verdant bosom
What glimmers there so white?
Have wreaths of snowy blossoms,
Soft-floating, fallen from heaven?

Ah, see! a tender infant!—
It plays with flowers, unwitting;
It strives to grasp morn's golden beams.
O where, sweet stranger, where's your home?
Afar from unknown shores
The waves have wafted hither
This helpless little one.

Nay, clasp not, tender darling,
With tiny hand the flowers!
No hand returns the pressure,
The flowers are strange and mute.

They clothe themselves in beauty,
They breathe a rich perfume;
But cannot fold around you
A mother's loving arms;—
Far, far away that mother's fond embrace.

Life's early dawn just opening faint,
Your eye yet beaming Heaven's own smile,
So soon your tenderest guardians gone;
Severe, poor child, your fate,—
All, all to you unknown,

A noble duke has cross'd the mead,
And near you check'd his steed's career:
Wonder and pity touch his heart;
With knowledge high, and manners pure,
He rears you,—makes his castle-home your own.

How great, how infinite your gain!
Of all the land you bloom the loveliest;
Yet, ah! the priceless blessing,
The bliss of parents' fondness.
You left on strands unknown!"

Undine let fall her lute with a melancholy smile. The eyes of Bertalda's noble foster-parents were filled with tears.

"Ah yes, it was so,—such *was* the morning on which I found you, poor orphan!" cried the duke, with deep emotion; "the beautiful singer is certainly right: still

'The priceless blessing,
The bliss of parents' fondness,'

it was beyond our power to give you."

"But we must hear, also, what happened to the poor parents," said Undine, as she struck the chords, and sung:

"Through her chambers roams the mother,
Searching, searching every where;
Seeks, and knows not what, with yearning,
Childless house still finding there.

Childless house!—O sound of anguish!
She alone the anguish knows,
There by day who led her dear one,
There who rock'd its night-repose.

Beechen buds again are swelling,
  Sunshine warms again the shore;
Ah, fond mother, cease your searching!
  Comes the lov'd and lost no more.

Then when airs of eve are fresh'ning,
  Home the father wends his way,
While with smiles his woe he's veiling,
  Gushing tears his heart betray.

Well he knows, within his dwelling,
  Still as death he'll find the gloom,
Only hear the mother moaning,—
  No sweet babe to *smile* him home."

"O tell me, in the name of Heaven tell me, Undine, where are my parents?" cried the weeping Bertalda. "You certainly know; you must have discovered them, you wonderful being; for otherwise you would never have thus torn my heart. Can they be already here? May I believe it possible?" Her eye glanced rapidly over the brilliant company, and rested upon a lady of high rank who was sitting next to her foster-father.

Then, bending her head, Undine beckoned toward the door, while her eyes overflowed with the sweetest emotion. "Where, then, are the poor parents waiting?" she asked; and the old fisherman, hesitating, advanced, with his wife, from the crowd of spectators. They looked inquiringly, now at Undine, and now at the beautiful lady who was said to be their daughter.

"It is she! it is she there before you!" exclaimed the restorer of their child, her voice half choked with rapture. And both the aged parents embraced their recovered daughter, weeping aloud and praising God.

But, terrified and indignant, Bertalda tore herself from their arms. Such a discovery was too much for her proud spirit to bear,—especially at the moment when she had doubtless expected to see her former splendour increased, and when hope was picturing to her nothing less brilliant than a royal canopy and a crown. It seemed to her as if her rival had contrived all this on purpose to humble her before Huldbrand and the whole world. She reproached Undine; she reviled the old people; and even such offensive words as "deceiver, bribed and perjured impostors," burst from her lips.

The aged wife of the fisherman then said to herself, in a low voice: "Ah, my God, she has become wicked! and yet I feel in my heart that she is my child."

The old fisherman had meanwhile folded his hands, and offered up a silent prayer that she might *not* be his daughter.

Undine, faint and pale as death, turned from the parents to Bertalda, from Bertalda to the parents. She was suddenly cast down from all that heaven of happiness in which she had been dreaming, and plunged into an agony of terror and disappointment which she had never known even in dreams.

"Have you, then, a soul? Have you indeed a soul, Bertalda?" she cried again and again to her angry friend, as if with vehement effort she would rouse her from a sudden delirium or some distracting dream of night, and restore her to recollection.

But when Bertalda became every moment only more and more enraged—when the disappointed parents began to weep aloud—and the company, with much warmth of dispute, were espousing opposite sides,—she begged, with such earnestness and dignity, for the liberty of speaking in this her husband's hall, that all around her were in an instant hushed to silence. She then advanced to the upper end of the table, where, both humbled and haughty, Bertalda had seated herself, and, while every eye was fastened upon her, spoke in the following manner:

"My friends, you appear dissatisfied and disturbed; and you are interrupting, with your strife, a festivity I had hoped would bring joy to you and to me. Ah! I knew nothing of your heartless ways of thinking; and never shall I understand them. I am not to blame for the mischief this disclosure has done. Believe me, little as you may imagine this to be the case, it is wholly owing to yourselves. One word more, therefore, is all I have to add; but this is one that must be spoken:—I have uttered nothing but truth. Of the certainty of the fact, I give you the strongest assurance. No other proof can I or will I produce; but this I will affirm in the presence of God. The person who gave me this information was the very same who decoyed the infant Bertalda into the water, and who, after thus taking her from her parents, placed her on the green grass of the meadow, where he knew the duke was to pass."

"She is an enchantress!" cried Bertalda; "a witch, that has intercourse with evil spirits. She acknowledges it herself."

"Never! I deny it!" replied Undine, while a whole heaven of innocence and truth beamed from her eyes. "I am no witch; look upon me, and say if I am."

"Then she utters both falsehood and folly," cried Bertalda; "and she is unable to prove that I am the child of these low people. My noble parents, I entreat you to take me from this company, and out of this city, where they do nothing but shame me."

But the aged duke, a man of honourable feeling, remained unmoved; and his wife remarked: "We must thoroughly examine into this matter. God forbid that we should move a step from this hall before we do so."

Then the aged wife of the fisherman drew near, made a low obeisance to the duchess, and said: "Noble and pious lady, you have opened my heart. Permit me to tell you, that if this evil-disposed maiden is my daughter, she has a mark like a violet between her shoulders, and another of the same kind on the instep of her left foot. If she will only consent to go out of the hall with me—"

"I will not consent to uncover myself before the peasant woman," interrupted Bertalda, haughtily turning her back upon her.

"But before me you certainly will," replied the duchess, gravely. "You will follow me into that room, maiden; and the old woman shall go with us."

The three disappeared; and the rest continued where they were, in breathless expectation. In a few minutes the females returned—Bertalda pale as death; and the duchess said: "Justice must be done; I therefore declare that our lady hostess has spoken exact truth. Bertalda is the fisherman's daughter; no further proof is required; and this is all of which, on the present occasion, you need to be informed."

The princely pair went out with their adopted daughter; the fisherman, at a sign from the duke, followed them with his wife. The other guests retired in silence, or suppressing their murmurs; while Undine sank weeping into the arms of Huldbrand.

The lord of Ringstetten would certainly have been more gratified, had the events of this day been different; but even such as they now were, he could by no means look upon them as unwelcome, since his lovely wife had shewn herself so full of goodness, sweetness, and kindliness.

"If I have given her a soul," he could not help saying to himself, "I have assuredly given her a better one than my own;" and now he only thought of soothing and comforting his weeping wife, and of removing her even so early as the morrow from a place which, after this cross accident, could not fail to be distasteful to her. Yet it is certain that the opinion of the public concerning her was not changed. As something extraordinary had long before been expected of her, the mysterious discovery of Bertalda's parentage had occasioned little or no surprise; and every one who became acquainted with Bertalda's story, and with the violence of her behaviour on that occasion, was only disgusted and set against her. Of this state of things, however, the knight and his lady were as yet ignorant; besides, whether the public condemned Bertalda or herself, the one view of the affair would have been as distressing to Undine as the other; and thus they came to the conclusion, that the wisest course they could take, was to leave behind them the walls of the old city with all the speed in their power.

With the earliest beams of morning, a brilliant carriage for Undine drove up to the door of the inn; the horses of Huldbrand and his attendants stood near, stamping the pavement, impatient to proceed. The knight was leading his beautiful wife from the door, when a fisher-girl came up and met them in the way.

"We have no need of your fish," said Huldbrand, accosting her; "we are this moment setting out on a journey."

Upon this the fisher-girl began to weep bitterly; and then it was that the young couple first perceived it was Bertalda. They immediately returned with her to their apartment, when she informed them, that, owing to her unfeeling and violent conduct of the preceding day, the duke and duchess had been so displeased with her, as entirely to withdraw from her their protection, though not before giving her a generous portion. The fisherman, too, had received a handsome gift, and had, the evening before, set out with his wife for his peninsula.

"I would have gone with them," she pursued, "but the old fisherman, who is said to be my father—"

"He is, in truth, your father, Bertalda," said Undine, interrupting her. "See, the stranger whom you took for the master of the water-works gave me all the particulars. He wished to dissuade me from taking you with me to Castle Ringstetten, and therefore disclosed to me the whole mystery."

"Well then," continued Bertalda, "my father,—if it must needs be so,—my father said: 'I will not take you with me until you are changed. If you will venture to come to us alone through the ill-omened forest, that shall be a proof of your having some regard for us. But come not to me as a lady; come merely as a fisher-girl.' I do as he bade me; for since I am abandoned by all the world, I will live and die in solitude, a poor fisher-girl, with parents equally poor. The forest, indeed, appears very terrible to me. Horrible spectres make it their haunt, and I am so fearful. But how can I help it? I have only come here at this early hour to beg the noble lady of Ringstetten to pardon my unbecoming behaviour of yesterday.—Sweet lady, I have the fullest persuasion that you meant to do me a kindness, but you were not aware how severely you would wound me; and then, in my agony and surprise, so many rash and frantic expressions burst from my lips. Forgive me, ah forgive me! I am in truth so unhappy already. Only consider what I was but yesterday morning, what I was even at the beginning of your yesterday's festival, and what I am to-day!"—

Her words now became inarticulate, lost in a passionate flow of tears, while Undine, bitterly weeping with her, fell upon her neck. So powerful was her emotion, that it was a long time before she could utter a word. At length she said:

"You shall still go with us to Ringstetten; all shall remain just as we lately arranged it; but say 'thou' to me again, and do not call me 'noble lady' any more. Consider, we were changed for each other when we were children; even then we were united by a like fate, and we will strengthen this union with such close affection as no human power shall dissolve. Only first of all you must go with us to Ringstetten. How we shall share all things as sisters, we can talk of after we arrive."

Bertalda looked up to Huldbrand with timid inquiry. He pitied her in her affliction, took her hand, and begged her, tenderly, to entrust herself to him and his wife.

"We will send a message to your parents," continued

he, "giving them the reason why you have not come;"—and he would have added more about his worthy friends of the peninsula, when, perceiving that Bertalda shrank in distress at the mention of them, he refrained. He took her under the arm, lifted her first into the carriage, then Undine, and was soon riding blithely beside them; so persevering was he, too, in urging forward their driver, that in a short time they had left behind them the limits of the city, and a crowd of painful recollections; and now the ladies could take delight in the beautiful country which their progress was continually presenting.

After a journey of some days, they arrived, on a fine evening, at Castle Ringstetten. The young knight being much engaged with the overseers and menials of his establishment, Undine and Bertalda were left alone. They took a walk upon the high rampart of the fortress, and were charmed with the delightful landscape which the fertile Suabia spread around them. While they were viewing the scene, a tall man drew near, who greeted them with respectful civility, and who seemed to Bertalda much to resemble the director of the city fountain. Still less was the resemblance to be mistaken, when Undine, indignant at his intrusion, waved him off with an air of menace; while he, shaking his head, retreated with rapid strides, as he had formerly done, then glided among the trees of a neighbouring grove and disappeared.

"Do not be terrified, Bertalda," said Undine; "the hateful master of the fountain shall do you no harm this time."—And then she related to her the particulars of her history, and who she was herself,—how Bertalda had been taken away from the people of the peninsula, and Undine left in her place. This relation at first filled the young maiden with amazement and alarm; she imagined her friend must be seized with a sudden madness. But, from the consistency of her story, she became more and more convinced that all was true, it so well agreed with former occurrences, and still more convinced from that inward feeling with which truth never fails to make itself known to us. She could not but view it as an extraordinary circumstance that she was herself now living, as it were, in the midst of one of those wild tales which she had formerly heard related. She gazed upon Undine with reverence, but could not keep from a shuddering feeling which seemed to come between her and her friend; and she could not but wonder when the knight, at their evening repast, shewed himself so kind and full of love towards a being who appeared to her, after the discoveries just made, more to resemble a phantom of the spirit-world than one of the human race.

CHAPTER VII.

THE writer of this tale, both because it moves his own heart and he wishes it to move that of others, asks a favour of you, dear reader. Forgive him if he passes over a considerable space of time in a few words, and only tells you generally what therein happened. He knows well that it might be unfolded skilfully, and step by step, how Huldbrand's heart began to turn from Undine and towards Bertalda—how Bertalda met the young knight with ardent love, and how they both looked upon the poor wife as a mysterious being, more to be dreaded than pitied—how Undine wept, and her tears stung the conscience of her husband, without recalling his former love; so that though at times he shewed kindness to her, a cold shudder soon forced him to turn from her to his fellow-mortal Bertalda; —all this, the writer knows, might have been drawn out fully, and perhaps it ought to have been. But it would have made him too sad; for he has witnessed such things, and shrinks from recalling even their shadow. Thou knowest, probably, the like feeling, dear reader; for it is the lot of mortal man. Happy art thou if thou hast received the injury, not inflicted it; for in this case it is more blessed to receive than to give. Then only a soft sorrow at such a recollection passes through thy heart, and perhaps a quiet tear trickles down thy cheek over the faded flowers in which thou once so heartily rejoiced. This is enough: we will not pierce our hearts with a thousand separate stings, but only bear in mind that all happened, as I just now said.

Poor Undine was greatly troubled; and the other two were very far from being happy. Bertalda in particular, whenever she was in the slightest degree opposed in her wishes, attributed the cause to the jealousy and oppression of the injured wife. She was therefore daily in the habit of shewing a haughty and imperious demeanour, to which Undine yielded with a sad submission; and which was generally encouraged strongly by the now blinded Huldbrand.

What disturbed the inmates of the castle still more, was the endless variety of wonderful apparitions which assailed Huldbrand and Bertalda in the vaulted passages of the building, and of which nothing had ever been heard before within the memory of man. The tall white man, in whom Huldbrand but too plainly recognised Undine's uncle Kühleborn, and Bertalda the spectral master of the water-works, often passed before them with threatening aspect and gestures; more especially, however, before Bertalda, so that, through terror, she had several times already fallen sick, and had, in consequence, frequently thought of quitting the castle. Yet partly because Huldbrand was but too dear to her, and she trusted to her innocence, since no words of love had passed between them, and partly also because she knew not whither to direct her steps, she lingered where she was.

The old fisherman, on receiving the message from the lord of Ringstetten that Bertalda was his guest, returned answer in some lines almost too illegible to be deciphered, but still the best his advanced life and long disuse of writing permitted him to form.

"I have now become," he wrote, "a poor old widower, for my beloved and faithful wife is dead. But lonely as I now sit in my cottage, I prefer Bertalda's remaining where she is, to her living with me. Only let her do nothing to hurt my dear Undine, else she will have my curse."

The last words of this letter, Bertalda flung to the winds; but the permission to remain from home, which her father had granted her, she remembered, and clung to,—just as we are all of us wont to do in similar circumstances.

One day, a few moments after Huldbrand had ridden out, Undine called together the domestics of the family, and ordered them to bring a large stone, and carefully to cover with it a magnificent fountain, that was situated in the middle of the castle court. The servants objected that it would oblige them to bring water from the valley below. Undine smiled sadly.

"I am sorry, my friends," replied she, "to increase your labour; I would rather bring up the water-vessels myself: but this fountain must indeed be closed. Believe me when I say that it must be done, and that only by doing it we can avoid a greater evil."

The domestics were all rejoiced to gratify their gentle mistress; and making no further inquiry, they seized the enormous stone. While they were raising it in their hands, and were now on the point of adjusting it over the fountain, Bertalda came running to the place, and cried, with an air of command, that they must stop; that the water she used, so improving to her complexion, was brought from this fountain, and that she would by no means allow it to be closed.

This time, however, Undine, while she shewed her usual gentleness, shewed more than her usual resolution:

she said it belonged to her, as mistress of the house, to direct the household according to her best judgment; and that she was accountable in this to no one but her lord and husband.

"See, O pray see," exclaimed the dissatisfied and indignant Bertalda, "how the beautiful water is curling and curving, winding and waving there, as if disturbed at being shut out from the bright sunshine, and from the cheerful view of the human countenance, for whose mirror it was created!"

In truth the water of the fountain was agitated, and foaming, and hissing in a surprising manner; it seemed as if there were something within possessing life and will, that was struggling to free itself from confinement. But Undine only the more earnestly urged the accomplishment of her commands. This earnestness was scarcely required. The servants of the castle were as happy in obeying their gentle lady, as in opposing the haughty spirit of Bertalda; and however the latter might scold and threaten, still the stone was in a few minutes lying firm over the opening of the fountain. Undine leaned thoughtfully over it, and wrote with her beautiful fingers on the flat surface. She must, however, have had something very sharp and corrosive in her hand, for when she retired, and the domestics went up to examine the stone, they discovered various strange characters upon it, which none of them had seen there before.

When the knight returned home, toward evening, Bertalda received him with tears, and complaints of Undine's conduct. He cast a severe glance of reproach at his poor wife, and she looked down in distress; yet she said very calmly:

"My lord and husband, you never reprove even a bond-slave before you hear his defence; how much less, then, your wedded wife!"

"Speak, what moved you to this singular conduct?" said the knight, with a gloomy countenance.

"I could wish to tell you when we are entirely alone," said Undine, with a sigh.

"You can tell me equally well in the presence of Bertalda," he replied.

"Yes, if you command me," said Undine; "but do not command me—pray, pray do not!"

She looked so humble, affectionate, and obedient, that the heart of the knight was touched and softened, as if it felt the influence of a ray from better times. He kindly took her arm within his, and led her to his apartment, where she spoke as follows:

"You already know something, my beloved lord, of Kühleborn, my evil-disposed uncle, and have often felt displeasure at meeting him in the passages of this castle. Several times has he terrified Bertalda even to swooning. He does this because he possesses no soul, being a mere elemental mirror of the outward world, while of the world within he can give no reflection. Then, too, he sometimes observes that you are displeased with me, that in my childish weakness I weep at this, and that Bertalda, it may be, laughs at the same moment. Hence it is that he imagines all is wrong with us, and in various ways mixes with our circle unbidden. What do I gain by reproving him, by shewing displeasure, and sending him away? He does not believe a word I say. His poor nature has no idea that the joys and sorrows of love have so sweet a resemblance, and are so intimately connected that no power on earth is able to separate them. A smile shines in the midst of tears, and a smile calls forth tears from their dwelling-place."

She looked up at Huldbrand, smiling and weeping; and he again felt within his heart all the magic of his former love. She perceived it, and pressed him more tenderly to her, while with tears of joy she went on thus:

"When the disturber of our peace would not be dismissed with words, I was obliged to shut the door upon him; and the only entrance by which he has access to us is that fountain. His connexion with the other water-spirits here in this region is cut off by the valleys that border upon us; and his kingdom first commences farther off on the Danube, in whose tributary streams some of his good friends have their abode. For this reason I caused the stone to be placed over the opening of the fountain, and inscribed characters upon it, which baffle all the efforts of my suspicious uncle; so that he now has no power of intruding either upon you, or me, or Bertalda. Human beings, it is true, notwithstanding the characters I have inscribed there, are able to raise the stone without any extraordinary trouble; there is nothing to prevent them. If you choose, therefore, remove it, according to Bertalda's desire; but she assuredly knows not what she asks. The rude Kühleborn looks with peculiar ill-will upon her; and should those things come to pass that he has predicted to me, and which may happen without your meaning any evil, ah! dearest, even you yourself would be exposed to peril."

Huldbrand felt the generosity of his gentle wife in the depth of his heart, since she had been so active in confining her formidable defender, and even at the very moment she was reproached for it by Bertalda. He pressed her in his arms with the tenderest affection, and said, with emotion:

"The stone shall remain unmoved; all remains, and ever shall remain, just as you choose to have it, my sweetest Undine!"

At these long-withheld expressions of tenderness, she returned his caresses with lowly delight, and at length said: "My dearest husband, since you are so kind and indulgent to-day, may I venture to ask a favour of you? See now, it is with you as with summer. Even amid its highest splendour, summer puts on the flaming and thundering crown of glorious tempests, in which it strongly resembles a king and god on earth. You, too, are sometimes terrible in your rebukes; your eyes flash lightning, while thunder resounds in your voice; and although this may be quite becoming to you, I in my folly cannot but sometimes weep at it. But never, I entreat you, behave thus toward me on a river, or even when we are near any water. For if you should, my relations would acquire a right over me. They would inexorably tear me from you in their fury, because they would conceive that one of their race was injured; and I should be compelled, as long as I lived, to dwell below in the crystal palaces, and never dare ascend to you again; or should *they send* me up to you!—O God! that would be far worse still. No, no, my beloved husband; let it not come to that, if your poor Undine is dear to you."

He solemnly promised to do as she desired; and, inexpressibly happy and full of affection, the married pair returned from the apartment. At this very moment, Bertalda came with some work-people whom she had meanwhile ordered to attend her, and said with a fretful air, which she had assumed of late:

"Well, now the secret consultation is at an end, the stone may be removed. Go out, workmen, and see to it."

The knight, however, highly resenting her impertinence, said, in brief and very decisive terms: "The stone remains where it is!" He reproved Bertalda also for the vehemence that she had shewn towards his wife. Whereupon the workmen, smiling with secret satisfaction, withdrew; while Bertalda, pale with rage, hurried away to her room.

When the hour of supper came, Bertalda was waited for in vain. They sent for her; but the domestic found her apartments empty, and brought back with him only a sealed letter, addressed to the knight. He opened it in alarm, and read:

"I feel with shame that I am only the daughter of a poor fisherman. That I for one moment forgot this, I will make expiation in the miserable hut of my parents. Farewell to you and your beautiful wife!"

Undine was troubled at heart. With eagerness she entreated Huldbrand to hasten after their friend, who had flown, and bring her back with him. Alas! she had no occasion to urge him. His passion for Bertalda again burst forth with vehemence. He hurried round the castle, inquiring whether any one had seen which way the fair fugitive had gone. He could gain no information; and was already in the court on his horse, determining to take at a venture the road by which he had conducted Bertalda to the castle, when there appeared a page, who assured him that he had met the lady on the path to the Black Valley. Swift as an arrow, the knight sprang through the gate in the direction pointed out, without hearing Undine's voice of agony, as she cried after him from the window:

"To the Black Valley? O, not there! Huldbrand, not there! Or if you will go, for Heaven's sake take me with you!"

But when she perceived that all her calling was of no avail, she ordered her white palfrey to be instantly saddled, and followed the knight, without permitting a single servant to accompany her.

The Black Valley lies secluded far among the mountains. What its present name may be, I am unable to say. At the time of which I am speaking, the country-people gave it this appellation from the deep obscurity produced by the shadows of lofty trees, more especially by a crowded growth of firs that covered this region of moorland. Even the brook, which bubbled between the rocks, assumed the same dark hue, and shewed nothing of that cheerful aspect which streams are wont to wear that have the blue sky immediately over them.

It was now the dusk of evening; and between the heights it had become extremely wild and gloomy. The knight, in great anxiety, skirted the border of the brook;

He was at one time fearful that, by delay, he should allow the fugitive to advance too far before him; and then again, in his too eager rapidity, he was afraid he might somewhere overlook and pass by her, should she be desirous of concealing herself from his search. He had in the mean time penetrated pretty far into the valley, and might hope soon to overtake the maiden, provided he were pursuing the right track. The fear, indeed, that he might not as yet have gained it, made his heart beat with more and more of anxiety. In the stormy night which was now approaching, and which always fell more fearfully over this valley, where would the delicate Bertalda shelter herself, should he fail to find her? At last, while these thoughts were darting across his mind, he saw something white glimmer through the branches on the ascent of the mountain. He thought he recognised Bertalda's robe; and he directed his course toward it. But his horse refused to go forward; he reared with a fury so uncontrollable, and his master was so unwilling to lose a moment, that (especially as he saw the thickets were altogether impassable on horseback) he dismounted, and, having fastened his snorting steed to an elm, worked his way with caution through the matted underwood. The branches, moistened by the cold drops of the evening dew, struck against his forehead and cheeks; distant thunder muttered from the further side of the mountains; and every thing put on so strange an appearance, that he began to feel a dread of the white figure, which now lay at a short distance from him upon the ground. Still he could see distinctly that it was a female, either asleep or in a swoon, and dressed in long white garments such as Bertalda had worn the past day. Approaching quite near to her, he made a rustling with the branches and a ringing with his sword; but she did not move.

"Bertalda!" he cried, at first low, then louder and louder; yet she heard him not. At last, when he uttered the dear name with an energy yet more powerful, a hollow echo from the mountain-summits around the valley returned the deadened sound, "Bertalda!" Still the sleeper continued insensible. He stooped down; but the duskiness of the valley and the obscurity of twilight would not allow him to distinguish her features. While, with painful uncertainty, he was bending over her, a flash of lightning suddenly shot across the valley. By this stream of light, he saw a frightfully distorted visage close to his own; and a hoarse voice reached his ear:

"You enamoured swain, give me a kiss!" Huldbrand sprang upon his feet with a cry of horror; and the hideous figure rose with him.

"Go home!" it cried, with a deep murmur: "the fiends are abroad. Go home! or I have you!" And it stretched toward him its long white arms.

"Malicious Kühleborn!" exclaimed the knight, with restored energy; "if Kühleborn you are, what business have you here?—what's your will, you goblin? There, take your kiss!" And in fury he struck his sword at the form. But it vanished like vapour; and a rush of water, which wetted him through and through, left him in no doubt with what foe he had been engaged.

"He wishes to frighten me back from my pursuit of Bertalda," said he to himself; "he imagines that I shall be terrified at his senseless tricks, and resign the poor distressed maiden to his power, so that he can wreak his vengeance upon her at will. But that he shall not, weak spirit of the flood! What the heart of man can do, when it exerts the full force of its will and of its noblest powers, the poor goblin cannot fathom."

He felt the truth of his words, and that they had inspired his heart with fresh courage. Fortune, too, appeared to favour him; for, before reaching his fastened steed, he distinctly heard the voice of Bertalda, weeping not far before him, amid the roar of the thunder and the tempest, which every moment increased. He flew swiftly toward the sound, and found the trembling maiden, just as she was attempting to climb the steep, hoping to escape from the dreadful darkness of this valley. He drew near her with expressions of love; and bold and proud as her resolution had so lately been, she now felt nothing but joy that the man whom she so passionately loved should rescue her from this frightful solitude, and thus call her back to the joyful life in the castle. She followed almost unresisting, but so spent with fatigue, that the knight was glad to bring her to his horse, which he now hastily unfastened from the elm, in order to lift the fair wanderer upon him, and then to lead him carefully by the reins through the uncertain shades of the valley.

But, owing to the wild apparition of Kühleborn, the horse had become wholly unmanageable. Rearing and wildly snorting as he was, the knight must have used uncommon effort to mount the beast himself; to place the trembling Bertalda upon him was impossible. They were compelled, therefore, to return home on foot. While with one hand the knight drew the steed after him by the bridle, he supported the tottering Bertalda with the other. She exerted all the strength in her power, in order to escape speedily from this vale of terrors. But weariness weighed her down like lead; and all her limbs trembled, partly in consequence of what she had suffered from the extreme terror which Kühleborn had already caused her, and partly from her present fear at the roar of the tempest and thunder amid the mountain-forest.

At last she slid from the arm of the knight; and sinking upon the moss, she said: "Only let me lie here, my noble lord. I suffer the punishment due to my folly; and I must perish here through faintness and dismay."

"Never, gentle lady, will I leave you," cried Huldbrand, vainly trying to restrain the furious animal he was leading; for the horse was all in a foam, and began to chafe more ungovernably than before, till the knight was glad to keep him at such a distance from the exhausted maiden as to save her from a new alarm. But hardly had he withdrawn five steps with the frantic steed, when she began to call after him in the most sorrowful accents, fearful that he would actually leave her in this horrible wilderness. He was at a loss what course to take. He would gladly have given the enraged beast his liberty; he would have let him rush away amid the night and exhaust his fury, had he not feared that in this narrow defile his iron-shod hoofs might come thundering over the very spot where Bertalda lay.

In this extreme peril and embarrassment, he heard with delight the rumbling wheels of a wagon, as it came slowly descending the stony way behind them. He called out for help: answer was returned in the deep voice of a man, bidding them have patience, but promising assistance; and two grey horses soon after shone through the bushes, and near them their driver in the white frock of a carter; and next appeared a great sheet of white linen, with which the goods he seemed to be conveying were covered. The greys, in obedience to a shout from their master, stood still. He came up to the knight, and aided him in checking the fury of the foaming charger.

"I know well enough," said he, "what is the matter with the brute. The first time I travelled this way, my horses were just as wilful and headstrong as yours. The reason is, there is a water-spirit haunts this valley,—and a wicked wight they say he is,—who takes delight in mischief and witcheries of this sort. But I have learned a charm; and if you will let me whisper it in your horse's ear, he will stand just as quiet as my silver greys there."

"Try your luck, then, and help us as quickly as possible!" said the impatient knight.

Upon this the wagoner drew down the head of the rearing courser close to his own, and spoke some words in his ear. The animal instantly stood still and subdued; only his quick panting and smoking sweat shewed his recent violence.

Huldbrand had little time to inquire by what means

this had been effected. He agreed with the man that he should take Bertalda in his wagon, where, as he said, a quantity of soft cotton was stowed, and he might in this way convey her to Castle Ringstetten: the knight could accompany them on horseback. But the horse appeared to be too much exhausted to carry his master so far. Seeing this, the man advised him to mount the wagon with Bertalda. The horse could be attached to it behind.

"It is down hill," said he, "and the load for my greys will therefore be light."

The knight accepted his offer, and entered the wagon with Bertalda. The horse followed patiently after; while the wagoner, sturdy and attentive, walked beside them.

Amid the silence and deepening obscurity of the night; the tempest sounding more and more remote, in the comfortable feeling of their security, a confidential conversation arose between Huldbrand and Bertalda. He reproached her in the most flattering words for her resentful flight. She excused herself with humility and feeling; and from every tone of her voice it shone out, like a lamp guiding to the beloved through night and darkness, that Huldbrand was still dear to her. The knight felt the *sense* of her words, rather than heard the words themselves, and answered simply to this sense.

Then the wagoner suddenly shouted, with a startling voice: "Up, my greys, up with your feet! Hey, now together!—shew your spirit!—remember who you are!"

The knight bent over the side of the wagon, and saw that the horses had stepped into the midst of a foaming stream, and were indeed almost swimming; while the wheels of the wagon were rushing round and flashing like mill-wheels; and the wagoner had got on before, to avoid the swell of the flood.

"What sort of a road is this? It leads into the middle of the stream!" cried Huldbrand to his guide.

"Not at all, sir," returned he, with a laugh; "it is

just the contrary. The stream is running in the middle of our road. Only look about you, and see how all is overflowed!"

The whole valley, in fact, was in commotion, as the waters, suddenly raised and visibly rising, swept over it.

"It is Kühleborn, that evil water-spirit, who wishes to drown us!" exclaimed the knight. "Have you no charm of protection against him, friend?"

"I have one," answered the wagoner; "but I cannot and must not make use of it, before you know who I am."

"Is this a time for riddles?" cried the knight. "The flood is every moment rising higher; and what does it concern *me* to know who *you* are?"

"But mayhap it does concern you, though," said the guide; "for *I* am Kühleborn."

Thus speaking, he thrust his head into the wagon, and laughed with a distorted visage. But the wagon remained a wagon no longer; the grey horses were horses no longer; all was transformed to foam—all sank into the waters that rushed and hissed around them; while the wagoner himself, rising in the form of a gigantic wave, dragged the vainly struggling courser under the waters, then rose again huge as a liquid tower, swept over the heads of the floating pair, and was on the point of burying them irrecoverably beneath it. Then the soft voice of Undine was heard through the uproar; the moon emerged from the clouds; and by its light Undine was seen on the heights above the valley. She rebuked, she threatened the floods below her. The menacing and tower-like billow vanished, muttering and murmuring; the waters gently flowed away under the beams of the moon; while Undine, like a hovering white dove, flew down from the hill, raised the knight and Bertalda, and bore them to a green spot, where, by her earnest efforts, she soon restored them and dispelled their terrors.

She then assisted Bertalda to mount the white palfrey on which she had herself been borne to the valley; and thus all three returned homeward to Castle Ringstetten.

CHAPTER VIII.

After this last adventure, they lived at the castle undisturbed and in peaceful enjoyment. The knight was more and more impressed with the heavenly goodness of his wife, which she had so nobly shewn by her instant pursuit, and by the rescue she had effected in the Black Valley, where the power of Kühleborn again commenced. Undine herself enjoyed that peace and security which never fails the soul as long as it knows distinctly that it is on the right path; and besides, in the newly awakened love and regard of her husband, a thousand gleams of hope and joy shone upon her.

Bertalda, on the other hand, shewed herself grateful, humble, and timid, without taking to herself any merit for so doing. Whenever Huldbrand or Undine began to explain to her their reason for covering the fountain, or their adventures in the Black Valley, she would earnestly entreat them to spare her the recital, for the recollection of the fountain occasioned her too much shame, and that of the Black Valley too much terror. She learnt nothing more about either of them; and what would she have gained from more knowledge? Peace and joy had visibly taken up their abode at Castle Ringstetten. They enjoyed their present blessings in perfect security, and now imagined that life could produce nothing but pleasant flowers and fruits.

In this happiness, winter came and passed away; and spring, with its foliage of tender green, and its heaven of softest blue, succeeded, to gladden the hearts of the three inmates of the castle. The season was in harmony with their minds, and their minds imparted their own hues to the season. What wonder, then, that its storks and swallows inspired them also with a disposition to travel? On a bright morning, while they were wandering down to one of the sources of the Danube, Huldbrand spoke of the magnificence of this noble stream, how it continued swelling as it flowed through countries enriched by its waters, with what splendour Vienna rose and sparkled on its banks, and how it grew lovelier and more imposing throughout its progress.

"It must be glorious to trace its course down to Vienna!" Bertalda exclaimed, with warmth; but immediately resuming the humble and modest demeanour she had recently shewn, she paused and blushed in silence.

This much moved Undine; and with the liveliest wish to gratify her friend, she said, "What hinders our taking this little voyage?"

Bertalda leapt up with delight, and the two friends at the same moment began painting this enchanting voyage on the Danube in the most brilliant colours. Huldbrand, too, agreed to the project with pleasure; only he once whispered, with something of alarm, in Undine's ear:

"But at that distance Kühleborn becomes possessed of his power again!"

"Let him come, let him come," she answered with a laugh; "I shall be there, and he dares do none of his mischief in my presence."

Thus was the last impediment removed: they prepared for the expedition, and soon set out upon it with lively spirits and the brightest hopes.

But be not surprised, O man, if events almost always happen very differently from what you expect. That malicious power which lies in ambush for our destruction delights to lull its chosen victim asleep with sweet songs and golden delusions; while, on the other hand, the messenger of Heaven often strikes sharply at our door, to alarm and awaken us.

During the first days of their passage down the Danube, they were unusually happy. The farther they advanced upon the waters of this proud river, the views became more and more fair. But amid scenes otherwise most delicious, and from which they had promised themselves the purest delight, the stubborn Kühleborn, dropping all disguise, began to shew his power of annoying them. He had no other means of doing this, indeed, than by tricks,—for Undine often rebuked the swelling waves or the contrary winds, and then the insolence of the enemy was instantly humbled and subdued; but his attacks were renewed, and Undine's reproofs again became necessary; so that the pleasure of the fellow-travellers was completely destroyed. The boatmen, too, were continually whispering to one another in dismay, and eyeing their three superiors with distrust; while even the servants began more and more to form dismal surmises, and to watch their master and mistress with looks of suspicion.

Huldbrand often said in his own mind, "This comes when like marries not like—when a man forms an unnatural union with a sea-maiden." Excusing himself, as we all love to do, he would add: "I did not, in fact, know that she *was* a maid of the sea. It is my misfortune that my steps are haunted and disturbed by the wild humours of her kindred, but it is not my crime."

By reflections like these, he felt himself in some measure strengthened; but, on the other hand, he felt the more ill-humour, almost dislike, towards Undine. He would look angrily at her, and the unhappy wife but too well understood his meaning. One day, grieved by this unkindness, as well as exhausted by her unremitted exertions to frustrate the artifices of Kühleborn, she toward evening fell into a deep slumber, rocked and soothed by the gentle motion of the bark. But hardly had she closed her eyes, when every person in the boat, in whatever direction he might look, saw the head of a man, frightful beyond imagination: each head rose out of the waves, not like that of a person swimming, but quite perpendicular, as if firmly fastened to the watery mirror, and yet moving on with the bark. Every one wished to shew to his companion what terrified himself, and each perceived the same expression of horror on the face of the other, only hands and eyes were directed to a different quarter, as if to a point where the monster, half laughing and half threatening, rose opposite to each.

When, however, they wished to make one another understand the sight, and all cried out, "Look there!" "No, there!" the frightful heads all became visible to each, and the whole river around the boat swarmed with the most horrible faces. All raised a scream of terror at the sight, and Undine started from sleep. As she opened her eyes, the deformed visages disappeared. But Huldbrand was made furious by so many hideous visions. He would have burst out in wild imprecations, had not Undine with the meekest looks and gentlest tone of voice said:

"For God's sake, my husband, do not express displeasure against me here,—we are on the water."

The knight was silent, and sat down absorbed in deep thought. Undine whispered in his ear: "Would it not be better, my love, to give up this foolish voyage, and return to Castle Ringstetten in peace?"

But Huldbrand murmured wrathfully: "So I must become a prisoner in my own castle, and not be allowed to breathe a moment but while the fountain is covered? Would to Heaven that your cursed kindred" . . . .

Then Undine pressed her fair hand on his lips caressingly. He said no more; but in silence pondered on all that Undine had before said.

Bertalda, meanwhile, had given herself up to a crowd of thronging thoughts. Of Undine's origin she knew a good deal, but not the whole; and the terrible Kühleborn especially remained to her an awful, an impenetrable mystery—never, indeed, had she once heard his name. Musing upon these wondrous things, she unclasped, without being fully conscious of what she was doing, a golden necklace, which Huldbrand, on one of the preceding days of their passage, had bought for her of a travelling trader; and she was now letting it float in sport just over the surface of the stream, while in her dreamy mood she enjoyed the bright reflection it threw on the water, so clear beneath the glow of evening. That instant a huge hand flashed suddenly up from the Danube, seized the necklace in its grasp, and vanished with it beneath the flood. Bertalda shrieked aloud, and a scornful laugh came pealing up from the depth of the river.

The knight could now restrain his wrath no longer. He started up, poured forth a torrent of reproaches, heaped curses upon all who interfered with his friends and troubled his life, and dared them all, water-spirits or mermaids, to come within the sweep of his sword.

Bertalda, meantime, wept for the loss of the ornament so very dear to her heart, and her tears were to Huldbrand as oil poured upon the flame of his fury; while Undine held her hand over the side of the boat, dipping it in the waves, softly murmuring to herself, and only at times interrupting her strange mysterious whisper to entreat her husband:

"Do not reprove me here, beloved; blame all others as you will, but not me. You know why!" And in truth, though he was trembling with excess of passion, he kept himself from any word directly against her.

She then brought up in her wet hand, which she had been holding under the waves, a coral necklace, of such exquisite beauty, such sparkling brilliancy, as dazzled the eyes of all who beheld it. "Take this," said she, holding it out kindly to Bertalda; "I have ordered it to be brought, to make some amends for your loss; so do not grieve any more, poor child."

But the knight rushed between them, and, snatching the beautiful ornament out of Undine's hand, hurled it back into the flood; and, mad with rage, exclaimed: "So, then, you have still a connexion with them! In the name of all witches, go and remain among them with your presents, you sorceress, and leave us human beings in peace!"

With fixed but streaming eyes, poor Undine gazed on him, her hand still stretched out, just as when she had so lovingly offered her brilliant gift to Bertalda. She then began to weep more and more, as if her heart would break, like an innocent, tender child, cruelly aggrieved. At last, wearied out, she said: "Farewell, dearest, farewell. They shall do you no harm; only remain true, that I may have power to keep them from you. But I must go hence! go hence, even in this early youth! Oh, woe, woe! what have you done! Oh, woe, woe!"

And she vanished over the side of the boat. Whether she plunged into the stream, or whether, like water melting into water, she flowed away with it, they knew not, —her disappearance was like both and neither. But she was lost in the Danube, instantly and completely; only little waves were yet whispering and sobbing around the boat, and they could almost be heard to say, "Oh, woe, woe! Ah, remain true! Oh, woe!"

But Huldbrand, in a passion of burning tears, threw himself upon the deck of the bark; and a deep swoon soon wrapped the wretched man in a blessed forgetfulness of misery.

Shall we call it a good or an evil thing, that our mourning has no long duration? I mean that deep mourning which comes from the very well-springs of our being, which so becomes one with the lost objects of our love, that we hardly realise their loss, while our grief devotes itself religiously to the honouring of their image, until we reach that bourne which they have already reached!

Truly all good men observe in a degree this religious devotion: but yet it soon ceases to be that first deep grief. Other and new images throng in, until, to our sorrow, we experience the vanity of all earthly things. Therefore I must say: Alas, that our mourning should be of such short duration!

The lord of Ringstetten experienced this; but whether for his good, we shall discover in the sequel of this history. At first he could do nothing but weep—weep as bitterly as the poor gentle Undine had wept, when he snatched out of her hand that brilliant ornament, with which she so kindly wished to make amends for Bertalda's loss. And then he stretched his hand out, as she had done, and wept again like her, with renewed violence. He cherished a secret hope, that even the springs of life would at last become exhausted by weeping. And has not the like thought passed through the minds of many of us with a painful pleasure in times of sore affliction? Bertalda wept with him; and they lived together a long while at the castle of Ringstetten in undisturbed quiet, honouring the memory of Undine, and having almost wholly forgotten their former attachment. And therefore the good Undine, about this time, often visited Huldbrand's dreams: she soothed him with soft and affectionate caresses, and then went away again, weeping in silence; so that when he awoke, he sometimes knew not how his cheeks came to be so wet, —whether it was caused by *her* tears, or only by his own.

But as time advanced, these visions became less frequent, and the sorrow of the knight less keen; still he might never, perhaps, have entertained any other wish than thus quietly to think of Undine, and to speak of her, had not the old fisherman arrived unexpectedly at the castle, and earnestly insisted on Bertalda's returning with him as his child. He had received information of Undine's disappearance; and he was not willing to allow Bertalda to continue longer at the castle with the widowed knight. "For," said he, "whether my daughter loves me or not is at present what I care not to know; but her good name is at stake; and where that is the case, nothing else may be thought of."

This resolution of the old fisherman, and the fearful solitude that, on Bertalda's departure, threatened to oppress the knight in every hall and passage of the deserted castle, brought to light what had disappeared in his sorrow for Undine,—I mean, his attachment to the fair Bertalda; and this he made known to her father.

The fisherman had many objections to make to the proposed marriage. The old man had loved Undine with exceeding tenderness, and it was doubtful to his mind that the mere disappearance of his beloved child could be properly viewed as her death. But were it even granted that her corpse were lying stiff and cold at the bottom of the Danube, or swept away by the current to the ocean, still Bertalda had had some share in her death; and it was unfitting for her to step into the place of the poor injured wife. The fisherman, however, had felt a strong regard also for the knight: this, and the entreaties of his daughter, who had become much more gentle and respectful, as well as her tears for Undine, all exerted their influence; and he must at last have been forced to give up his opposition, for he remained at the castle without objection, and a messenger was sent off express to Father Heilmann, who in former and happier days had united Undine and Huldbrand, requesting him to come and perform the ceremony at the knight's second marriage.

Hardly had the holy man read through the letter from the lord of Ringstetten, ere he set out upon the journey, and made much greater despatch on his way to the castle than the messenger from it had made in reaching him. Whenever his breath failed him in his rapid progress, or his old limbs ached with fatigue, he would say to himself:

"Perhaps I shall be able to prevent a sin; then sink

iot, withered body, before I arrive at the end of my journey!" And with renewed vigour he pressed forward, iurrying on without rest or repose, until, late one evening, he entered the shady court-yard of the castle of Ringtetten.

The betrothed pair were sitting side by side under the rees, and the aged fisherman in a thoughtful mood sat iear them. The moment they saw Father Heilmann, hey rose with a spring of joy, and pressed round him vith eager welcome. But he, in a few words, asked the oridegroom[1] to return with him into the castle; and when Huldbrand stood mute with surprise, and delayed comolying with his earnest request, the pious priest said to iim:

"I do not know why I should want to speak to you in orivate; what I have to say as much concerns Bertalda ind the fisherman as yourself; and what we must at some ime hear, it is best to hear as soon as possible. Are you, then, so very certain, Knight Huldbrand, that your irst wife is actually dead? I can hardly think it. I will ay nothing, indeed, of the mysterious state in which she nay be now existing; I know nothing of it with certainty. But that she was a most devoted and faithful wife, is beyond all dispute. And for fourteen nights past, she has appeared to me in a dream, standing at my bedside, wringing her tender hands in anguish, and sighing out, 'Ah, prevent him, dear father! I am still living! Ah, save his life! Ah, save his soul!'

"I did not understand what this vision of the night could mean, then came your messenger; and I have now hastened hither, not to unite, but, as I hope, to separate what ought not to be joined together. Leave her, Huldbrand! leave him, Bertalda! He still belongs to another; and do you not see on his pale cheek his grief for his lost wife? That is not the look of a bridegroom; and the

[1] The *betrothed* are called *bride* and *bridegroom* in Germany.

spirit says to me, that 'if you do not leave him, you will never be happy!'"

The three felt in their inmost hearts that Father Heilmann spoke the truth; but they would not believe it. Even the old fisherman was so infatuated, that he thought it could not be otherwise than as they had latterly settled amongst themselves. They all, therefore, with a determined and gloomy eagerness, struggled against the representations and warnings of the priest, until, shaking his head and oppressed with sorrow, he finally quitted the castle, not choosing to accept their offered shelter even for a single night, or indeed so much as to taste a morsel of the refreshment they brought him. Huldbrand persuaded himself, however, that the priest was a mere visionary; and sent at daybreak to a monk of the nearest monastery, who, without scruple, promised to perform the ceremony in a few days.

p. 81.

CHAPTER IX.

It was between night and dawn of day that Huldbrand was lying on his couch, half waking and half sleeping. Whenever he attempted to compose himself to sleep, a terror came upon him and scared him, as if his slumbers were haunted with spectres. But he made an effort to rouse himself fully. He felt fanned as by the wings of a swan, and lulled as by the murmuring of waters, till in sweet confusion of the senses he sunk back into his state of half consciousness.

At last, however, he must have fallen perfectly asleep; for he seemed to be lifted up by wings of the swans, and to be wafted far away over land and sea, while their music swelled on his ear most sweetly. "The music of the swan! the song of the swan!" he could not but repeat to himself every moment; "is it not a sure foreboding of death?" Probably, however, it had yet another meaning. All at once he seemed to be hovering over the Mediterranean Sea. A swan sang melodiously in his ear, that this *was* the Mediterranean Sea. And while he was looking down upon the waves, they became transparent as crystal, so that he could see through them to the very bottom.

At this a thrill of delight shot through him, for he could see Undine where she was sitting beneath the clear crystal dome. It is true she was weeping very bitterly, and looked much sadder than in those happy days when they lived together at the castle of Ringstetten, both on their arrival and afterward, just before they set out upon their fatal passage down the Danube. The knight could not help thinking upon all this with deep emotion, but it did not appear that Undine was aware of his presence.

Kühleborn had meanwhile approached her, and was about to reprove her for weeping, when she drew herself up, and looked upon him with an air so majestic and commanding, that he almost shrunk back.

"Although I now dwell here beneath the waters," said she, "yet I have brought my soul with me. And therefore I may weep, little as you can know what such tears are. They are blessed, as every thing is blessed to one gifted with a true soul."

He shook his head incredulously; and after some thought, replied: "And yet, niece, you are subject to our laws, as a being of the same nature with ourselves; and should *he* prove unfaithful to you, and marry again, you are obliged to take away his life."

"He remains a widower to this very hour," replied Undine; "and I am still dear to his sorrowful heart."

"He is, however, betrothed," said Kühleborn, with a laugh of scorn; "and let only a few days wear away, and then comes the priest with his nuptial blessing; and then you must go up to the death of the husband with two wives."

"I have not the power," returned Undine, with a smile. "I have sealed up the fountain securely against myself and all of my race."

"Still, should he leave his castle," said Kühleborn, "or should he once allow the fountain to be uncovered, what then? for he thinks little enough of these things."

"For that very reason," said Undine, still smiling amid her tears, "for that very reason he is at this moment hovering in spirit over the Mediterranean Sea, and dreaming of the warning which our discourse gives him. I thoughtfully planned all this."

That instant, Kühleborn, inflamed with rage, looked up at the knight, wrathfully threatened him, stamped on the ground, and then shot like an arrow beneath the waves. He seemed to swell in his fury to the size of a whale. Again the swans began to sing, to wave their wings, and fly; the knight seemed to soar away over mountains and streams, and at last to alight at Castle Ringstetten, and to awake on his couch.

Upon his couch he actually did awake; and his attendant, entering at the same moment, informed him that Father Heilmann was still lingering in the neighbourhood; that he had the evening before met with him in the forest, where he was sheltering himself under a hut, which he had formed by interweaving the branches of trees, and covering them with moss and fine brushwood; and that to the question, "What he was doing there, since he would not give the marriage-blessing?" his answer was:

"There are many other blessings than those given at marriages; and though I did not come to officiate at the wedding, I may still officiate at a very different solemnity. All things have their seasons; we must be ready for them all. Besides, marrying and mourning are by no means so very unlike; as every one, not wilfully blinded, must know full well."

The knight made many bewildered reflections on these words and on his dream. But it is very difficult to give up a thing which we have once looked upon as certain; so all continued as had been arranged previously.

Should I relate to you how passed the marriage-feast at Castle Ringstetten, it would be as if you saw a heap of bright and pleasant things, but all overspread with a black mourning crape, through whose darkening veil their brilliancy would appear but a mockery of the nothingness of all earthly joys.

It was not that any spectral delusion disturbed the scene of festivity; for the castle, as we well know, had been secured against the mischief of water-spirits. But the knight, the fisherman, and all the guests, were unable to banish the feeling that the chief personage of the feast was still wanting, and that this chief personage could be no other than the gentle and beloved Undine.

Whenever a door was heard to open, all eyes were involuntarily turned in that direction; and if it was nothing but the steward with new dishes, or the cup-bearer with a supply of wine of higher flavour than the last, they again looked down in sadness and disappointment; while the flashes of wit and merriment which had been passing at times from one to another, were extinguished by tears of mournful remembrance.

The bride was the least thoughtful of the company, and therefore the most happy; but even to her it sometimes seemed strange that she should be sitting at the head of the table, wearing a green wreath and gold-embroidered robe, while Undine was lying a corpse, stiff and cold, at the bottom of the Danube, or carried out by the current into the ocean. For ever since her father had suggested something of this sort, his words were continually sounding in her ear; and this day, in particular, they would neither fade from her memory, nor yield to other thoughts.

Evening had scarcely arrived, when the company returned to their homes; not dismissed by the impatience of the bridegroom, as wedding parties are sometimes broken up, but constrained solely by heavy sadness and forebodings of evil. Bertalda retired with her maidens, and the knight with his attendants, to undress; but there was no gay laughing company of bridesmaids and bridesmen at this mournful festival.

Bertalda wished to awake more cheerful thoughts: she ordered her maidens to spread before her a brilliant set of jewels, a present from Huldbrand, together with rich apparel and veils, that she might select from among them the brightest and most beautiful for her dress in the morning. The attendants rejoiced at this opportunity of pouring forth good wishes and promises of happiness to their young mistress, and failed not to extol the beauty of the bride with the most glowing eloquence. This went on for a long time, until Bertalda at last, looking in a mirror, said with a sigh:

"Ah, but do you not see plainly how freckled I am growing? Look here on the side of my neck."

They looked at the place, and found the freckles, indeed, as their fair mistress had said; but they called them mere beauty-spots, the faintest touches of the sun, such as would only heighten the whiteness of her delicate complexion. Bertalda shook her head, and still viewed them as a blemish.

"And I could remove them," she said at last, sighing. "But the castle-fountain is covered, from which I formerly used to have that precious water, so purifying to the skin. Oh, had I this evening only a single flask of it!"

"Is that all?" cried an alert waiting-maid, laughing, as she glided out of the apartment.

"She will not be so foolish," said Bertalda, well-pleased and surprised, "as to cause the stone-cover of the fountain to be taken off this very evening?" That instant they heard the tread of men already passing along the court-yard, and could see from the window where the officious maiden was leading them directly up to the fountain, and that they carried levers and other instruments on their shoulders.

"It is certainly my will," said Bertalda, with a smile, "if it does not take them too long." And pleased with the thought, that a word from her was now sufficient to accomplish what had formerly been refused with a painful reproof, she looked down upon their operations in the bright moonlit castle-court.

The men raised the enormous stone with an effort; some one of the number indeed would occasionally sigh, when he recollected they were destroying the work of their former beloved mistress. Their labour, however, was much lighter than they had expected. It seemed as if some power from within the fountain itself aided them in raising the stone.

"It appears," said the workmen to one another in astonishment, "as if the confined water had become a springing fountain." And the stone rose more and more, and, almost without the assistance of the work-people, rolled slowly down upon the pavement with a hollow sound. But an appearance from the opening of the fountain filled them with awe, as it rose like a white column of water: at first they imagined it really to be a fountain, until they perceived the rising form to be a pale female, veiled in white. She wept bitterly, raised her hands above her head, wringing them sadly, as with slow and solemn step she moved toward the castle. The servants shrank back, and fled from the spring; while the bride, pale and motionless with horror, stood with her maidens at the window. When the figure had now come close beneath their room, it looked up to them sobbing, and Bertalda thought she recognised through the veil the pale features of Undine. But the mourning form passed on sad, reluctant, and lingering, as if going to the place of execution. Bertalda screamed to her maids to call the knight; not one of them dared to stir from her place; and even the bride herself became again mute, as if trembling at the sound of her own voice.

While they continued standing at the window, motionless as statues, the mysterious wanderer had entered the castle, ascended the well-known stairs, and traversed the well-known halls, in silent tears. Alas, how different had she once passed through these rooms!

The knight had in the mean time dismissed his attendants. Half-undressed and in deep dejection, he was standing before a large mirror; a wax taper burned dimly beside him. At this moment some one tapped at his door, very, very softly. Undine had formerly tapped in this way, when she was playing some of her endearing wiles.

"It is all an illusion!" said he to himself. "I must to my nuptial bed."

"You must indeed, but to a cold one!" he heard a voice, choked with sobs, repeat from without; and then he saw in the mirror, that the door of his room was slowly, slowly opened, and the white figure entered, and gently closed it behind her.

"They have opened the spring," said she in a low tone; "and now I am here, and you must die."

He felt, in his failing breath, that this must indeed be; but, covering his eyes with his hands, he cried: "Do not, in my death-hour, do not make me mad with terror. If that veil conceals hideous features, do not lift it! Take my life, but let me not see you."

"Alas!" replied the pale figure, "will you not then look upon me once more? I am as fair now as when you wooed me on the island!"

"O if it indeed were so," sighed Huldbrand, "and that I might die by a kiss from you!"

"Most willingly, my own love," said she. She threw back her veil; heavenly fair shone forth her pure countenance. Trembling with love and the awe of approaching death, the knight leant towards her. She kissed him with a holy kiss; but she relaxed not her hold, pressing him more closely in her arms, and weeping as if she would weep away her soul. Tears rushed into the knight's eyes, while a thrill both of bliss and agony shot through his heart, until he at last expired, sinking softly back from her fair arms upon the pillow of his couch, a corse.

"I have wept him to death!" said she to some domestics, who met her in the ante-chamber; and passing through the terrified group, she went slowly out, and disappeared in the fountain.

CHAPTER X.

FATHER HEILMANN had returned to the castle as soon as the death of the lord of Ringstetten was made known in the neighbourhood; and he arrived at the very hour when the monk who had married the unfortunate couple was hurrying from the door, overcome with dismay and horror.

When father Heilmann was informed of this, he replied: "It is all well; and now come the duties of my office, in which I have no need of an assistant."

He then began to console the bride, now a widow, though with little benefit to her worldly and thoughtless spirit.

The old fisherman, on the other hand, though severely afflicted, was far more resigned to the fate of his son-in-law and daughter; and while Bertalda could not refrain from accusing Undine as a murderess and sorceress, the old man calmly said: "After all, it could not happen otherwise. I see nothing in it but the judgment of God; and no one's heart was more pierced by the death of Huldbrand than she who was obliged to work it, the poor forsaken Undine!"

He then assisted in arranging the funeral solemnities as suited the rank of the deceased. The knight was to be interred in a village churchyard, in whose consecrated ground were the graves of his ancestors; a place which they, as well as himself, had endowed with rich privileges and gifts. His shield and helmet lay upon his coffin, ready to be lowered with it into the grave—for lord Huldbrand of Ringstetten had died the last of his race; the mourners began their sorrowful march, chanting their melancholy songs beneath the calm unclouded heaven; father Heilmann preceded the procession, bearing a high crucifix; while the inconsolable Bertalda followed, supported by her aged father.

Then they suddenly saw in the midst of the mourning

females, in the widow's train, a snow-white figure, closely veiled, and wringing its hands in the wild vehemence of sorrow. Those next to whom it moved, seized with a secret dread, started back or on one side; and owing to their movements, the others, next to whom the white stranger now came, were terrified still more, so as to produce confusion in the funeral train. Some of the military escort ventured to address the figure, and attempt to remove it from the procession, but it seemed to vanish from under their hands, and yet was immediately seen advancing again, with slow and solemn step, among the followers of the body. At last, in consequence of the shrinking away of the attendants, it came close behind Bertalda. It now moved so slowly, that the widow was not aware of its presence, and it walked meekly and humbly behind her undisturbed.

This continued until they came to the churchyard, where the procession formed a circle round the open grave. Then it was that Bertalda perceived her unbidden companion, and, half in anger and half in terror, she commanded her to depart from the knight's place of final rest. But the veiled female, shaking her head with a gentle denial, raised her hands towards Bertalda in lowly supplication, by which she was greatly moved, and could not but remember with tears how Undine had shewn such sweetness of spirit on the Danube when she held out to her the coral necklace.

Father Heilmann now motioned with his hand, and gave order for all to observe perfect stillness, that they might breathe a prayer of silent devotion over the body, upon which earth had already been thrown. Bertalda knelt without speaking; and all knelt, even the grave-diggers, who had now finished their work. But when they arose, the white stranger had disappeared. On the spot where she had knelt, a little spring, of silver brightness, was gushing out from the green turf, and it kept swelling and flowing onward with a low murmur, till it almost encircled the mound of the knight's grave; it then continued its course, and emptied itself into a calm lake, which lay by the side of the consecrated ground. Even to this day, the inhabitants of the village point out the spring; and hold fast the belief that it is the poor deserted Undine, who in this manner still fondly encircles her beloved in her arms.

p. 97.

THE TWO CAPTAINS.

p. 38.

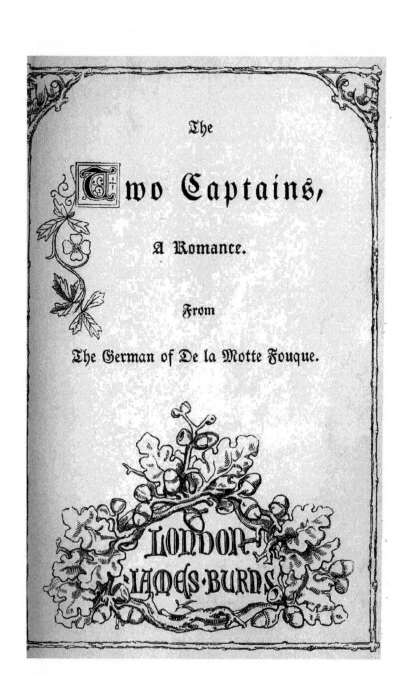

The Two Captains,

A Romance.

From

The German of De la Motte Fouque.

LONDON
JAMES BURNS

LONDON:
PRINTED BY ROBSON, LEVEY, AND FRANKLYN,
Great New Street, Fetter Lane

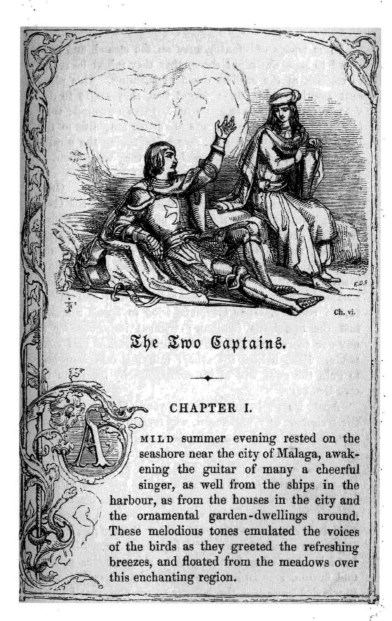

Ch. vi.

The Two Captains.

CHAPTER I.

A MILD summer evening rested on the seashore near the city of Malaga, awakening the guitar of many a cheerful singer, as well from the ships in the harbour, as from the houses in the city and the ornamental garden-dwellings around. These melodious tones emulated the voices of the birds as they greeted the refreshing breezes, and floated from the meadows over this enchanting region.

Some troops of infantry were on the strand, and purposed to pass the night there, that they might be ready to embark at the earliest dawn of morning. This pleasant evening made them forget that they ought to devote to sleep their last hours on European ground; they began to sing war-songs, and to drink long life to the mighty emperor Charles V., now beleaguering the pirate-nest of Tunis, and to whose assistance they were about to sail.

These happy soldiers were not all of one race. Only two banners waved for Spain; the third bore the German colours; and the difference of manners and speech had often previously given rise to much bantering. Now, however, thoughts of the approaching voyage, and the dangers they would share together, as well as the enjoyment which this lovely southern evening poured through soul and sense, united the comrades in full and undisturbed concord. The Germans tried to speak Spanish, and the Spaniards German; without its occurring to any one to remark the blunders and mistakes that were made. Each helped the other; thinking only how best to gain the good will of his companion by means of his own language.

Apart from this noisy group, a young German captain, Sir Heimbert of Waldhausen, was reclining under a cork-tree, and looking up to the stars with a stedfast and solemn gaze, very different from the frank, social spirit which his comrades knew and loved in him so well. A Spanish captain, named Don Frederigo Mendez, approached him. He was as young, and as much accustomed to martial exercises; but his disposition was as reserved and thoughtful as Heimbert's was gentle and frank. "Pardon me, señor," began the solemn Spaniard, "if I disturb your meditations; but I have so often known you as a courageous warrior and faithful companion in arms, in the many hot fights in which I have had the honour to see you, that I would choose you before all others for a knightly service, if it will not interfere with your own plans and projects for this evening."

"Dear sir," frankly returned Heimbert; "I have an affair of importance to transact before sunrise; but till midnight I am right willing and ready to render you any service as a brother in arms."

"Enough," said Frederigo; "for before midnight must the tones have long ceased, in which I take leave of the dearest creature I have known in my native city. But, that you may understand the whole affair, as my noble companion should, listen to me attentively for a few moments:—

"Some time before I left Malaga, to join our great emperor's army, and to assist in spreading the glory of his arms in Italy, I served, after the manner of young knights, a damsel of this city, the beautiful Lucilla. She stood hardly on the border that divides childhood from growing womanhood; and as I, then a mere boy, offered my homage with friendly childlike mind, so my young mistress in similar guise received it.

"At last I went to Italy, as you very well know, who were my companion in many a hot fight, as well as in many a magic and tempting scene in that luxurious land. Through all our changes I held the image of my gentle mistress stedfastly, and never once relinquished the service and faith I had vowed to her; though I will not conceal from you, that it was more to fulfil the word I had pledged at my departure than from any immoderate glowing feeling of my heart. When we returned to my native city, a few weeks since, I found my lady married to one of the richest and most distinguished knights of Malaga. Fiercer far than love, jealousy (that almost almighty child of heaven and hell) now spurred me on to follow Lucilla's steps. From her dwelling to the church—from thence to the houses of her friends, and, again to her home; and even, as far as possible, into the circle of knights and ladies which surrounds her, I unweariedly pursued her. I thus assured myself that no other young knight attended her, and that she had entirely devoted herself to the husband her parents had selected for her, although he was not the one of her heart's choice. This so fully contented me, that I should not have had occasion to trouble you at this moment, if Lucilla had not approached me the other day, and whispered in my ear, that I should not provoke her husband, for he was very passionate and bold; to herself it threatened no danger—not the least—because he loved and honoured her above all things; but upon that very account would his anger fall more fearfully upon me. You can now easily understand, my noble comrade, that to preserve my character for contempt of danger I must now pursue Lucilla's steps more closely than ever, and sing nightly serenades beneath her flowery window till the morning star makes its mirror in the sea. At midnight, Lucilla's husband sets out for Madrid, and after that hour I will carefully avoid the street in which she dwells; but until then, as soon as the evening is sufficiently advanced, I will not cease to sing love-romances before his house. I have learnt that not only he, but also Lucilla's brothers have engaged in the quarrel; and it is this, señor, which makes me request for a short time the assistance of your good sword."

Heimbert warmly seized the Spaniard's hand, and said, "To shew you, dear sir, how willingly I undertake what you wish, I will meet your confidence with like frankness, and relate a pleasant incident which happened to me in this city, and beg you, after midnight, to render me a little service. My story is short, and will not detain you longer than we must wait for the twilight to become deep enough to begin your serenade.

"The day after we arrived here, I was amusing myself in one of the beautiful gardens which surround us. I have now been long in these southern lands, but I believe the dreams which every night carry me back to my German home are the cause of my finding every thing about me here so strange and astonishing still. At all events, wnen I wake each morning I wonder anew, as if I was just arrived. I was then wandering among the aloes, and under the laurel and oleander trees, as one bewildered. Suddenly I heard a cry near me, and a young lady, dressed in white, flew into my arms and fainted away, while her companions separated in every direction. A soldier has always his senses about him, and I soon perceived a furious bull pursuing the beautiful damsel. Quickly I threw her over a flowery hedge, and sprang after myself, whilst the beast, blind with rage, passed us by; and I could afterwards hear no more of it, than that it had escaped from a neighbouring court-yard, where some youths were trying to commence a bull-fight, and had broken furiously into this garden.

"I was now alone with the senseless lady in my arms; and she was so wondrously beautiful that I have never in my whole life felt happier or sadder than at that moment. I laid her upon the grass, and sprinkled her angel-brow with water from a fountain near us. At last she came to herself, and as she opened her lovely eyes, I thought I now knew how the blessed spirits look in heaven.

"She thanked me with grateful and courteous words, and called me her knight. But I was so enchanted, I could not utter a word; and she must almost have thought me dumb. At length my speech returned; and I ventured to breathe a request—which came from my heart—that the lovely lady would often give me the happiness of seeing her in this garden, for the few weeks I should remain here, till the service of the emperor should drive me forth to the burning sands of Africa. She looked at me, half smiling, half sadly, and murmured, 'Yes.' And she has kept her word, and appeared there daily, without our having yet ventured to speak to one another. For though we were sometimes quite alone, I could not do more than enjoy the happiness of walking by her side. Often she has sung to me; and I have answered her in song. When I yesterday informed her that our departure was so near, I fancied there was a tear in her heavenly eye; and I must have looked very sorrowful also, for she said, consolingly, 'Ah, pious, childlike warrior! one may confide in you as in an angel. After midnight, before the twilight summons you to embark, I give you leave to say farewell to me in this place. If you could find a faithful friend, whose silence you could depend on, to watch the entrance from the street, it might be as well; for many soldiers will be at that time returning from their last carouse in the city.' Now God has sent me such a friend; and I shall go joyfully to the lovely maiden."

"I wish the service you require had more danger," answered Frederigo, "that I might better prove to you how faithfully I would serve you with life and limb. But come, noble brother! the hour of my adventure is arrived."

Frederigo took a guitar under his arm; and wrapping themselves in their mantles, the young captains hastily made their way to the city.

The night-violets before Lucilla's window were pouring forth their sweet perfume, when Frederigo, leaning in the angle of an old wide shadowing church opposite, began to tune his guitar. Heimbert placed himself behind a pillar, his drawn sword under his mantle, and his clear blue eyes, like two watching stars, quietly penetrating around.

Frederigo sang:—

"Fair in the spring-bright meadows grew
A little flower in May,
And rosy-tinted petals threw
A blush upon its snowy hue,
Beneath the sunny ray.

To me, a youth, that little flower
My soul's delight became;
And often then, in happy hour,
I taught my tongue with courteous power
Some flattering lay to frame.

But ah! from where the floweret stood
  In delicate array,
Was I to distant scenes of blood,
To foreign lands, o'er field and flood,
  Soon summoned far away.

And now I am returned again,
  I seek my lovely flower:
But all my hopeful search is vain;
Transplanted from its grassy plain,
  My flower is free no more.

A gardener has the treasure found,
  And claimed it for his prize:
Now cherished in a guarded bound,
And hedged with golden lattice round,
  She is denied mine eyes.

His lattice he may freely twine,
  His jealous bars I grant:
But *all* I need not yet resign;
For still this pure delight is mine,
  Her wondrous praise to chant.

And, wandering in the coolness there,
  I'll touch my cithern's string,
Still celebrate the floweret fair;
While e'en the gardener shall not dare
  Forbid my voice to sing."

"That remains to be proved, señor," said a man, stepping close, and, as he thought, unobserved, to Frederigo. He had been apprised of the stranger's approach by a signal from his watchful friend, and answered with the greatest coolness: "If you wish to commence a suit with my guitar, señor, you will find she has a tongue of steel, which has already on many occasions done her excellent service. With which do you wish to speak?—with the guitar, or with the advocate?"

While the stranger hesitated what to reply to this bold

speech, Heimbert perceived two mantled figures draw near, and remain standing a few steps from him—one behind the other, so as to cut off Frederigo's flight, if he had intended to escape.

"I believe, dear sirs," said Sir Heimbert, in a friendly manner, "we are here on the same errand: to take care that no one intrudes upon the conference of yonder knights. At least, that is my business. And I can assure you, that any one who attempts to interfere with their affair shall receive my dagger in his heart. You see we shall best fulfil our duty by remaining still." The two gentlemen bowed courteously, and were silent.

So astonishing was the quiet self-possession with which the two soldiers carried on their affair, that their three companions were at a loss to imagine how they would commence their quarrel. At last Frederigo again touched his guitar, and appeared about to begin another song. At this mark of contempt and unconsciousness of danger, Lucilla's husband (for it was he who had taken his stand by Don Frederigo) was so enraged, that he, without further delay, snatched his sword from its sheath, and called out in a voice of suppressed rage: "Draw! or I shall stab you!"

"Very willingly, señor," answered Frederigo, composedly. "You have no need to threaten me, and might quite as well have spoken quietly." So saying, he laid his guitar in a niche in the church-wall, seized his weapon, and, bowing gracefully to his adversary, the fight began.

For some time the two figures by Heimbert's side, who were Lucilla's brothers, remained quite quiet; but as Frederigo began to get the better of their brother-in-law, they made a movement, as if they would take part in the fight. At this, Heimbert made his good sword gleam in the moonlight, and said: "Dear sirs, you surely would not wish me to put my threat into execution. Pray do not oblige me to do so; for if it cannot be otherwise, doubt not I shall keep my word." The two young men remained from this time quite motionless, surprised at the cheerful, true-hearted friendliness of all Heimbert's words.

Meanwhile had Frederigo, though pressing hard upon his adversary, yet carefully avoided wounding him; and at last, by a dexterous movement, he wrested his weapon from him; so that Lucilla's husband, in the surprise and shock of this unexpected advantage, retreated a few steps. Frederigo threw the sword in the air, and adroitly catching it near the point as it descended, said, as he offered the ornamented hilt to his opponent: "Take it, señor; and I hope this matter is ended; and you now understand that I am only here to shew I fear no danger in the world. The bell tolls twelve from the old dome; and I give you my word of honour, as a knight and a soldier, that neither is Doña Lucilla pleased with my attentions, nor should I, if I lived a hundred years in Malaga, continue to serenade her. So pursue your journey in peace; and farewell." Then he once more greeted his conquered adversary with solemn, stern courtesy, and withdrew. Heimbert followed him, after he had cordially shaken hands with the two brothers, saying: "Never let it again enter your heads, dear young gentlemen, to interfere in an honourable fight. Do you understand me?"

He soon overtook his companion, and walked by his side in silence—his heart beating with joy, sorrow, and expectation. Don Frederigo Mendez was also silent, till Heimbert stopped before a garden-door overhung with fruitful orange-boughs, and pointing to a pomegranate-tree laden with fruit, said: "We are at the place, dear comrade." Then the Spaniard appeared about to ask a question; but he checked himself, and merely said: "Understand me: you have my word of honour to protect this entrance for you till the hour of dawn." He began walking to and fro before the gate with drawn sword, like a sentinel; whilst Heimbert, trembling with joy, hastened through the dark groves within.

CHAPTER II.

He had not far to seek the lovely star which he so deeply felt was the one destined to shed its light over his whole life. The full moon revealed to him the slender form of the lady walking near the entrance. She wept softly, and yet smiled with such composure, that her tears seemed rather to resemble a decoration of pearls than a veil of sorrow.

The lovers wandered silently beside one another through the flowery pathway, half in sorrow, half in joy; while sometimes the night-air touched the guitar on the lady's arm so lightly, that a slight murmur blended with the song of the nightingale; or her delicate fingers on the strings awoke a few fleeting chords, and the shooting stars seemed as if they would pursue the retreating tones of the guitar.

O how truly blessed was this hour to the youth and maiden! for now neither rash wishes nor impure desires had any place in their minds. They walked side by side, satisfied that the good God had granted them this happiness; and so little desiring any thing farther, that the fleeting and perishable nature of the present floated away in the background of their thoughts. In the midst of this beautiful garden they found a large open lawn, ornamented with statues, and surrounding a fountain. On the edge of this the lovers sat down, alternately fixing their eyes on the water sparkling in the moonlight and on one another. The maiden touched her guitar; and Heimbert, compelled by some irresistible impulse, sang the following words to it:

"A sweet, sweet life have I,
But cannot name its charm;
Oh! would it teach me consciously,
That so my lips, in calm,
Soft, gentle songs, should ever praise
What my fond spirit endless says."

He suddenly stopped, and blushed, for he feared he had said too much. The lady blushed also; and after playing some time, half abstractedly, on the strings, she sang as if still in a dream:—

"Who beside the youth is singing,
 Seated on the tender grass,
Where the moon her light is flinging,
 And the sparkling waters pass?

Shall the maid reveal her name,
 When, though still unknown it be,
Glows her trembling cheek with shame,
 And her heart beats anxiously?

First let the knight be nam'd—'tis he
 Who, in his bright array,
With Spaniards stood triumphantly
 Upon the glorious day.

Who before Pavia bravely fought,
 A boy of sixteen years:
Pride to his country hath he brought,
 And to his foemen fears.

Heimbert is his noble name;
 Victor he in many a fight:
Dona Clara feels no shame,
 Sitting by so brave a knight,

In her name's soft sound revealing,
 Seated on the tender grass,
Where the moonbeams' light is stealing,
 And the sparkling waters pass."

"Ah," said Heimbert, blushing more deeply than before,—"oh, Doña Clara, that affair at Pavia was a very insignificant feat of arms; and if it had deserved a reward, what could better serve as one than the surpassing bliss which I now enjoy? Now I know what your name is, and dare address you by it, you angel bright, Doña Clara! you blessed and beautiful Doña Clara! Only tell me who has made so favourable a report of my youthful deeds, that I may ever think of him gratefully."

"Can the noble Heimbert of Waldhausen suppose," replied Clara, "that the warriors of Spain sent no sons where he stood in battle? You have surely seen them near you in the fight; and how, then, can it surprise you that your glories are known here?"

They now heard the silvery tones of a little bell from the neighbouring palace, and Clara whispered, "It is time to part: adieu, my hero!" And she smiled on Heimbert through her tears; and as she bent towards him, he almost fancied he felt a gentle kiss breathed on his lips. When he looked around, Clara had disappeared: the morning clouds began to assume the rosy tint of dawn, and he rejoined his watchful friend at the entrance-door, with a whole heaven of love's proud happiness in his heart.

"Stand! no further!" exclaimed Frederigo, as Heimbert appeared from the garden, holding, at the same time, his drawn sword towards him.

"Oh, you are mistaken, my good comrade," said the German, laughing,—"it is I whom you see before you."

"Don't imagine, Sir Heimbert of Waldhausen, that I mistake you," said Frederigo; "but I have kept my word, and honourably fulfilled my promise to be your guard in this place; and now I demand of you to draw without further delay, and fight for your life."

"Alas!" sighed Heimbert, "I have often heard that there are witches in these southern lands, who have the power to deprive people of their senses with their magic arts and charms, but till to-day I have never experienced any thing of the sort. Think better of it, my dear comrade, and go with me to the shore."

Frederigo smiled scornfully, and answered, "Leave off your silly nonsense; and if one must explain every thing to you, word by word, before you understand it, I will tell you that the lady you came to meet in this my garden, Doña Clara Mendez, is my only and dearest sister. Now lose no further time, and draw, señor."

"God forbid!" exclaimed the German, without touching his weapon: "you shall be my brother-in-law, Frederigo, and not my murderer, still less will I be yours."

Frederigo shook his head angrily, and advanced with measured steps towards his companion. Heimbert, however, continued motionless, and said, "No, Frederigo, I can never do *you* any harm; for not only do I love your sister, but you must certainly be the person who has spoken to her so honourably of my battle-deeds in Italy."

"If I did so," answered Frederigo, "I was a fool. But thou, thou weak coward, draw thy sword, or—"

Frederigo had hardly spoken these words, before Heimbert, glowing with indignation, snatched his sword from its sheath, exclaiming, "This the devil himself could not bear!" And now the two young captains fiercely closed upon one another.

This was quite another battle to that which Frederigo had previously fought with Lucilla's husband. The two soldiers well understood their weapons, and boldly strove with one another; the light gleamed from their swords, as first one and then the other made a deadly thrust with the speed of lightning, which his adversary as speedily turned aside. Firmly they planted the left foot, as if rooted in the earth, the right advanced one step to make each onset, and then quickly withdrawn to recover their footing. From the resolution and quiet self-possession with which both combatants fought, it was easy to see that one or other of them must find his grave beneath the orange-trees, whose overhanging boughs were now illuminated by the glow of morning. This would certainly have been the case, had not the report of a cannon from the harbour reached them.

The combatants stopped as at an understood signal,

and silently counted till thirty, when a second gun was heard. "That is the signal for embarkation, señor," said Frederigo; "we are now in the emperor's service, and all fighting is unlawful which is not against the foes of Charles the Fifth. We must defer our combat until the termination of the war."

The two captains hastened to the shore, and were engaged in the embarkation of their troops. The sun, rising from the sea, shone at once on the ships and the water.

CHAPTER III.

The voyagers had for some time to contend with contrary winds; and when, at last, the coast of Barbary became visible, the evening closed so deeply over the sea, that no pilot in the little squadron would venture nearer land, and they anchored in the calm sea. They crossed themselves, and anxiously waited for the morning; while the soldiers, full of hope and anticipation of honour, assembled in groups upon the decks, straining their eyes to see the long-desired scene of their glory.

Meanwhile the heavy firing of besiegers and besieged thundered unceasingly from the fortress of Goletta; and as the heavy clouds of night thickened over the shore, the flames of the burning houses in the city became more visible, and the course of the fiery shots could be distinctly traced as they crossed each other in their path of frightful devastation. It was evident that the Musselmans had sallied forth, for a sharp fire of musketry was suddenly heard amidst the roaring of the cannon. The fight now approached the trenches of the Christians; and from the ships they could hardly see whether the besiegers were in danger or not. At last they perceived that the Turks were driven back into the fortress: thither the Christian host pursued them, and loud shouts of victory were heard from the Spanish camp—Goletta was taken!

The troops on board the ships were composed of young courageous men; and how their hearts glowed and beat high at this glorious spectacle need not be detailed to those who carry a brave heart in their own bosoms; while to any other, all description would be thrown away.

Heimbert and Frederigo stood near one another. "I know not," said the latter, "what it is which tells me that to-morrow I must plant my standard upon yonder height, which is so brightly lighted up by the burning brands in Goletta." "That is just my feeling," said Heimbert. Then the two captains were silent, and turned angrily away.

The wished-for morning at last arose, the ships neared the shore, and the troops landed, while an officer was immediately despatched to apprise the mighty general Alva of the arrival of this reinforcement. The soldiers hastily ranged themselves on the beach, and were soon in battle-order, to await the inspection of their great leader.

Clouds of dust appeared in the grey twilight, and the officer, hastening back, announced the approach of the general. And because, in the language of Castile, *Alva* signifies 'morning,' the Spaniards raised a shout of triumph at the happy omen they perceived in the first beams of the rising sun and the head of the general's staff becoming visible together.

Alva's stern pale face soon appeared: he was mounted upon a large Andalusian charger of the deepest black, and galloped up and down the lines once; then, halting in the middle, looked over the ranks with a scrutinising eye, and said, with evident satisfaction, "You pass muster well. 'Tis as it should be. I like to see you in such order, and can perceive that, notwithstanding your youth, you are tried soldiers. We will first hold a review, and then I will lead you to something more interesting."

He dismounted, and, walking to the right wing, began

to inspect one troop after another in the closest manner, summoning each captain to his side, and exacting from him an account of the most minute particulars. Sometimes a cannon-ball from the fortress whistled over the heads of the soldiers; and then Alva would stand still, and closely observe their countenances. When he saw that no eye moved, a contented smile spread itself over his solemn face.

When he had thus examined both divisions, he remounted his horse, and again placed himself in the middle. Stroking his long beard, he said, "You are in such good order, soldiers, that you shall take your part in the glorious day which now dawns for our Christian Armada. We will take Barbarossa! Do you hear the drums and fifes in the camp? and see him sally forth to meet the emperor? Yonder is the place for you!"

"Vivat Carolus Quintus!" resounded through the ranks. Alva beckoned the captains to him, and appointed to each his duty. He was used to mingle the German and Spanish troops together, that emulation might increase their courage; and on the present occasion it happened that Heimbert and Frederigo were commanded to storm the height which, now illumined by the beams of morning, they recognised as the very same that had appeared so inviting the night before.

The cannons roared, and the trumpets sounded, the colours waved proudly in the breeze, and the leaders gave the word "March!" when the troops rushed on all sides to the battle.

Thrice had Frederigo and Heimbert almost forced their way through a breach in the wall of the fortifications on the height, and thrice were they repulsed by the fierce resistance of the Turks into the valley below. The Musselmans shouted after the retreating foe, clashed their weapons furiously together, and contemptuously laughing, asked whether any one would again venture to give heart and brain to the scimitar, and his body to the rolling stones. The two captains, gnashing their teeth with fury, rearranged their ranks, in order to fill the places of the slain and mortally wounded in these three fruitless attacks. Meanwhile a murmur ran through the Christian host, that a witch fought for the enemy, and helped them to conquer.

At this moment Duke Alva rode up to them; he looked sharply at the breach they had made. "Could you not break through the foe *here?*" said he, shaking his head. "This surprises me; for from you two youths and your troops I expected better things."

"Do you hear, do you hear *that?*" cried the captains, pacing through their lines.

The soldiers shouted loudly, and demanded to be led once more against the enemy. Even those mortally wounded exerted their last breath to cry, "Forward, comrades!"

Swift as an arrow had the great Alva leapt from his horse, and, seizing a partisan from the stiff hand of one of the slain, he placed himself before them, and cried, "I will have part in your glory! In the name of God and of the Blessed Virgin, forwards, my children!"

They rushed joyfully up the hill, all hearts reanimated, and raising their war-cry to heaven, while a few already cried, "Victoria! Victoria!" and the Musselmans seemed to give way. Then, like the vision of an avenging angel, a maiden, dressed in richly embroidered garments of purple and gold, appeared in the Turkish ranks; and those who were terrified before, now shouted, "Allah!" and accompanied that name with "Zelinda, Zelinda!" The maiden drew a small box from beneath her arm; and after opening and breathing into it, threw it among the Christian army. A wild explosion from this destructive engine scattered through the host a whole fire of rockets, grenades, and other fearful messengers of death. The astounded troops held on through the storm. "On, on!" cried Alva; and "On!" echoed the two captains. But at that moment a flaming bolt fastened on the duke's high-plumed cap, and burnt and crackled about his head, so that the general fell fainting down the height. Then the Spanish and German troops were generally routed, and fled hurriedly from the fearful height before the storm. The Musselmans again shouted; and Zelinda's beauty shone over the conquering host like a baleful star.

When Alva opened his eyes, he saw Heimbert standing over him, his clothes, face, and arms scorched by the fire he had with much difficulty extinguished on his commander's head, when a second body of flame rolled down the height in the same manner. The duke was thanking the youth for his preservation, when some soldiers came by, who told him the Saracen power had commenced an attack on the opposite wing of the army. Alva threw himself on the first horse they brought him, and without losing a word, dashed to the place where the threatened danger called him.

Frederigo's glowing eye was fixed on the rampart where the brilliant lady stood, with her snow-white arm extended in the act of hurling a two-edged spear; sometimes encouraging the Musselmans in Arabic, then again speaking scornfully to the Christians in Spanish. Don Frederigo exclaimed, "Oh, foolish lady! she thinks to daunt me, and yet places herself before me,—so tempting, so irresistible a war-prize!"

And as if magic wings had grown from his shoulders, he began to fly up the height with such swiftness, that Alva's storm-flight from thence appeared a lazy snail's pace. Before any one could see how he had gained the height, and wresting spear and shield from the lady, he seized her in his arms, and attempted to bear her away as his prize, while Zelinda clung with both hands to the palisade in anxious despair. Her cries for help were unavailing; partly because the Turks were stupified with astonishment to see the magic power of the lady overcome by the almost magic deed of the youth, and partly because the faithful Heimbert, immediately on perceiving his companion's enterprise, had led both troops to his support, and now stood by his side, fighting hand to hand with the besieged. This time the fury of the Musselmans, overcome as they were by surprise and superstition, availed nothing against the prowess of the Christian soldiers.

The Spaniards and Germans broke through the enemy, assisted by fresh squadrons of their army. The Mohammedans fled with frightful howling; and the banner of the holy German empire, and that of the imperial house of Castile, united by joyful Victorias, waved over the glorious battle-field before the walls of Tunis.

CHAPTER IV.

ZELINDA had escaped from Frederigo's arms in the confusion of the conquerors and conquered, and flew so swiftly through the well-known ground, that though love and desire added wings to his feet, she was soon out of sight. This kindled the fury of the enchanted Spaniard so much the more against the infidel foe. Wherever they collected their scattered force to withstand the progress of the Christians, he hastened with the troops, which ranged themselves around him as about a victorious banner; while Heimbert was ever at his side like a faithful shield, often warding off from his friend dangers which were unperceived by the infatuated youth.

They learnt that Barbarossa had fled the day before, and pushed onwards with little opposition through the gates of Tunis.

Frederigo's and Heimbert's troops were always together.

Thick clouds of smoke began to roll through the streets, and the soldiers had frequently to shake off the sparks and burning fragments which fell upon their coats and richly plumed helmets. "Suppose the enemy has set fire to the powder-magazine in despair!" exclaimed the thoughtful Heimbert. And Frederigo, to whom a word or sign was sufficient, hastened to the spot from whence the smoke proceeded. Their troops pressed closely after them.

A sudden turn in the street brought them upon a magnificent palace, out of whose beautifully ornamented windows the flames were already bursting. Their fitful splendour seemed to make them like death-torches, prepared to do honour to the costly building in the hour of its ruin, as they illuminated first one part and then another of the massy edifice, and then sunk down again into fearful darkness of smoke and vapour.

And like a faultless statue, the crowning glory of the whole, Zelinda stood upon a giddy projection, wreathed around with gleaming tongues of flame, calling upon the faithful to assist her in securing from destruction the wisdom of many centuries, which was laid up in this building. The pinnacle tottered with the effects of the fire beneath, and a few stones gave way. Frederigo anxiously cried to the endangered lady; and hardly had she withdrawn her lovely foot, when the whole came crashing down on the pavement. Zelinda disappeared within the burning palace, and Frederigo rushed up the marble steps; Heimbert, his ever-faithful friend, immediately following.

Their swift feet led them into a vast saloon, where they saw high arches over their heads, and a labyrinth of chambers opening one into another around them. The walls were all ranged with splendid shelves, in which were stored rolls of parchment, papyrus, and palm-leaf, inscribed with the long-forgotten characters of past ages, which had now reached the end of their designs; for the flames were creeping in destruction among them, and stretched their serpent-like heads from one repository of learning to another; while the Spanish soldiers, who had hoped for plunder, were enraged at finding this mighty building filled only with these parchments, and the more so, because they discerned in them nothing but what appeared to them magical characters.

Frederigo flew, as in a dream, through the strange halls, now half consumed, ever calling Zelinda; not thinking or caring for any thing but his enchanting beauty. Long did Heimbert remain at his side, till they reached a cedar staircase which led to a higher story, where Frederigo listened a moment, and then said: "She is speaking there aloud! she needs my help!" and sprung up the glowing steps. Heimbert hesitated an instant, for he saw them giving way, and thought to warn his companion; but at that moment they broke down, and left nothing but a fiery path. Still he could see that Frederigo had clung to an iron grating, over which he soon swung himself. The way was inaccessible to Heimbert: quickly recollecting himself, he lost no time in idly gazing, but hastily sought another flight of stairs in the neighbouring halls, which would conduct him to his friend.

Meanwhile Frederigo, following the enchanting voice, had reached a gallery, in the midst of which was a fearful abyss of flames, while the pillars on each side were yet standing. He soon perceived the lovely figure of Zelinda, who clung to a pillar with one hand, while with the other she threatened some Spanish soldiers, who seemed every moment about to seize her, and already had her delicate foot advanced to the edge of the glowing gulf. It was impossible for Frederigo to join her, for the breadth of the separating flames was far too great to spring across. Trembling lest his voice should make the maiden, through either terror or anger, precipitate herself into the abyss, he spoke quite softly over the fiery grave: "Ah, Zelinda! have no such frightful thoughts; your preserver is here!" The maiden bowed her queenly head. And when Frederigo saw her so calm and composed, he cried with all the thunder of a warrior's voice, "Back! you rash plunderers! whoever advances one step nearer to that lady shall feel the weight of my anger!" They started, and appeared willing to retire, till one among them said, "The knight can do us no harm — the gulf is a little too broad for that; and as for the lady's throwing herself in, it is evident that the young knight is her lover; and whoever has a lover is not so inclined to throw herself away." At this they laughed, and again advanced. Zelinda neared the flaming edge; but Frederigo, with the fury of a lion, had torn his target from his arm, and now flung it across with so sure an aim, that the rash leader fell senseless to the ground. The rest again stood still. "Away with you!" cried Frederigo, authoritatively; "or my dagger shall strike the next as surely; nor will I ever rest till I have found you out, and made you feel the force of my vengeance." The dagger gleamed in the youth's hand, and yet more fearfully gleamed the rage in his eyes. The soldiers fled. Then Zelinda bowed courteously to her preserver; and taking a roll of palm-leaves which lay at her feet, she hastily disappeared at a side-door of the gallery. In vain did Frederigo seek her in the burning palace.

The great Alva held a council with his officers in an open place in the midst of the conquered city, and, by means of an interpreter, questioned the Moorish prisoners what had become of the beautiful enchantress who had been seen encouraging them on the walls, and who, he said, was the most lovely sorceress the world ever saw. Nothing could be gained from the answers; for though all knew her to be a noble lady, well versed in magic lore, none seemed able to tell from whence she had entered Tunis, or whither she had now fled. At last, when they had begun to think their ignorance was the pretence of obstinacy, an old dervish, who had been hitherto unnoticed, pressed forward, and said, with a scornful smile: "Whoever wishes to seek the lady, the way is open for him. I will not conceal what I know of her destination; and I *do* know something. Only you must first promise me I shall not be compelled to guide any one to her, or my lips shall remain closed for ever; and you may do what you will with me." He looked like one who would keep his word; and Alva, who was pleased with the man's resolute spirit (so akin to his own), gave him the desired assurance. The dervish began his relation.

He was once, he said, wandering in the endless desert of Sahara—perhaps from empty curiosity, and perhaps for a better reason. He lost his way; and at last, when wearied to death, he reached one of those fruit-bearing islands which they call an oasis. Now followed a description of the things he saw there, clothed in all the warmth of oriental imagery; so that the hearts of his hearers sometimes melted within them, and sometimes their hair stood on end at the horrors he related; though, from the strange pronunciation of the speaker, and from his hurried way of speaking, they could hardly understand half he said. The end of all was, that Zelinda dwelt upon this blooming island, surrounded on all sides by the pathless desert, and protected by magic terrors. On her way thither, as the old dervish very well knew, she had left the city half an hour before. The contemptuous words with which he closed his speech shewed plainly that he desired nothing more than that some Christian would undertake the journey, which would inevitably lead him to destruction. At the same time he solemnly affirmed he had uttered nothing but undoubted truth, as a man would do who knows that things are just as he related them. Thoughtful and astonished were the circle of officers around him.

Heimbert had just joined the party, after seeking his friend in the burning palace, and collecting and arranging their troops in such a manner as to prevent the possibility of any surprise from the robber-hordes. He now advanced before Alva, and humbly bowed.

"What wilt thou, my young hero?" said Alva, greeting the young captain in the most friendly manner. "I know your smiling, blooming countenance well. The last time I saw you, you stood like a protecting angel over me. I am so sure that you can make no request but what is knightly and honourable, that I grant it, whatever it may be."

"My gracious general," said Heimbert, whose cheeks glowed at this praise, "if I may venture to ask a favour, it is, that you will give me permission to follow the lady Zelinda in the way this strange dervish has pointed out."

The great general bowed assentingly, and added: "To a more noble knight could not this honourable adventure be consigned."

"I do not know that," said an angry voice in the crowd; "but this I do know, that to me, above all other men, this adventure belongs, as a reward for the capture of Tunis. For who was the first on the height and in the city?"

"That was Don Frederigo Mendez," said Heimbert, taking the speaker by the hand, and leading him before Alva. "In his favour I will willingly resign my reward; for he has done the emperor and the army better service than I have."

"Neither of you shall lose his reward," said Alva. "Each has now permission to seek the maiden in whatever way he thinks best."

Swift as lightning the two young captains escaped from the circle on opposite sides.

CHAPTER V.

Like a vast trackless sea, without one object to break the dreary monotony of its horizon, ever white and ever desolate, the great desert of Sahara stretches itself before the eyes of the unhappy wanderer who has lost himself in this frightful region. And, in another way, it resembles the ocean. It throws up waves; and often a burning mist is seen on its surface. Not, indeed, the gentle play of the waves which unite all the coasts of the earth; where each wave, as it rolls onward, brings you a message of love from the far island-kingdoms, and carries your answer with it in a love-flowing dance. These waves are only the wild toying of the hot wind with the faithless dust, which always falls back again upon its joyless plain, and never reaches the solid land, where happy men dwell. It is not the lovely cool sea-breeze in which the friendly fays sport themselves, and form their blooming gardens and stately grottoes: it is the suffocating vapour rebelliously given back to the glowing sun by the unfruitful sands.

Hither the two captains arrived at the same time, and stood struck with astonishment at the pathless chaos before them. Traces of Zelinda, which were not easily hidden, had hitherto compelled them to travel almost always together, however displeased Frederigo might be, and whatever angry glances he cast upon his unwelcome companion. Each had hoped to overtake Zelinda before she reached the desert, well knowing how almost impossible it would be to find her, if she had once entered it. And now they had failed in this, and could obtain no further information from the few Arabs they met, than that there existed a tradition that any one who would travel in a southerly direction, guiding his course by the stars, would, the sages maintained, arrive at a wonderfully blooming oasis, the dwelling of a heavenly beautiful enchantress. But all this appeared to the speakers to be highly uncertain and mysterious.

The young men looked troubled; and their horses snorted and started back at the treacherous sand, while even the riders were uneasy and perplexed. Then they sprang from their saddles suddenly, as at some word of command; and taking the bridles from their horses, and slackening the girths, they turned them loose on the plain, to find their way back to the habitation of man. They took some provision from their saddle-bags, placed it on their shoulders, and, casting from their feet their heavy riding-boots, they plunged, like two courageous swimmers, into the endless waste.

With no other guide than the sun by day, and by night the host of stars, the two captains soon lost sight of one another; for Frederigo had avoided the object of his displeasure; while Heimbert, thinking of nothing but the end of his journey, and firmly relying upon God's protection pursued his course in a due southerly direction.

The night had many times succeeded the day, when, one evening, Heimbert was quite alone on the endless desert, without one fixed object for his eye to rest upon; the light flask he carried was empty; and the evening brought with it, instead of the desired coolness, only suffocating columns of sand; so that the exhausted wanderer was obliged to press his burning face to the scorching plain to escape the death-bringing cloud. Sometimes he thought he heard footsteps near him, and the sound of a wide mantle rustling over him; but when he raised himself with anxious haste, he only saw what he had already too often seen in the daytime—the wild beasts of the wilderness roaming about the desert in undisturbed freedom. Now it was a frightful camel, then a long-necked ungainly giraffe, or a great ostrich with its wings outspread. They all appeared to scoff at him; and he resolved to open his eyes no more, but rather perish, without allowing these hateful and strange creatures to disturb his soul in the hour of death.

Soon he heard the sound of horse's hoofs and neighing, and saw a shadow on the sand, and heard a man's voice close to him. Half unwilling, he yet could not resist raising himself wearily; when he saw a rider in an Arab's dress on a slender Arabian horse. Overcome with joy at the sight of a human being, he exclaimed: "Welcome, O man, in this frightful waste! and succour, if thou canst, thy fellow-man, who must otherwise perish with thirst." And then remembering that the tones of his dear German mother-tongue were not intelligible in this joyless land, he repeated these words in that common language, the *lingua*

Romana, which is universally used by Mohammedans and Christians in this part of the world.

The Arab was silent some time, and looked with scorn upon his strange discovery. At last he replied in the same language: "I was in Barbarossa's fight, sir knight, as well as you; and if our overthrow affected me bitterly, I now find no little satisfaction at seeing one of our conquerors lying so pitifully before me."

"Pitifully!" angrily repeated Heimbert; and his wounded feelings of honour for the moment giving him back all his strength, he seized his sword, and stood in battle order.

"Oh, oh!" laughed the Arab; "is the Christian viper so strong? Then it only remains for me to put spurs to my good steed, and leave thee to perish here, thou lost creeping worm."

"Ride where thou list, dog of a heathen!" retorted Heimbert. "Before I accept a crumb from thee, I *will* perish, unless the dear God sends me manna in this wilderness."

The Arab spurred his fleet horse, and galloped two hundred paces, laughing long and loud. He stopped, however, and, trotting back to Heimbert, said: "Thou art rather too good a knight to leave to die of hunger and thirst. Have a care, now: my good sabre shall reach thee."

Heimbert, who had again stretched himself in hopeless despair on the burning sand, was quickly roused by these words to his feet, sword in hand; and as the Arab's horse flew past him, with a sudden spring the stout German avoided the blow and parried the cut which the rider aimed at him with his Turkish scimitar.

Repeatedly did the Arab make similar attacks, vainly hoping to give his antagonist the death-blow. At last, overcome by impatience, he came so near, that Heimbert was able to seize him by the girdle and tear him from the fast-galloping horse. With this violent exertion, Heimbert also fell to the ground, but he lay above his adversary; and holding a dagger he had pulled from his girdle before his face, he said: "Wilt thou have mercy or death?"

The Arab closed his eyes before the murderous steel, and answered: "Have pity on me, thou brave warrior! I surrender to thee."

Heimbert commanded him to throw away the sabre he still held in his right hand. He did so; and both combatants rose from the ground, to sink again immediately upon the sand; for the conqueror felt himself far weaker than the conquered.

The Arab's good horse had returned to his master, as is the custom of those noble animals, who never forsake even a fallen lord, and now stood behind them, stretching his long slender neck over them with a friendly look.

"Arab," said Heimbert, with exhausted voice, "take from thy horse what provision thou hast, and place it before me."

The subdued Arab did humbly what was commanded him, now submitting to the will of his conqueror, as he had before treated him with revengeful anger.

After taking some draughts of palm-wine from the skin, Heimbert looked at the youth with new eyes. He partook of some fruits, drank again of the wine, and said, "Have you much farther to ride this night, young man?"

"Yes, indeed," answered the Arab, sorrowfully. "Upon a very distant oasis dwells my aged father and my blooming bride. Now, even if you leave me my freedom, I must perish in this waste desert before I can reach my lovely home."

"Is that the oasis," asked Heimbert, "on which the powerful magic lady, Zelinda, dwells?"

"Allah forbid!" exclaimed the Arab, clasping his hands together. "Zelinda's wondrous island receives none but magicians, and lies far to the scorching south; while our friendly home stretches towards the cooler west."

"I only asked the question to see if we could be companions by the way," said Heimbert, kindly. "As that cannot be, we must divide every thing; for I would not have so good a soldier perish with hunger and thirst."

Saying this, the young captain began to divide the fruits and wine into two portions, placing the greater at his left hand, the smaller at his right, and desired the Arab to take the former. He listened with astonishment as Heimbert added: "See, good sir, I have either not much further to pursue my journey, or I shall die in this desert; of that I have a strong presentiment. Besides, I cannot carry so much on foot as you can on horseback."

"Knight! victorious knight!" cried the amazed Musselman, "do you give me my horse?"

"It would be a sin and shame to deprive so noble a rider of such a faithful beast," replied Heimbert, smiling. "Ride on, in God's name! and may you safely reach your destination."

He assisted him to mount; and just as the Arab was thanking him, he suddenly exclaimed, "The magic lady!" and, putting spurs to his horse, flew over the dusty plain swift as the wind; while Heimbert, on looking round, saw close beside him, in the bright moonlight, a shining figure, which he easily recognised to be Zelinda.

CHAPTER VI.

The lady looked fixedly at the young soldier, and appeared thinking how she should address him, while he, with astonishment at suddenly finding her he had so long sought, was equally at a loss for words. At length she said in Spanish, "Thou wonderful enigma, I have been witness to all that has passed between thee and the Arab; and the affair perplexes my head as a whirlwind. Tell me plainly, that I may know whether thou art a madman or an angel."

"I am neither one or other, dear lady," answered Heimbert, with his wonted friendliness. "I am only a poor wanderer, who have been obeying one of the commands of his dear Lord Jesus Christ."

"Sit down," said Zelinda, "and relate to me the history of thy lord, who must be an unheard-of person, if he has such servants as thee. The night is cool and still, and beside me thou hast nothing to fear from the dangers of the waste."

"Lady," replied Heimbert, smiling, "I am not of a fearful disposition, and when I am speaking of my blessed Lord and Redeemer, I know not the least anxiety."

So saying, they both sat down on the now cooled sand, and began a wondrous conversation, while the clear moon shone upon them like a magic lamp from the high blue heavens. Heimbert's words, full of love, and truth, and simplicity, sank like soft sunbeams into Zelinda's heart, driving away the unholy magic power which ruled her, and wrestling with that for possession of the noble territory of her soul. When the morning dawned, she said, "Thou wouldst not be called an angel, but surely thou art one; for what are the angels but messengers of the most high God?"

"In that sense," returned Heimbert, "I am content to be so called. My hope is, to bear His message at all times; and if He bestows further grace and strength upon me, it will give me pleasure if you become my companion in this pious work."

"That is not impossible," said Zelinda, thoughtfully. "But first come with me to my island, where thou shalt be entertained as beseems such an ambassador, far better than here on the desert sand, with miserable palm-wine, which thou must obtain with difficulty."

"Pardon me," answered Heimbert; "it is difficult to refuse a lady any request, but it is unavoidable on this occasion. In your island, many glorious things are brought together by forbidden arts, and their forms are changed from those the Almighty One created. These might dazzle my senses, and in the end enslave them. If you wish to hear more of those best and purest things which I can relate to you, you must come out to me on this barren sand. The Arab's dates and palm-wine will suffice for many a day yet."

"You would do much better to come with me," said Zelinda, shaking her head with a dissatisfied smile. "You were surely neither born nor educated for a hermit, and there is nothing upon my oasis so very mysterious as you suppose. What is there so strange in birds, and beasts, and flowers, being collected together from different parts of the world, and perhaps a little changed, so that one partakes of the nature of another, as you must have seen in our Arabian pictures? A moving changing flower, a bird growing on a branch, a fountain emitting fiery sparks, a singing bough—these truly are not such frightful, hateful things?"

"He must avoid temptation, who will not be overcome by it," answered Heimbert, very gravely. "I shall remain in the wilderness: is it your pleasure to visit me here again?"

Zelinda looked down, somewhat displeased, then lowly bending her head, she answered, "Yes; to-morrow evening I will be here." She turned away, and immediately disappeared in the rising storm-blast of the desert.

With the return of evening the lovely lady appeared, and watched the night through in holy converse with the inspired youth, leaving him in the morning humbler, purer, and more pious; and this went on for several days. "Thy palm-wine and dates must be consumed," said Zelinda one evening; and placed before Heimbert a flask of rich wine and some costly fruits. He, however, softly put the gifts aside, and answered, "Noble lady, I thank you from my heart, but I fear these have been made by your magic arts; or could you assure me that they are not, by Him whom you are beginning to know?" Zelinda's eyes sank in silent confusion, and she took back her gifts. The next evening she brought some similar provisions, and, smiling confidently, gave the desired assurance. Then Heimbert partook of them without scruple; and henceforth the pupil hospitably provided for the sustenance of her teacher in the wilderness.

And now, as the knowledge of the truth sank more deeply in Zelinda's soul, so that she often sat till morning listening to the young man with glowing cheeks, flowing hair, sparkling eyes, and folded hands, he carefully observed to make her understand that it was on account of his friend he had sought her in this dreary region, and that it was Frederigo's love for her which was the means of the highest good to her soul. She well remembered the handsome fearless young captain who had stormed the height and clasped her in his arms, and related to their friend how he had saved her in the burning library. Heimbert had many pleasant things to say of Frederigo; of his knightly deeds, his serious mind, and of his love to Zelinda, which, since the capture of Tunis, would not be hidden within his troubled breast, but betrayed itself in a thousand ways, sleeping or waking, to the young German. The godly truth, and the image of her loving hero, entered Zelinda's heart together, and both took root there. Heimbert's presence, and the almost adoring admiration with which his pupil regarded him, did not disturb this state of mind; for from the first moment, his appearance had something too pure and heavenly to allow of any thoughts of earthly love. When Heimbert was alone, he often smiled to himself, and said in his own beloved German language, "How delightful it is to be able, consciously, to repay Frederigo the service he did me, unconsciously, with his angelic sister!" Then he would sing such lovely German songs of Clara's beauty and pious grace, as sounded strangely pleasant in the wilderness, and beguiled his long and lonely hours.

As once Zelinda came in the evening light, her steps

airy and graceful, and carrying a basket of food for Heimbert on her lovely head, he smiled and shook his head, saying, "It is quite incomprehensible to me, lovely maiden, why you continue to come to me in this waste. You cannot find pleasure in magic arts now that the spirit of truth and love dwells within you; and if you changed all things in your oasis into the natural forms which the merciful God gave them, I could go thither with you, and we should have much more time for holy converse."

"Sir knight," answered Zelinda, "you speak truly, and I have thought of doing what you say for many days, but a strange visitor deprives me of the power. The dervish whom you saw in Tunis, is with me; and because in past days we have performed many magic works together, he thinks to usurp his former authority over me now. He perceives the alteration in me, and on that account is the more importunate."

"We must either expel or convert him," said Heimbert, girding on his sword, and taking up his shield from the ground. "Lead me, dear lady, to your wonderful island."

"You avoided it before," answered the astonished damsel, "and it still remains quite unchanged."

"Formerly it would have been only rashness to venture," returned Heimbert. "You came out to me here, which was better for us both. Now, however, the old serpent might destroy in you the work the Lord has done, and it is therefore a knightly duty to go. In God's name, then, to the work." And they hastened together across the darkening plain to the blooming island.

Magic airs began to play about their heads, and bright stars sparkled from the waving boughs beside their path. Heimbert fixed his eyes on the ground, and said, "Go before me, lovely lady, and guide me at once to the place where I shall find the dervish, for I will see as little of these distracting magic forms as is possible."

Zelinda did as he desired; and so, for the moment,

each performed the other's part. The maiden was the guide, while Heimbert followed, with confiding friendliness, in the unknown path.

Branches stooped as if to caress their cheeks; wonderful singing-birds grew from the bushes; golden and green serpents, with little golden crowns, crept on the velvet-turf, on which Heimbert stedfastly bent his eyes, and brilliant stones gleamed from the moss. When the serpents touched these jewels, they gave forth a silvery sound. The soldier let the serpents creep, and the precious stones sparkle, without caring for any thing save to follow hastily the footsteps of his guide.

"We are at the place," said she, with suppressed voice; and looking up, he saw a shining grotto of shells, and perceived within a man asleep, clad in a complete suit of gold scale-armour, of the old Numidian fashion.

"Is that also a phantom, in golden scales?" asked Heimbert, smiling.

"Oh, no," answered Zelinda, very gravely, "it is the dervish himself; and I see, from his having clothed himself in that coat of mail, which has been made invulnerable by being dipped in dragon's blood, that he has, by his magic, made himself aware of our intentions."

"What does that signify?" said Heimbert; "he must know them at last." And he began to call with cheerful voice, "Awake, old man! awake! here is an acquaintance of yours, to whom you must speak."

As the dervish opened his great rolling eyes, all the wondrous things in this magic region began to move: the water to dance, the branches to strike one another in wild confusion, and, at the same time, the jewels, and corals, and shells gave forth strange perplexing melodies.

"Roll and turn, thunder and play, as you will," cried Heimbert, looking stedfastly around him, "you shall not turn me from my good purpose; and to overpower all this tumult, God has given me a strong far-sounding soldier's voice." Then he turned to the dervish, saying, "It appears, old man, that you already know what has passed between Zelinda and me. If you do not know the whole matter, I will tell you, in a few words, that already she is as good as a Christian, and the bride of a noble Spanish knight. For your own sake, do not put any hindrance in the way; but it would be far better for you, if you would also become a Christian. Talk to me of this, and command all these devilries to cease; for see, dear sir, our religion speaks of such divine and heavenly things, that one must lay aside all rough and violent passions."

But the dervish, whose hatred glowed towards all Christians, hardly waited to hear the knight's last words before he pressed upon him with drawn scimitar. Heimbert put aside his thrust, saying, "Take care of yourself, sir: I have heard that your weapons are charmed; but that avails nought before my good sword, which has been consecrated in holy places." The dervish recoiled from the sword wildly, but as wildly sprang to the other side of his adversary, who only caught the deadly cuts with his target. Like a golden scaly dragon, the Mohammedan swung himself round Heimbert, with a ferocity which, with his long flowing white beard, had something ghastly and horrible in it. Heimbert was prepared to oppose him on all sides, only watching carefully for some opening in the scales made by his violent movements. At last it happened as he expected: he saw between the breast and arm the dark garments of the dervish, and there the German made his deadly thrust. The old man cried, "Allah! Allah!" and fell, fearful even in his fall, senseless to the ground.

"Yet I pity him," sighed Heimbert, leaning on his sword, and looking down on his fallen foe; "he fought nobly, and in his death he called upon his Allah, whom he believes to be the true God. We must give him honourable burial." He dug a grave with the broad scimitar of his adversary, laid the corpse in it, covering it with turf, and knelt in silent heartfelt prayer for the soul of the departed.

CHAPTER VII.

When Heimbert rose from his pious duty, his first glance fell on the smiling Zelinda, who stood by his side; the second, upon the completely changed scene around. Grottoes and caverns had vanished, and with them also the half-terrible, half-charming caricatures of trees and beasts; a gentle hillock of the softest green sloped on each side from the point where he stood to the sandy plain. Several little springs of water murmured in refreshing beauty, and date-trees overhung the pleasant spot, all now smiling with simple sweet peace in the beams of the rising sun.

"Lady," said Heimbert to his companion, "you can now feel how immeasurably greater and more beautiful is all that the dear Father of us all has created than any work of man's highest art. To assist Him in His gracious works has the Heavenly Gardener, in His abundant mercy, granted to us, His beloved children, that we may become thereby better and happier; but we should be especially careful not to walk in our own rash wilful ways: this it is which drives us a second time from Paradise."

"It shall not happen again," said Zelinda, humbly kneeling before the youth. "Wouldst thou dare, in this desolate region, where we can meet with no priest of our faith, to bestow upon me, who am now changed, without farther delay, the blessing of Holy Baptism?"

Heimbert answered, after a thoughtful pause, "I hope I may do this: if I am wrong, God will pardon what is surely done in zeal to bring to Him so worthy a soul as soon as possible."

They walked side by side to one of the springs of the oasis, silently praying, and their souls filled with peaceful hope. By the time they had reached it, and addressed themselves to the holy work, the sun had risen in glory, as if to confirm and strengthen them in their purpose; so that their beaming countenances looked joyful and confiding to one another. Heimbert had not thought of what Christian name he would bestow upon his neophyte; but as he sprinkled the water over her, and saw the desert-sea, so solemn in the glow of morning, he remembered the pious hermit Antonius in his Egyptian waste, and baptised the lovely convert—Antonia.

They passed the day in holy conversation, and Antonia shewed her friend a little cave where she used to keep her provisions, when she first dwelt on this oasis. "For," said she, "the good God is my witness that my motive for coming hither was to become better acquainted with Him and His works in solitude, without the least thought of learning magic arts. Then came the dervish tempting me; and he drew, by his horrible power, the evil spirits of the desert into a league against me, and they allured me to make all the things they shewed me either in dreams or awake."

Heimbert had no scruple to take with him from this store whatever of wine and dried fruits would be useful for their journey. Antonia assured him that the way, which was very well known to her, would lead them in a few days to the fruitful shore of this waterless ocean. With the approach of evening coolness they began their wanderings.

The travellers had almost traversed this pathless plain, when, one day, they saw a wandering figure at a very great distance; for in the boundless Sahara every object is visible an immense way off, if the whirlwind of the desert raises no sandy columns to intercept the view. This unfortunate man seemed uncertain which way to direct his steps, sometimes taking one direction, and then changing to the opposite one. Antonia's oriental falcon-eyes could discover that it was no Arab, but a man in knightly garb.

"Oh, dear sister," said Heimbert, with eager joy, "it

must be poor Frederigo seeking thee! For God's sake, let us hasten, lest he lose us, and perhaps his own life also, in this immeasurable waste."

They strove with all their power to reach him, but, owing to the burning sun (for it was now midday), Antonia could not long support these hasty steps; and soon the fearful storm-blast raised the cloud of sand, which completely obscured the object of their search.

With the rising moon they renewed their pursuit, calling loudly upon Frederigo, and making signal-flags of their white handkerchiefs tied to their walking-staffs; but all in vain. The object which had disappeared remained invisible. Only a few giraffes sprang timidly before them, and the ostriches crossed their path with winged speed.

At last, when morning dawned, Antonia stopped, and said, "Thou canst not leave me alone, brother, in this wilderness, and I cannot go one step further. God will protect the noble Frederigo; for how can a Father forsake so excellent a child?"

"The pupil shames the tutor," returned Heimbert, his sorrowful face brightening into a smile. "We have done our parts, and may confidently leave the rest to God, hoping He will assist our helplessness." He spread his mantle on the sand, that Antonia might rest more comfortably; but suddenly looked up, exclaiming, "Oh, God! there is a man quite buried in the sand! oh that he may not be already dead!"

Immediately he began to sprinkle wine from their little flask upon his forehead, and to chafe his temples with it. At length he slowly opened his eyes, and said, "Oh that the morning-dew had not again fallen on me, then I should have perished unknown and unlamented in this desert, as it must happen at last!" With these words he closed his eyes again, like one drunken with sleep; but Heimbert unceasingly continued his endeavours to restore him, and after some time the wearied wanderer half raised himself on the sand.

He looked from Heimbert to his companion, and again at Heimbert, and suddenly exclaimed, gnashing his teeth with rage, "It is even so: I shall not perish in the dim obscurity of forgetfulness; I have lived to see the success of my rival, and my sister's shame!" He sprang eagerly to his feet, and rushed on Heimbert with drawn sword. The German moved neither sword nor arm, but answered, with a friendly voice, "So exhausted as thou art, I cannot possibly take advantage of thee; besides, I must first place this lady in security."

Antonia, who had looked at first with much emotion on the angry knight, now stepped between the two, and said, "Oh, Frederigo, neither misery nor anger can entirely disfigure thee; but in what has my noble brother offended thee?"

"*Brother!*" repeated Frederigo, with astonishment.

"Or godfather, or confessor," said Heimbert: "call me which you please; only call this lady no longer Zelinda—her name is Antonia; she is a Christian, and thy bride!"

Frederigo stood lost in astonishment; but Heimbert's true-hearted words and Antonia's lovely blushes interpreted the enigma for him. He sank before the long-cherished image of his lady; and here, in this inhospitable desert, there bloomed to heaven a flower of love, gratitude, and faith.

The excitement of this overpowering happiness at last gave way to bodily fatigue. Antonia reposed her delicate limbs on the now scorching sand, like a drooping flower, and slept under the protection of her lover and chosen brother.

"Sleep thou also," said Heimbert softly to Frederigo; "thou must have wandered far, for weariness is stamped upon thine eyelids, while I am quite fresh, and will watch beside thee."

"Ah, Heimbert," sighed the noble Castilian, "my

sister is thine, thou messenger of heaven—that is an understood thing; but for our unfinished quarrel—"

"Certainly," interrupted Heimbert, very gravely, "thou must satisfy me for every hasty word when we are again in Spain. But, till then, I beg thou wilt never mention it, for it is no fit topic of conversation."

Frederigo sorrowfully reposed on the sand, overpowered by long-resisted sleep; and Heimbert knelt to thank God for so many gracious blessings already bestowed, and for placing so joyful a future before him.

The next day the three travellers reached the border of the desert, and refreshed themselves with a week's rest at a little village hard by; which, with its shadowing trees and soft green pastures, seemed like a little Paradise compared to the joyless Sahara. Frederigo's condition made this rest particularly necessary; for he had not once left the desert, and was often compelled to fight with the wandering Arabs for his subsistence, and sometimes he had suffered the total want of food and drink. At length he became so perplexed, that the stars no longer sufficed to guide him, and he was driven about, sorrowful and aimless, like the whirlwind of the desert.

Even now, when he fell asleep after the noon-day meal, and Antonia and Heimbert watched his slumbers like two smiling angels, he would suddenly awake in terror, and look round him with horror, till, reassured by their friendly faces, he sunk back again to rest. In answer to the questions they put to him when he was fully awake, he said that, in his wanderings, nothing had been more horrible to him than the deceitful dreams which sometimes carried him to his own home, sometimes into the merry camp of his comrades, and sometimes even into Zelinda's neighbourhood, and doubled, by contrast, the helpless misery of the frightful desert. This it was which always gave to the moment of waking something fearful, and even in sleep he retained a dim consciousness of past sufferings.

"You cannot think," added he, "what it was to be suddenly banished from the well-known scenes to the endless waste, where, instead of the long-desired enchanting countenance of my beloved, I only saw the long neck of a hateful camel curiously stretched over me, and with yet more hateful timidity springing away as I rose."

This, together with other effects of his misfortunes, soon passed away from Frederigo's mind, and they continued their journey to Tunis. Yet the remembrance of his conduct to Heimbert, and its unavoidable consequences, spread like a cloud over the noble Spaniard's brow, and softened the natural sternness of his character, so that Antonia could cling more closely to him with her loving heart.

Tunis, which had been the scene of Zelinda's magic power, and of her zeal against the Christians, now witnessed her solemn baptism in a newly-consecrated edifice; and immediately afterwards the three companions embarked with favourable winds for Malaga.

CHAPTER VIII.

Beside the fountain where she had parted from Heimbert, Doña Clara sat one evening in deep thought. The guitar on her arm gave forth a few solitary chords, which her delicate hand dreamily enticed from it; and at last they formed themselves into a melody, while the following words were murmured from her half-opened lips:

"Say who, by Tunis' walls afar,
Where with grim bands of Paynim might
The Spaniard and the German fight,—
From lilies dark with gory dew,
And roses of death's pallid hue,
Say, who hath won the prize of war?

Of Alva ask the tale of fame,
And he two knights of pride will name:
One was my brother, tried and brave;
One, he to whom my heart I gave:
And fain I hoped, in joyous light,
To weave their garlands doubly bright.

But sadly o'er my eyes and brow
A widow's veil falls doubly now;
The knights are gone, and ne'er again
Shall they be found 'mid living men."

The guitar was silent, and soft dew-drops fell from her heavenly eyes. Heimbert, who was hidden behind the neighbouring orange-tree, felt sympathetic tears roll down his cheeks; and Frederigo, who had led him and Antonia in by the garden-way, would no longer keep the cup of joy from the restored ones, but disclosed himself, with a dear form on either arm, as a messenger from heaven to his sister.

But such moments of high overpowering delight, like the most precious and long-expected heavenly blessings, are better imagined than described. It is only doing an ill service to recount what this one said, and that one did. Picture it then to thyself, dear reader, after thine own fancy, if the two pairs in my story have become dear to thee, and thou art now intimate with them. If this be not the case, my words would be lost upon thee. For those, then, who with hearty pleasure have dwelt on the re-union of sister and lover, I will proceed with increased satisfaction.

When Heimbert, casting a significant look at Frederigo, wished to retire, after having placed Antonia in Doña Clara's protection, the noble Spaniard would not permit him. He detained his companion with the most courteous and brotherly kindness, entreating him to remain till the evening banquet, at which many distinguished persons of the family of Mendez were present. In their presence Frederigo declared that the brave Heimbert of Waldhausen was Doña Clara's bridegroom: at the same time calling them to witness the sealing it with the most solemn words, in order that whatever might afterwards happen, which should seem inimical to their contract, it might yet remain indissoluble. The spectators were somewhat astonished at these strange precautionary measures, though no one opposed Frederigo's desire, but unhesitatingly gave him their word that they would carry out his wishes. Their ready compliance was greatly caused by Duke Alva's having, during his late sojourn in Malaga, filled the whole city with his praises of the two heroic young captains.

When the generous wines were circulating round the table, Frederigo stepped behind Heimbert's chair, and whispered, "If it please you, señor, the moon is now risen and shining bright as day: I am ready to meet you." Heimbert bowed assentingly, and the youths left the hall, followed by the sweet salutations of their unsuspecting brides.

As they passed through the blooming gardens, Frederigo said, "Ah! how happily we might have walked together here, had it not been for my rashness!"

"Yes, truly," answered Heimbert; "but as it has happened, and cannot now be otherwise, we will proceed, and only look upon one another as soldiers and noblemen."

"Even so," replied Frederigo; and they hastened on to the farthest part of the gardens, where the sound of their clashing arms might not reach the high banqueting hall.

Silent and enclosed amid dark groves was the chosen spot. No sounds could be heard there from the joyous company, no noise from the populous streets of the city. Only high in heaven the full moon shone down with bright beams upon the solemn circle. It was the right place. Both captains drew their shining blades, and stood opposite to one another, ready for the combat; but before they began, a kindlier feeling drew them to each another; they lowered their weapons, and embraced in the most brotherly manner, then they tore themselves away, and the fearful fight began.

They were now no more brothers in arms—no more friends—no more brothers in law, who raised the sharp swords against each other. With firm boldness, but with cool collectedness, they fell upon one another, whilst each guarded his own breast at the same time. After a few hot deadly passes, the combatants were compelled to rest, and they regarded one another with increased love; each rejoicing to find his dear comrade so stout and courageous. Then the fierce strife began anew.

Heimbert dashed aside Frederigo's sword with his left hand as it was thrust at his side, but the keen edge had penetrated through his leathern glove, and the rosy blood gushed out.

"Halt!" cried Frederigo; and they searched for the wound; but finding it of no importance, they bound it up, and with undiminished ardour renewed the fight. It was not long before Heimbert's sword pierced Frederigo's shoulder, and the German, conscious that it had done so, cried in his turn, "Halt." At first Frederigo would not acknowledge that there was a wound; but when the blood streamed forth, he accepted his friend's assistance. This wound also seeming of no consequence, and the noble Spaniard finding himself strong enough in arm and hand to wield the sword, they pursued the deadly contest.

Then they heard a garden-door open, and the tread as of a horse from the groves. Both combatants stayed their stern work, and turned to the unwelcome visitant. The next moment they saw through the slender pines some one approaching whose bearing and dress shewed that he was a warrior, mounted on a stately charger; and Frederigo, as master of the house, said to him, "Señor, why you have intruded into a strange garden, we will inquire another time. I shall now only beg of you to retire from it at once, and to leave me your name."

"I shall not retire at present," answered the stranger; "but my name I will gladly tell you. I am the Duke of Alva."

At this moment the moonbeams fell upon his stern pale face—that dwelling-place of all that was noble, and great, and majestic. The two captains bowed low and sank their arms.

"I surely know you," said Alva, looking at them fixedly with his dark eyes. "Yes, truly, I do know you, you two young heroes of the battle of Tunis. God be blessed and praised, that I find two such noble warriors alive, whom I had almost given up for lost. But tell me now, what has turned your brave swords against each other? I trust you will not object to lay open before me the cause of this knightly encounter."

They complied with the great duke's behest. Both the youths related their history, from the evening before the embarkation till the present moment; whilst Alva remained motionless before them in deep meditation, looking almost like an equestrian statue.

The captains had already long ended their story, and the duke still remained silent and motionless in deep meditation. At last he addressed them in the following manner:—

"May God and His holy word help me, my young knights, as I tell you, with my best wisdom and truth of heart, that I believe this affair of yours to be now perfectly settled. Twice have you fought with one another on account of the irritating words which escaped Don Frederigo's lips: and if indeed the slight wounds which you have hitherto received are not sufficient, still, your having been comrades in the fight at Tunis, and Sir Heimbert of Waldhausen having saved Don Frederigo Mendez' life in the desert, after he had rescued his bride for him in battle, all this gives the knight of Waldhausen the privilege of forgiving an enemy every offence, to whom he has shewn himself so well inclined. The old Roman history tells us of two centurions under the great Julius Cæsar who settled a dispute, and contracted a hearty brotherly friendship, from fighting side by side, and delivering one another out of the midst of the Gallic army. But I affirm that you two have done more for each other; and therefore I declare this affair to be entirely settled and at an end. Sheathe your swords, then, and embrace in my presence."

Obedient to their general's command, the young knights

for the present put up their swords; but, anxious lest the slightest shade should fall upon their honour, they yet delayed the reconciling embrace.

The great Alva looked somewhat sternly upon them, and said, "Do you suppose, young knights, that I could desire to save the lives of two soldiers at the expense of their good name? Sooner than that, I would rather see you both struck dead at once. But I see that with such obstinate men, one must proceed to more effective measures." And leaping from his horse, which he bound to a tree, he stepped between the two captains with a drawn sword in his right hand, crying out, "Whoever takes upon him to deny that the quarrel between Sir Heimbert of Waldhausen and Don Frederigo Mendez is nobly and honourably settled, shall have to do with Duke Alva for life or death. And should either of the aforenamed knights object to this, let him declare it. I stand as champion for my own opinion."

The youths bowed to their great umpire, and sank into one another's arms. The duke embraced them with heartfelt affection, which appeared the more charming and refreshing, as any outward demonstration of it was seldom to be seen in this strong-minded man.

Then he led the reconciled ones back to their brides; and when these, after the first joyful surprise at the presence of the much-honoured general was over, started back on perceiving drops of blood on the youths' garments, the duke said laughingly, "Oh! the brides-elect of soldiers must not shrink from such medals of honour."

The Duke Alva took on himself to stand as father to both the happy brides, and to fix the festival of their betrothal for the very next day. From this time forth they all lived in undisturbed concord; and when Sir Heimbert was recalled with his lovely spouse to the bosom of his native Germany, the two families yet continued near each other by letters and constant communications. And in after times the descendants of the lord of Waldhausen boasted their connexion with the family of Mendez, while the latter ever preserved the tradition of the brave and magnanimous Heimbert of Waldhausen.

ASLAUGA'S KNIGHT.

Aslauga's Knight,

A Romance.

Ch. iii.

From the German of Fouque.

London: James Burns.

LONDON:
PRINTED BY ROBSON, LEVEY, AND FRANKLYN,
Great New Street, Fetter Lane.

Aslauga's Knight.

CHAPTER I.

MANY years ago there lived in the island of Führen a noble knight, called Froda the friend of the Skalds, who was so named because he not only offered free hospitality in his fair castle to every renowned and noble bard, but likewise strove with all his might to discover those ancient songs, and tales, and legends, which, in Runic writings or elsewhere, were still to be found; he had even made some voyages to Iceland in search of them, and had fought many a hard battle with the pirates of those seas—for he was also a right valiant knight, and he followed his great ancestors not only in their love of song, but also in their bold deeds of arms. Although he was still scarcely beyond the prime of youth, yet all the other nobles in the island willingly submitted themselves to him, whether in council or in war; nay, his renown had even been carried ere now over the sea to the neighbouring land of Germany.

One bright autumn evening this honour-loving knight sat before his castle, as he was often wont to do, that he might look far and wide over land and sea, and that he might invite any travellers who were passing by, as was his custom, to share in his noble hospitality. But on this day he saw little of all that he was accustomed to look upon; for on his knees there lay an ancient book with skilfully and richly painted characters, which a learned Icelander had just sent to him across the sea: it was the history of Aslauga, the fair daughter of Sigurd, who at first, concealing her high birth, kept goats among the simple peasants of the land, clothed in mean attire; then, in the golden veil of her flowing hair, won the love of King Ragnar Lodbrog; and at last shone brightly on the Danish throne as his glorious queen, till the day of her death.

To the Knight Froda it seemed as though the gracious Lady Aslauga rose in life and birth before him, so that his calm and stedfast heart, true indeed to ladies' service, but never yet devoted to one particular female image, burst forth in a clear flame of love for the fair daughter of Sigurd. "What matters it," thought he to himself, "that it is more than a hundred years since she disappeared from earth? She sees so clearly into this heart of mine—and what more can a knight desire? wherefore she shall henceforth be my honoured love, and shall inspire me in battle and in song." And therewith he sang a lay on his new love, which ran in the following manner:

"They ride over hill and dale apace
To seek for their love the fairest face—
They search through city and forest-glade
To find for their love the gentlest maid—
They climb wherever a path may lead
To seek the wisest dame for their meed.
Ride on, ye knights; but ye never may see
What the light of song has shewn to me:

Loveliest, gentlest, and wisest of all,
Bold be the deeds that her name shall recall;
What though she ne'er bless my earthly sight?
Yet death shall reveal her countenance bright.
Fair world, good night! Good day, sweet love!
Who seeks here in faith shall find above."

"Such purpose may come to good," said a hollow voice near the knight; and when he looked round, he saw the form of a poor peasant-woman, so closely wrapped in a grey mantle that he could not discern any part of her countenance. She looked over his shoulder on the book, and said, with a deep sigh, "I know that story well; and it fares no better with me than with the princess of whom it tells." Froda looked at her with astonishment. "Yes, yes," pursued she, with strange becks and nods; "I am the descendant of the mighty Rolf, to whom the fairest castles and forests and fields of this island once belonged; your castle and your domains, Froda, amongst others, were his. We are now cast down to poverty; and because I am not so fair as Aslauga, there is no hope that my possessions will be restored to me; and therefore I am fain to veil my poor face from every eye." It seemed that she shed warm tears beneath her mantle. At this Froda was greatly moved, and begged her, for God's sake, to let him know how he could help her, for that he was a descendant of the famous northern heroes of the olden time; and perhaps yet something more than they—namely, a good Christian. "I almost think," murmured she from beneath her covering, "that you are that very Froda whom men call the Good, and the friend of the Skalds, and of whose generosity and mildness such wonderful stories are told. If it be so, there may be help for me. You need only give up to me the half of your fields and meadows, and I should be in a condition to live, in some measure, such a life as befits the descendant of the mighty Rolf." Then Froda looked thoughtfully on the ground; partly because she had asked for so very much; partly, also, because he was considering whether she could really be descended from the powerful Rolf. But the veiled form said, after a pause, "I must have been mistaken, and you are not indeed that renowned, gentle-hearted Froda: for how could he have doubted so long about such a trifle? But I will try the utmost means. See now! for the sake of the fair Aslauga, of whom you have both read and sung—for the sake of the honoured daughter of Sigurd, grant my request!" Then Froda started up eagerly, and cried, "Let it be as you have said!" and gave her his knightly hand to confirm his words. But he could not grasp the hand of the peasant-woman, although her dark form remained close before him. A secret shudder began to run through his limbs, whilst suddenly a light seemed to shine forth from the apparition—a golden light—in which she became wholly wrapped; so that he felt as though Aslauga stood before him in the flowing veil of her golden hair, and smiling graciously on him. Transported and dazzled, he sank on his knees. When he rose up once more, he only saw a cloudy mist of autumn spreading over the meadow, fringed at its edges with lingering evening lights, and then vanishing far over the waves. The knight scarcely knew what had happened to him. He returned to his chamber buried in thought, and sometimes feeling sure that he had beheld Aslauga; sometimes, again, that some goblin had risen before him with deceitful tricks, mocking in spiteful wise the service which he had vowed to his dead mistress. But henceforth, wherever he roved, over valley or forest or heath, or whether he sailed upon the waves of the sea, the like appearances met him. Once he found a lute lying in a wood, and drove a wolf away from it; and when sounds burst from the lute without its being touched, a fair child rose up from it, as of old Aslauga herself had done. At another time he would see goats clambering among the highest cliffs by the sea-shore; and it was a golden form who tended them. Then, again, a bright queen, resplendent in a dazzling bark, would seem to glide past him, and salute him graciously;

—and if he strove to approach any of these, he found nothing but cloud, and mist, and vapour. Of all this many a lay might be sung. But so much he learnt from them all,—that the fair Lady Aslauga accepted his service, and that he was now in deed and in truth become her knight.

Meanwhile the winter had come and gone. In northern lands this season never fails to bring to those who understand and love it many an image full of beauty and meaning, with which a child of man might well be satisfied, so far as earthly happiness can satisfy, through all his time on earth. But when the spring came glancing forth with its opening buds and flowing waters, there came also bright and sunny tidings from the land of Germany to Fühnen.

There stood on the rich banks of the Maine, where it pours its waters through the fertile land of Franconia, a castle of almost royal magnificence, whose orphan-mistress was a relation of the German emperor. She was named Hildegardis; and was acknowledged far and wide as the fairest of maidens. Therefore her imperial uncle wished that she should wed none but the bravest knight who could any where be met with. Accordingly he followed the example of many a noble lord in such a case, and proclaimed a tournament, at which the chief prize should be the hand of the peerless Hildegardis, unless the victor already bore in his heart a lady wedded or betrothed to him; for the lists were not to be closed to any brave warrior of equal birth, that the contest of strength and courage might be so much the richer in competitors.

Now the renowned Froda had tidings of this from his German brethren in arms; and he prepared himself to appear at the festival. Before all things, he forged for himself a splendid suit of armour; as, indeed, he was the most excellent armourer of the north, far-famed as it is for skill in that art. He worked the helmet out in pure gold, and formed it so that it seemed to be covered with bright flowing locks, which called to mind Aslauga's tresses. He also fashioned on the breastplate of his armour, overlaid with silver, a golden image in half relief, which represented Aslauga in her veil of flowing locks, that he might make known, even at the beginning of the tournament—"This knight, bearing the image of a lady upon his breast, fights not for the hand of the beautiful Hildegardis, but only for the joy of battle and for knightly fame." Then he took out of his stables a beautiful Danish steed, embarked it carefully on board a vessel, and sailed prosperously to the opposite shore.

CHAPTER II.

In one of those fair beech-woods, which abound in the fertile land of Germany, he fell in with a young and courteous knight of delicate form, who asked the noble northman to share the meal which he had invitingly spread out upon the greensward, under the shade of the pleasantest boughs. Whilst the two knights sat peacefully together at their repast, they felt drawn towards each other; and rejoiced when, on rising from it, they observed that they were about to follow the same road. They had not come to this good understanding by means of many words; for the young knight Edwald was of a silent nature, and would sit for hours with a quiet smile upon his lips without opening them to speak. But even in that quiet smile there lay a gentle, winning grace; and when from time to time a few simple words of deep meaning sprang to his lips, they seemed like a gift deserving of thanks. It was the same with the little songs which he sang ever and anon; they were ended almost as soon as begun: but in each short couplet there dwelt a deep and winning spirit, whether it called forth a kindly sigh or a peaceful smile. It seemed to the noble Froda as if a younger brother rode beside him, or even a tender, blooming son. They travelled thus many days together; and it appeared as if their path were marked out for them in inseparable union: and much as they rejoiced at this, yet they looked sadly at each other whenever they set out afresh, or where cross-roads met, on finding that neither took a different direction; nay, it seemed at times as if a tear gathered in Edwald's downcast eye.

It happened on a time, that at their hostelry they met an arrogant, overbearing knight, of gigantic stature and powerful frame, whose speech and carriage proved him to be not of German but foreign birth. He appeared to come from the land of Bohemia. He cast a contemptuous smile on Froda, who, as usual, had opened the ancient book of Aslauga's history, and was attentively reading in it. "You must be a ghostly knight?" he said, inquiringly; and it appeared as if a whole train of unseemly jests were ready to follow. But Froda answered so firmly and seriously with a negative, that the Bohemian stopped short suddenly; as when the beasts, after venturing to mock their king the lion, are subdued to quietness by one glance of his eye. But not so easily was the Bohemian knight subdued; rather the more did he begin to mock young Edwald for his delicate form and for his silence—all which he bore for some time with great patience; but when at last the stranger used an unbecoming phrase, he arose, girded on his sword, and bowing gracefully, he said, "I thank you, Sir Knight, that you have given me this opportunity of proving that I am neither a slothful nor unpractised knight; for only thus can your behaviour be excused, which otherwise must be deemed most unmannerly. Are you ready?"

With these words he moved towards the door; the Bohemian knight followed, smiling scornfully; while Froda was full of care for his young and slender companion, although his honour was so dear to him that he could in no way interpose.

But it soon appeared how needless were the northman's fears. With equal vigour and address did Edwald assault his gigantic adversary, so that to look upon, it was almost like one of those combats between a knight and some monster of the forest, of which ancient legends tell. The issue too was not unlike. While the Bohemian was collecting himself for a decisive stroke, Edwald rushed in upon him, and, with the force of a wrestler, cast him to the ground. But he spared his conquered foe, helped him courteously to rise, and then turned to mount his own steed. Soon after he and Froda left the hostelry, and once more their journey led them on the same path as before.

"From henceforth this gives me pleasure," said Froda, pointing with satisfaction to their common road. "I must own to you, Edchen"—he had accustomed himself, in loving confidence, to call his young friend by that childlike name —"I must own to you, that hitherto, when I have thought that you might perhaps be journeying with me to the tournament held in honour of the fair Hildegardis, a heaviness came over my heart. Your noble knightly spirit I well knew, but I feared lest the strength of your slender limbs might not be equal to it. Now I have learned to know you as a warrior who may long seek his match; and God be praised if we still hold on in the same path, and welcome our earliest meeting in the lists!"

But Edwald looked at him sorrowfully, and said, "What can my skill and strength avail, if they be tried against you, and for the greatest earthly prize, which one of us alone can win? Alas! I have long foreboded with a heavy heart the sad truth, that you also are journeying to the tournament of the fair Hildegardis."

"Edchen," answered Froda, with a smile, "my gentle, loving youth, see you not that I already wear on my breastplate the image of a liege lady? I strive but for renown in arms, and not for your fair Hildegardis."

"*My* fair Hildegardis!" answered Edwald, with a sigh. "*That* she is not, nor ever will be,—or should she, ah! Froda, it would pierce your heart. I know well the northland faith is deep-rooted as your rocks, and hard to dissolve as their summits of snow; but let no man think that he can look unscathed into the eyes of Hildegardis. Has not she, the haughty, the too haughty maiden, so bewitched my tranquil, lowly mind, that I forget the gulf which lies between us, and still pursue her; and would rather perish than renounce the daring hope to win that eagle spirit for my own?"

"I will help you to it, Edchen," answered Froda, smiling still. "Would that I knew how this all-conquering lady looks! She must resemble the Valkyrien of our heathen forefathers, since so many mighty warriors are overcome by her."

Edwald solemnly drew forth a picture from beneath his breastplate, and held it before him. Fixed, and as if enchanted, Froda gazed upon it, with glowing cheeks and sparkling eyes; the smile passed away from his countenance, as the sunlight fades away from the meadows before the coming darkness of the storm.

"See you not now, my noble comrade," whispered Edwald, "that for one of us two, or perhaps for both, the joy of life is gone?"

"Not yet," replied Froda, with a powerful effort; "but hide your magic picture, and let us rest beneath this shade. You must be somewhat spent with your late encounter, and a strange weariness oppresses me with leaden weight." They dismounted from their steeds, and stretched themselves upon the ground.

The noble Froda had no thought of sleep; but he wished to be undisturbed whilst he wrestled strongly with himself, and strove, if it might be, to drive from his mind that image of fearful beauty. It seemed as if this new influence had already become a part of his very life, and at last a restless dreamy sleep did indeed overshadow the exhausted warrior. He fancied himself engaged in combat with many knights, whilst Hildegardis looked on smiling from a richly-adorned balcony; and just as he thought he had gained the victory, the bleeding Edwald lay groaning beneath his horse's feet. Then again it seemed as if Hildegardis stood by his side in a church, and they were about to receive the marriage-blessing. He knew well that this was not right, and the "yes," which he was to utter, he pressed back with resolute effort into his heart, and forthwith his eyes were moistened with burning tears. From yet stranger and more bewildering visions, the voice of Edwald at last awoke him. He raised himself up, and heard his young companion saying courteously, as he looked towards a neighbouring thicket, "Only return, noble maiden; I will surely help you, if I can; and I had no wish to scare you away, but that the slumbers of my brother in arms might not be disturbed by you." A golden gleam shone through the branches as it vanished.

"For heaven's sake, my faithful comrade," cried Froda, "to whom are you speaking, and who has been here by me?"

"I cannot myself rightly understand," said Edwald. "Hardly had you dropped asleep, when a figure came forth from the forest, closely wrapped in a dark mantle. At first I took her for a peasant. She seated herself at your head; and though I could see nothing of her countenance, I could well observe that she was sorely troubled, and even shedding tears. I made signs to her to depart, lest she should disturb your sleep; and would have offered her a piece of gold, supposing that poverty must be the cause of her deep distress. But my hand seemed powerless, and a shudder passed through me, as if I had entertained such a purpose towards a queen. Immediately glittering locks of gold waved here and there between the folds of her close-wrapped mantle, and the thicket began almost to shine in the light which they shed. "Poor youth," said she then, "you love truly, and can well understand how a lofty woman's heart burns in keenest sorrow, when a noble knight, who vowed himself to be her own, withdraws his heart, and, like a weak bondman, is led away to meaner hopes." Hereupon she arose, and, sighing, disappeared in yonder thicket. It almost seemed to me, Froda, as though she uttered your name."

"Yes, it was me she named," answered Froda; "and not in vain she named me.—Aslauga, thy knight comes, and enters the lists, and all for thee and thy reward alone! —At the same time, my Edchen, we will win for you your haughty bride." With this he sprang upon his steed, full of the proud joy of former times; and when the magic of Hildegardis' beauty, dazzling and bewildering, would rise up before him, he said smiling, "Aslauga!" and the sun of his inner life shone forth again cloudless and serene.

CHAPTER III.

From a balcony of her castle on the Maine Hildegardis was wont to refresh herself in the cool of the evening by gazing on the rich landscape below, but gazing more eagerly on the glitter of arms, which often came in sight from many a distant road; for knights were approaching singly, or with a train of followers, all eager to prove their courage and their strength in striving for the high prize of the tournament. She was in truth a proud and high-minded maiden,—perhaps more so than became even her dazzling beauty and her princely rank. As she now gazed with a proud smile on the glittering roads, a damsel of her train began the following lay:—

The joyous song of birds in spring
Upon the wing
Doth echo far through wood and dell,
And freely tell
Their treasures sweet of love and mirth,
Too gladsome for this lowly earth.

The gentle breath of flowers in May,
O'er meadows gay,

Doth fill the pure and balmy air
With perfume rare;
Still floating round each slender form,
Though scorch'd by sun, or torn by storm.

But every high and glorious aim,
And the pure flame
That deep abiding in my heart
Can ne'er depart,
Too lofty for my falt'ring tongue,
Must die with me, unknown, unsung.

"Wherefore do you sing that song, and at this moment?" said Hildegardis, striving to appear scornful and proud, though a deep and secret sadness was plainly enough seen to overshadow her countenance. "It came into my head unawares," replied the damsel, "as I looked upon the road by which the gentle Edwald with his pleasant lays first approached us; for it was from him I learnt it. But seems it not to you, my gracious lady, and to you too, my companions, as if Edwald himself were again riding that way towards the castle?" "Dreamer!" said Hildegardis scornfully,—and yet could not for some space withdraw her eyes from the knight, till at length, with an effort, she turned them on Froda, who rode beside him, saying: "Yes, truly, that knight is Edwald; but what can you find to notice in the meek-spirited, silent boy? Here, fix your eyes, my maidens, on this majestic figure, if you would behold a knight indeed." She was silent. A voice within her, as though of prophecy, said, "Now the victor of the tournament rides into the courtyard;" and she, who had never feared the presence of any human being, now felt humbled, and almost painfully awed, when she beheld the northern knight.

At the evening meal the two newly-arrived knights were placed opposite to the royal Hildegardis. As Froda, after the northern fashion, remained in full armour, the golden image of Aslauga gleamed from his silver breastplate full before the eyes of the haughty lady. She smiled scornfully, as if conscious that it depended on her will to drive that image from the breast and from the heart of the stranger-knight. Then suddenly a clear golden light passed through the hall, so that Hildegardis said, "O, the keen lightning!" and covered her eyes with both her hands. But Froda looked into the dazzling radiance with a joyful gaze of welcome. At this Hildegardis feared him yet more, though at the same time she thought, "This loftiest and most mysterious of men must be born for me alone." Yet could she not forbear, almost against her will, to look from time to time in friendly tenderness on the poor Edwald, who sat there silent, and with a sweet smile seemed to pity and to mock his own suffering and his own vain hopes.

When the two knights were alone in their sleeping-chamber, Edwald looked for a long time in silence into the dewy balmy night. Then he sang to his lute:

A hero wise and brave,
  A lowly tender youth,
Are wandering through the land
  In stedfast love and truth.

The hero, by his deeds,
  Both bliss and fame hath won,
And still, with heartfelt joy,
  The faithful child looked on.

But Froda took the lute from his hands, and said, "No, Edchen, I will teach you another song; listen!—

There's a gleam in the hall, and like morning's light
Hath shone upon all her presence bright.
Suitors watch as she passes by—
She may gladden their hearts by one glance of her eye:
But coldly she gazeth upon the throng,
And they that have sought her may seek her long.
She turns her away from the richly clad knight,
She heeds not the words of the learned wight;

The prince is before her in all his pride,
But other the visions around her that glide.
Then tell me, in all the wide world's space,
Who may e'er win that lady's grace?
In sorrowful love there sits apart
The gentle squire who hath her heart;
They all are deceived by fancies vain,
And he knows it not who the prize shall gain.

Edwald thrilled. "As God wills," said he, softly to himself. "But I cannot understand how such a thing could be. "As God wills," repeated Froda. The two friends embraced each other, and soon after fell into a peaceful slumber.

Some days afterwards, Froda sat in a secluded bower of the castle-garden, and was reading in the ancient book of his lovely mistress Aslauga. It happened at that very time that Hildegardis passed by. She stood still, and said, thoughtfully, "Strange union that you are of knight and sage, how comes it that you bring forth so little out of the deep treasures of your knowledge? And yet I think you must have many a choice history at your command, even such as that which now lies open before you; for I see rich and bright pictures of knights and ladies painted amongst the letters." "It is, indeed, the most surpassing and enchanting history in all the world," said Froda; "but you have neither patience nor thoughtfulness to listen to our wonderful legends of the north."

"Why think you so?" answered Hildegardis, with that pride which she rejoiced to display towards Froda, when she could find courage to do so; and, placing herself on a stone-seat opposite, she commanded him at once to read something to her out of that fair book.

Froda began; and in the very effort which he made to change the old heroic speech of Iceland into the German tongue, his heart and mind were stirred more fervently and solemnly. As he looked up from time to time, he beheld the countenance of Hildegardis beaming in ever-growing beauty with joy, wonder, and interest; and the thought passed through his mind whether this could indeed be his destined bride, to whom Aslauga herself was guiding him.

Then suddenly the characters became strangely confused; it seemed as if the pictures began to move, so that he was obliged to stop. While he fixed his eyes with a strong effort upon the book, endeavouring to drive away this strange confusion, he heard a well-known sweetly solemn voice, which said, "Leave a little space for me, fair lady. The history which that knight is reading to you relates to me; and I hear it gladly."

Before the eyes of Froda, as he raised them from his book, sat Aslauga in all the glory of her flowing golden locks beside Hildegardis, on the seat. With tears of affright in her eyes, the maiden sank back and fainted. Solemnly, yet graciously, Aslauga warned her knight with a motion of her fair right hand, and vanished.

"What have I done to you," said Hildegardis, when recovered from her swoon by his care, "what have I done to you, evil-minded knight, that you call up your northern spectres before me, and well nigh destroy me through terror of your magic arts?" "Lady," answered Froda, "may God help me, as I have not called hither the wondrous lady who but now appeared to us. But now her will is known to me, and I commend you to God's keeping."

With that he walked thoughtfully out of the bower. Hildegardis fled in terror from the gloomy shade; and, rushing out on the opposite side, reached a fair open grass-plot, where Edwald, in the soft glow of twilight, was gathering flowers; and, meeting her with a courteous smile, offered her a nosegay of narcissus and pansies.

CHAPTER IV.

At length the day fixed for the tournament arrived; and a distinguished noble, appointed by the German emperor, arranged all things in the most magnificent and sumptuous guise for the solemn festival. The field-combat opened wide, and fair, and level; thickly strewn with the finest sand, so that both man and horse might find sure footing; and, like a pure field of snow, it shone forth from the midst of the flowery plain. Rich hangings of silk from Arabia, curiously embroidered with Indian gold, adorned with their various colours the lists enclosing the space, and hung from the lofty galleries which had been erected for the ladies and the nobles who were to behold the combat. At the upper end, under a canopy of majestic arches richly wrought in gold, was the place of the Lady Hildegardis. Green wreaths and garlands waved gracefully between the glittering pillars in the soft breezes of July. And with impatient eyes the multitude, who crowded beyond the lists, gazed upwards, expecting the appearance of the fairest maiden of Germany; and were only at times drawn to another part by the stately approach of the combatants. O, how many a bright suit of armour, how many a silken richly-embroidered mantle, how many a lofty waving plume was here to be seen! The splendid troop of knights moved within the lists, greeting and conversing with each other, as a bed of flowers stirred by a breath of wind:—but the flower-stems had grown to lofty trees, the yellow and white flower-leaves had changed to gold and silver, and the dew-drops to pearls and diamonds. For whatever was most fair and costly, most varied and full of meaning, had these noble knights collected in honour of this day. Many an eye was turned on Froda, who, without scarf, plume, or mantle, with his shining silver breastplate, on which appeared the golden image of Aslauga, and with his well-wrought helmet of golden locks, shone, in the midst of the crowd, like polished brass. Others, again, there were, who took pleasure in looking at the young Edwald; his whole armour was covered by a mântle of white silk, embroidered in azure and silver, as his whole helmet was concealed by a waving plume of white feathers. He was arrayed with almost feminine elegance; and yet the conscious power with which he controlled his fiery, snow-white steed made known the victorious strength and manliness of the warlike stripling.

In strange contrast appeared the tall and almost gigantic figure of a knight clothed in a mantle of black glossy bear-skin, bordered with costly fur, but without any ornament of shining metal. His very helmet was covered with dark bear-skin; and, instead of plumes, a mass of blood-red horsehair hung like a flowing mane profusely on every side. Well did Froda and Edwald remember that dark knight; for he was the uncourteous guest of the hostelry: he also seemed to remark the two knights; for he turned his unruly steed suddenly round, forced his way through the crowd of warriors, and, after he had spoken over the enclosure to a hideous bronze-coloured woman, sprang with a wild leap across the lists, and, with the speed of an arrow, vanished out of sight. The old woman looked after him with a friendly nod. The assembled people laughed as at a strange masquing device; but Edwald and Froda had their own almost shuddering thoughts concerning it, which, however, neither imparted to the other.

The kettle-drums rolled, the trumpets sounded, and, led by the aged duke, Hildegardis advanced, richly apparelled, but more dazzling through the brightness of her own beauty. She stepped forward beneath the arches of the golden bower, and bowed to the assembly. The knights bent low, and the feeling rushed into many a heart, "There is no man on earth who can deserve a bride so queenly." When Froda bowed his head, it seemed to him as if the golden radiance of Aslauga's tresses floated before his sight;

and his spirit rose in joy and pride that his lady held him worthy to be so often reminded of her.

And now the tournament began. At first the knights strove with blunted swords and battle-axes; then they ran their course with lances man to man; but at last they divided into two equal parties, and a general assault began, in which every one was allowed to use at his own will either sword or lance. Froda and Edwald equally surpassed their antagonists, as (measuring each his own strength and that of his friend) they had foreseen. And now it must be decided, by a single combat with lances, to whom the highest prize of victory should belong. Before this trial began, they rode slowly together into the middle of the course, and consulted where each should take his place. "Keep you your guiding-star still before your sight," said Froda, with a smile; "the like gracious help will not be wanting to me." Edwald looked round astonished for the lady of whom his friend seemed to speak; but Froda went on. "I have done wrong in hiding aught from you; but after the tournament you shall know all. Now lay aside all needless thoughts of wonder, dear Edchen, and sit firm in your saddle; for I warn you that I shall run this course with all my might: not my honour alone is at stake, but the far higher honour of my lady."

"So also do I purpose to demean myself," said Edwald, with a friendly smile. They shook each other by the hand, and rode to their places.

Amidst the sound of trumpets they met again, running their course with lightning speed; the lances shivered with a crash, the horses staggered, the knights, firm in their saddles, pulled them up, and rode back to their places. But as they prepared for another course, Edwald's white steed snorted in wild affright, and Froda's powerful chestnut reared up foaming.

It was plain that the two noble animals shrunk from a second hard encounter; but their riders held them fast with spur and bit, and, firm and obedient, they again dashed forward at the second call of the trumpet. Edwald, who by one deep, ardent gaze on the beauty of his mistress had stamped it afresh on his soul, cried aloud at the moment of encounter, "Hildegardis!" and so mightily did his lance strike his valiant adversary, that Froda sank backwards on his steed, with difficulty keeping his seat in his saddle, or holding firm in his stirrups; whilst Edwald flew by unshaken, lowered his spear to salute Hildegardis as he passed her bower, and then, amidst the loud applause of the multitude, rushed to his place, ready for the third course. And, ah! Hildegardis herself, overcome by surprise, had greeted him with a blush and a look of kindness; it seemed to him as if the overwhelming joy of victory were already gained. But it was not so; for the valiant Froda, burning with noble shame, had again tamed his affrighted steed, and, chastising him sharply with the spur for his share in this mischance, said in a low voice, "Beautiful and beloved lady, shew thyself to me,—the honour of thy name is at stake." To every other eye it seemed as if a golden rosy-tinted summer's cloud was passing over the deep-blue sky; but Froda beheld the heavenly countenance of his lady, felt the waving of her golden tresses, and cried, "Aslauga!" The two rushed together, and Edwald was hurled from his saddle far upon the dusty plain.

Froda remained for a time motionless, according to the laws of chivalry, as though waiting to see whether any one would dispute his victory, and appearing on his mailed steed like some lofty statue of brass. All around stood the multitude in silent wonderment. When at length they burst forth into shouts of triumph, he beckoned earnestly with his hand, and all were again silent. He then sprang lightly from his saddle, and hastened to the spot where the fallen Edwald was striving to rise. He pressed him closely to his breast, led his snow-white steed towards him, and would not be denied holding the stirrups of the youth whilst he mounted. Then he bestrode his own steed, and rode by Edwald's side towards the golden bower of Hildegardis, where with lowered spear and open vizor, he thus spoke: "Fairest of all living ladies, I bring you here Edwald your knightly bridegroom, before whose lance and sword all the knights of this tournament have fallen away, I only excepted, who can make no claim to the choicest prize of victory, since I, as the image on my breastplate may shew, already serve another mistress."

The duke was even now advancing towards the two warriors, to lead them into the golden bower; but Hildegardis restrained him with a look of displeasure, saying immediately, while her cheeks glowed with anger, "Then you seem, Sir Froda, the Danish knight, to serve your lady ill; for even now you openly styled me the fairest of living ladies."

"That did I," answered Froda, bending courteously; "because my fair mistress belongs to the dead."

A slight shudder passed at these words through the assembly, and through the heart of Hildegardis; but soon the anger of the maiden blazed forth again, and the more because the most wonderful and excellent knight she knew had scorned her for the sake of a dead mistress.

"I make known to all," she said with solemn earnestness, "that according to the just decree of my imperial uncle, this hand can never belong to a vanquished knight, however noble and honourable he may otherwise have proved himself. As the conqueror of this tournament, therefore, is bound to another service, this combat concerns me not; and I depart hence as I came, a free and unbetrothed maiden."

The duke seemed about to reply; but she turned haughtily away, and left the bower. Suddenly a gust of wind shook the green wreaths and garlands, and they fell untwined and rustling behind her. In this the people, displeased with the pride of Hildegardis, thought they beheld an omen of punishment, and with jeering words noticed it as they departed.

CHAPTER V.

The two knights had returned to their apartments in deep silence. When they arrived there, Edwald caused himself to be disarmed, and laid every piece of his fair shining armour together with a kind of tender care, almost as if he were burying the corpse of a beloved friend. Then he beckoned to his squires to leave the chamber, took his lute on his arm, and sang the following song to its notes:—

> "Bury them, bury them out of sight,
> For hope and fame are fled;
> And peaceful resting and quiet night
> Are all now left for the dead."

"You will stir up my anger against your lute," said Froda. "You had accustomed it to more joyful songs than this. It is too good for a passing-bell, and you too good to toll it. I tell you yet, my young hero, all will end gloriously."

Edwald looked awhile with wonder in his face, and he answered kindly: "Beloved Froda, if it displeases you, I will surely sing no more." But at the same time he struck a few sad chords, which sounded infinitely sweet and tender. Then the northern knight, much moved, clasped him in his arms, and said: "Dear Edchen, sing and say and do whatever pleases you; it shall ever rejoice me. But you may well believe me, for I speak not this without a spirit of presage—your sorrow shall change; whether to death or life I know not, but great and overpowering joy awaits you." Edwald rose firmly and cheerfully from his seat, seized his companion's arm with a strong grasp, and walked forth with him through the blooming alleys of the garden into the balmy air.

At that very hour, an aged woman, muffled in many a covering, was led secretly to the apartment of the lady Hildegardis. The appearance of the dark-complexioned stranger was mysterious; and she had gathered round her for some time, by many feats of jugglery, a part of the multitude returning home from the tournament, but had dispersed them at last in wild affright. Before this happened, the tire-woman of Hildegardis had hastened to her mistress, to entertain her with an account of the rare and pleasant feats of the bronze-coloured woman. The maidens in attendance, seeing their lady deeply moved, and wishing to banish her melancholy, bade the tire-woman bring the old stranger hither. Hildegardis forbade it not, hoping that she should thus divert the attention of her maidens, while she gave herself up more deeply and earnestly to the varying imaginations which flitted through her mind.

The messenger found the place already deserted; and the strange old woman alone in the midst, laughing immoderately. When questioned by her, she did not deny that she had all at once taken the form of a monstrous owl, announcing to the spectators in a screeching voice, that she was the Devil,—and that every one upon this rushed screaming home.

The tire-woman trembled at the fearful jest, but durst not return to ask again the pleasure of Hildegardis, whose discontented mood she had already remarked. She gave strict charge to the old woman, with many a threat and promise, to demean herself discreetly in the castle; after which she brought her in by the most secret way, that none of those whom she had terrified might see her enter.

The aged crone now stood before Hildegardis, and winked to her, in the midst of her low and humble salutation, in a strangely familiar manner, as though there were some secret between them. The lady felt an involuntary shudder, and could not withdraw her gaze from the features of that hideous countenance, hateful as it was to her. The curiosity which had led the rest to desire a sight of the strange woman was by no means gratified; for she performed none but the most common tricks of jugglery and related only well-known tales, so that the tire-woman felt wearied and indifferent; and, ashamed of having brought the stranger, she stole away unnoticed. Several other maidens followed her example; and as these withdrew, the old crone twisted her mouth into a smile, and repeated the same hideous confidential wink towards the lady. Hildegardis could not understand what attracted her in the jests and tales of the bronze-coloured woman; but so it was, that in her whole life she had never bestowed such attention on the words of any one. Still the old woman went on and on, and already the night looked dark without the windows; but the attendants who still remained with Hildegardis had sunk into a deep sleep, and had lighted none of the wax-tapers in the apartment.

Then, in the dusky gloom, the dark old crone rose from the low seat on which she had been sitting, as if she now felt herself well at ease, advanced towards Hildegardis, who sat as if spell-bound with terror, placed herself beside her on the purple couch, and embracing her in her long dry arms with a hateful caress, whispered a few words in her ear. It seemed to the lady as if she uttered the names of Froda and Edwald; and from them came the sound of a flute, which, clear and silvery as were its tones, seemed to lull her into a trance. She could indeed move her limbs, but only to follow those sounds, which like a silver net-work floated round the hideous form of the old woman. She moved from the chamber, and Hildegardis followed her through all her slumbering maidens, still singing softly as she went, "Ye maidens, ye maidens, I wander by night."

Without the castle, accompanied by squire and groom, stood the gigantic Bohemian warrior; he laid on the shoulders of the crone a bag of gold so heavy that she sank half whimpering, half laughing, on the ground; then lifted the entranced Hildegardis on his steed, and galloped with her silently into the ever-deepening gloom of night.

"All ye noble lords and knights, who yesterday contended gallantly for the prize of victory and the hand of the peerless Hildegardis, arise, arise! saddle your steeds, and to the rescue! The peerless Hildegardis is carried away!"

Thus proclaimed many a herald through castle and town, in the bright red dawn of the following day; and on all sides rose the dust from the tread of knights and noble squires along those roads by which so lately, in the evening twilight, Hildegardis in proud repose had gazed on her approaching suitors.

Two of them, well known to us, remained inseparably together; but they knew as little as the others whether they had taken the right direction; for how and when the adored lady could have disappeared from her apartments, was still to the whole castle a fearful and mysterious secret.

Edwald and Froda rode as long as the sun moved over their heads, unwearied as he; and now when he sank in the waves of the river, they thought to win the race from him, and still spurred on their jaded steeds. But the noble animals staggered and panted, and the knights were constrained to grant them some little refreshment in a grassy meadow. Secure of bringing them back at their first call, their masters removed both bit and curb, that they might be refreshed with the green pasture, and with the deep blue waters of the Maine, while they themselves reposed under the shade of a neighbouring thicket of alders.

And deep in the cool dark shade, there shone, as it were, a mild but clear sparkling light, and checked the speech of Froda, who at that moment was beginning to tell his friend the tale of his knightly service to his sovereign lady, which had been delayed hitherto, first by Edwald's sadness, and then by the haste of their journey. Ah, well did Froda know that lovely golden light! "Let us follow it, Edchen," said he in a low tone, "and leave the horses awhile to their pasture." Edwald in silence followed his companion's advice. A secret voice, half sweet, half fearful, seemed to tell him that here was the path, the only right path to Hildegardis. Once only he said in astonishment, "Never before have I seen the evening glow shine on the leaves so brightly." Froda shook his head with a smile, and they pursued in silence their unknown track.

When they came forth on the other side of the alder-thicket upon the bank of the Maine, which almost wound round it, Edwald saw well that another glow than that of evening was shining on them, for dark clouds of night already covered the heavens, and the guiding light stood fixed on the shore of the river. It lit up the waves, so that they could see a high woody island in the midst of the stream, and a boat on the hither side of the shore fast bound to a stake. But on approaching, the knights saw much more;—a troop of horsemen of strange and foreign appearance were all asleep, and in the midst of them, slumbering on cushions, a female form in white garments.

"Hildegardis!" murmured Edwald to himself, with a smile, and at the same time he drew his sword in readiness for the combat as soon as the robbers should awake, and beckoned to Froda to raise the sleeping lady, and convey her to a place of safety. But at this moment something like an owl passed whizzing over the dark squadron; and they all started up with clattering arms and hideous outcries. A wild unequal combat arose in the darkness of night, for that beaming light had disappeared. Froda and Edwald were driven asunder, and only at a distance heard each other's mighty war-cry. Hildegardis, startled from her magic sleep, uncertain whether she were waking or dreaming, fled bewildered and weeping bitterly into the deep shades of the alder-thicket.

CHAPTER VI.

FRODA felt his arm grow weary, and the warm blood was flowing from two wounds in his shoulder; he wished so to lie down in death that he might rise up with honour from his bloody grave to the exalted lady whom he served. He cast his shield behind him, grasped his sword-hilt with both hands, and rushed wildly, with a loud war-cry, upon the affrighted foe. Instantly he heard some voices cry, "It is the rage of the northern heroes which has come upon him." And the whole troop were scattered in dismay, while the exhausted knight remained wounded and alone in the darkness.

Then the golden hair of Aslauga gleamed once more in the alder-shade; and Froda said, leaning, through weariness, on his sword, "I think not that I am wounded to death; but whenever that time shall come, O beloved lady, wilt thou not indeed appear to me in all thy loveliness and brightness?" A soft "Yes" breathed against his cheek, and the golden light vanished.

But now Hildegardis came forth from the thicket, half fainting with terror, and said feebly, "Within is the fair and frightful spectre of the north—without is the battle;—O merciful heaven! whither shall I go?"

Then Froda approached to soothe the affrighted one, to speak some words of comfort to her, and to inquire after Edwald; but wild shouts and the rattling of armour announced the return of the Bohemian warriors. With haste Froda led the maiden to the boat, pushed off from the shore, and rowed her with the last effort of his failing strength towards the island which he had observed in the midst of the stream. But the pursuers had already kindled torches, and waved them sparkling here and there: by this light they soon discovered the boat; they saw that the dreaded Danish knight was bleeding, and gained fresh courage for their pursuit. Hardly had Froda pushed the boat to the shore of the island, before he perceived a Bohemian on the other side in another skiff; and soon afterwards the greater number of the enemy embarked to row towards the island. "To the wood, fair maiden," he whispered, as soon as he had landed Hildegardis on the shore: "there conceal yourself, whilst I endeavour to prevent the landing of the robbers." But Hildegardis, clinging to his arm, whispered again, "Do I not see that you are pale and bleeding? and would you have me expire with terror in the dark and lonely clefts of this rock? Ah! and if your northern gold-haired spectre were to appear again and seat herself beside me! Think you that I do not see her there now, shining through the thicket!" "She shines!" echoed Froda; and new strength and hope ran through every vein. He climbed the hill, following the gracious gleam; and Hildegardis, though trembling at the sight, went readily with her companion, saying only from time to time, in a low voice, "Ah, Sir Knight!—my noble wondrous knight—leave me not here alone; that would be my death." The knight, soothing her courteously, stepped ever onwards through the darkness of dell and forest; for already he heard the sound of the Bohemians landing on the shore of the island. Suddenly he stood before a cave thick-covered with underwood; and the gleam disappeared. "Here, then," he whispered, endeavouring to hold the branches asunder. For a moment she paused, and said, "If you should but let the branches close again behind me, and I were to remain alone with spectres in this cave! But, Froda, you will surely follow me—a trembling, hunted child as I am? Will you not?" Without more misgivings she passed through the branches; and the knight, who would willingly have remained without as a guard, followed her. Earnestly he listened through the stillness of night, whilst Hildegardis hardly dared to draw her breath. Then was heard the tramp of an armed man, coming ever nearer and nearer, and now close to the entrance of the cave. In vain did Froda strive to free himself from the trembling maiden. Already the branches before the entrance were cracking and breaking, and Froda sighed deeply. "Must I, then, fall like a lurking fugitive, entangled in a woman's garments? It is a base death to die. But can I cast this half-fainting creature away from me on the dark hard earth, perhaps into some deep abyss? Come, then, what will, thou, Lady Aslauga, knowest that I die an honourable death!"

"Froda! Hildegardis!" breathed a gentle, well-known voice at the entrance; and recognising Edwald, Froda bore the lady towards him into the starlight, saying, "She will die of terror in our sight in this deep cavern. Is the foe near at hand?" "Most of them lie lifeless on the shore, or swim bleeding through the waves," said Edwald. "Set your mind at rest, and repose yourself. Are you wounded, beloved Froda?" He gave this short account to his astonished companions—how, in the darkness, he had mixed with the Bohemians and pressed into the skiff, and that it had been easy to him on landing to disperse the robbers entirely, who supposed that they were attacked by one of their own crew, and thought themselves bewitched. "They began at last to fall on one another"—so he ended his history; "and we have only now to wait for the morning to conduct the lady home; for those who are wandering about of that owl-squadron will doubtless hide themselves from the eye of day." While speaking, he had skilfully and carefully arranged a couch of twigs and moss for Hildegardis; and when the wearied one, after uttering some gentle words of gratitude, had sunk into a slumber, he began, as well as the darkness would allow, to bind up the wounds of his friend. During this anxious task, while the dark boughs of the trees murmured over their heads, and the rippling of the stream was heard from afar, Froda, in a low voice, made known to his brother in arms to the service of what lady he was bound. Edwald listened with deep attention; but at last he said tenderly, "Trust me, the noble Princess Aslauga will not resent it, if you pledge yourself to this earthly beauty in faithful love. Ah! even now doubtless you are shining in the dreams of Hildegardis, richly-gifted and happy knight! I will not stand in your way with my vain wishes; I see now clearly that she can never, never love me. Therefore I will this very day hasten to the war which so many valiant knights of Germany are waging in the heathen land of Prussia; and the black cross, which distinguishes them for warriors of the Church, I will lay as the best balm on my throbbing heart. Take, then, dear Froda, that fair hand which you have won in battle, and live henceforth a life of surpassing happiness and joy."

"Edwald," said Froda, gravely, "this is the first time that I ever heard one word from your lips which a true knight could not fulfil. Do as it pleases you towards the fair and haughty Hildegardis; but Aslauga remains my mistress ever, and no other do I desire in life or death." The youth was startled by these stern words, and made no reply. Both, without saying more to each other, watched through the night in solemn thought.

The next morning, when the rising sun shone brightly over the flowery plains around the Castle of Hildegardis, the watchman on the tower blew a joyful blast from his horn; for his keen eye had distinguished far in the distance his fair lady, who was riding from the forest between her two deliverers; and from castle, town, and hamlet, came forth many a rejoicing train to assure themselves with their own eyes of the happy news.

Hildegardis turned to Edwald with eyes sparkling through tears, and said, "Were it not for you, young knight, they might have sought long and vainly before they found the lost maiden or the noble Froda, who would now be lying in that dark cavern a bleeding and lifeless corse." Edwald bowed lowly in reply, but persevered in his wonted silence. It even seemed as though an unusual grief restrained the smile which erewhile answered so readily, in childlike sweetness, to every friendly word.

The noble guardian of Hildegardis had, in the overflowing joy of his heart, prepared a sumptuous banquet, and invited all the knights and ladies present to attend it. Whilst Froda and Edwald, in all the brightness of their glory, were ascending the steps in the train of their rescued lady, Edwald said to his friend, "Noble, stedfast knight, you can never love me more!" And as Froda looked in astonishment, he continued—"Thus it is when children presume to counsel heroes, however well they may mean it. Now have I offended grievously against you, and yet more against the noble Lady Aslauga." "Because you would have plucked every flower of your own garden to gladden me with them?" said Froda: "no; you are my gentle brother in arms now, as heretofore, dear Edchen, and are perhaps become yet dearer to me."

Then Edwald smiled again in silent contentment, like a flower after the morning showers of May.

The eyes of Hildegardis glanced mildly and kindly on him, and she often conversed graciously with him, while, on the other hand, since yesterday, a reverential awe seemed to separate her from Froda. But Edwald also was much altered. However he welcomed with modest joy the favour of his lady, it yet seemed as if some barrier were between them which forbade him to entertain the most distant hope of successful love.

It chanced that a noble count, from the court of the Emperor, was announced, who being bound on an important embassy, had wished to pay his respects to the lady Hildegardis by the way. She received him gladly; and as soon as the first salutations were over, he said, looking at her and at Edwald, "I know not if my good fortune may not have brought me hither to a very joyful festivity. That would be right welcome news to the Emperor my master." Hildegardis and Edwald were lovely to look upon in their blushes and confusion; but the count, perceiving at once that he had been too hasty, inclined himself respectfully towards the young knight, and said, "Pardon me, noble Duke Edwald, my too great forwardness; but I know the wish of my sovereign, and the hope to find it already fulfilled prompted my tongue to speak." All eyes were fixed inquiringly on the young hero, who answered, in graceful confusion, "It is true; the Emperor, when I was last in his camp, through his undeserved favour, raised me to the rank of a duke. It was my good fortune, that in an encounter, some of the enemy's horse, who had dared to assault the sacred person of the Emperor, dispersed and fled on my approach." The count then, at the request of Hildegardis, related every circumstance of the heroic deed; and it appeared that Edwald had not only rescued the Emperor from the most imminent peril, but also, with the cool and daring skill of a general, had gained the victory which decided the event of the war.

Surprise at first sealed the lips of all; and even before their congratulations could begin, Hildegardis had turned towards Edwald, and said in a low voice, which yet, in that silence, was clearly heard by all, "The noble count has made known the wish of my imperial uncle; and I conceal it no longer, my own heart's wish is the same:—I am Duke Edwald's bride." And with that she extended to him her fair right hand; and all present waited only till he should take it, before they burst into a shout of congratulation. But Edwald forbore to do so; he only sunk on one knee before his lady, saying, "God forbid that the lofty Hildegardis should ever recall a word spoken solemnly to noble knights and dames. 'To no vanquished knight,' you said, 'might the hand of the Emperor's niece belong' —and behold there Froda the noble Danish knight, my conqueror." Hildegardis, with a slight blush, turned hastily away, hiding her eyes; and as Edwald arose, it seemed as though there were a tear upon his cheek.

In his clanging armour Froda advanced to the middle of the hall, exclaiming, "I declare my late victory over Duke Edwald to have been the chance of fortune, and I challenge the noble knight to meet me again to-morrow in the lists."

At the same time he threw his iron gauntlet ringing on the pavement.

But Edwald moved not to take it up. On the contrary, a glow of lofty anger was on his cheeks, and his eyes sparkled with indignation, so that his friend would hardly have recognised him; and after a silence he spoke:

"Noble Sir Froda, if I have ever offended you, we are now even. How durst you, a warrior gloriously wounded by two sword-strokes, challenge a man unhurt into the lists to-morrow, if you did not despise him?"

"Forgive me, Duke Edwald," answered Froda, somewhat abashed, but with cheerfulness; "I have spoken too boldly: not till I am completely cured do I call you to the field."

Then Edwald took up the gauntlet joyfully: he knelt once more before Hildegardis, who, turning away her face, gave him her fair hand to kiss, and walked, with his arm in that of his noble Danish friend, out of the hall.

CHAPTER VII.

While Froda's wounds were healing, Edwald would sometimes wander, when the shades of evening fell dark and silent around, on the flowery terraces beneath the windows of Hildegardis, and sing pleasant little songs; amongst others the following:—

"Heal fast, heal fast, ye hero-wounds;
O knight, be quickly strong;
Beloved strife
For fame and life,
O tarry not too long!"

But that one which the maidens of the castle loved best to learn from him was this; and it was perhaps the longest song that Edwald had ever sung in his whole life.

"Would I on earth were lying,
By noble hero slain;
So that love's gentle sighing
Breath'd me to life again!

Would I an emperor were,
  Of wealth and power!
Would I were gathering twigs
  In woodland bower!

Would that, in lone seclusion
  I lived a hermit's life!
Would, amid wild confusion,
  I led the battle-strife!

O would the lot were mine,
  In bower or field,
To which my lady fair
  Her smile would yield!"

At this time it happened, that a man, who held himself to be very wise, and who filled the office of secretary to the aged guardian of Hildegardis, came to the two knightly friends to propose a scheme to them. His proposal, in few words, was this, that as Froda could gain no advantage from his victory, he might in the approaching combat suffer himself to be thrown from his steed, and thus secure the lady for his comrade, at the same time fulfilling the wish of the emperor, which might turn to his advantage hereafter in many ways.

At this the two friends at first laughed heartily; but then Froda advanced gravely towards the secretary, and said, "Thou trifler, doubtless the old duke would drive thee from his service did he know of thy folly, and teach thee to talk of the emperor. Good night, worthy sir; and trust me that when Edwald and I meet each other, it will be with all our heart and strength."

The secretary hastened out of the room with all speed, and was seen next morning to look unusually pale.

Soon after this, Froda recovered from his wounds; the course was again prepared as before, but crowded by a still greater number of spectators; and in the freshness of a dewy morning the two knights advanced solemnly together to the combat.

"Beloved Edwald," said Froda, in a low voice, as they went, "take good heed to yourself, for neither this time can the victory be yours,—on that rose-coloured cloud appears Aslauga."

"It may be so," answered Edwald with a quiet smile; "but under the arches of that golden bower shines Hildegardis, and this time she has not been waited for."

The knights took their places,—the trumpets sounded, the course began, and Froda's prophecy seemed to be near its fulfilment, for Edwald staggered under the stroke of his lance, so that he let go the bridle, seized the mane with both hands, and thus hardly recovered his seat, whilst his high-mettled snow-white steed bore him wildly around the lists without control. Hildegardis also seemed to shrink at this sight; but the youth at length reined-in his steed, and the second course was run.

Froda shot like lightning along the plain, and it seemed as if the success of the young duke were now hopeless; but in the shock of their meeting, the bold Danish steed reared, starting aside as if in fear; the rider staggered, his stroke passed harmless by, and both steed and knight fell clanging to the ground before the stedfast spear of Edwald, and lay motionless upon the field.

Edwald did now as Froda had done before. In knightly wise he stood still awhile upon the spot, as if waiting to see whether any other adversary were there to dispute his victory; then he sprang from his steed, and flew to the assistance of his fallen friend.

He strove with all his might to release him from the weight of his horse; and presently Froda came to himself, rose on his feet, and raised up his charger also. Then he lifted up his vizor, and greeted his conqueror with a friendly smile, though his countenance was pale. The victor bowed humbly, almost timidly, and said, "You, my knight, overthrown—and by me! I understand it not."

"It was her own will," answered Froda, smiling. "Come now to your gentle bride."

The multitude around shouted aloud, each lady and knight bowed low, when the aged duke pointed out to them the lovely pair, and at his bidding, the betrothed, with soft blushes, embraced each other beneath the green garlands of the golden bower.

That very day were they solemnly united in the chapel of the castle, for so had Froda earnestly desired: a journey into a far-distant land, he said, lay before him, and much he wished to celebrate the marriage of his friend before his departure.

CHAPTER VIII.

The torches were burning clear in the vaulted halls of the castle, Hildegardis had just left the arm of her lover to begin a stately dance of ceremony with the aged duke, when Edwald beckoned to his companion, and they went forth together into the moonlit gardens of the castle.

"Ah, Froda, my noble lofty hero," exclaimed Edwald after a silence, "were you as happy as I am! But your eyes rest gravely and thoughtfully on the ground, or kindle almost impatiently heavenwards. It would be dreadful, indeed, had the secret wish of your heart been to win Hildegardis,—and I, foolish boy, so strangely favoured, had stood in your way."

"Be at rest, Edchen," answered the Danish hero with a smile. "On the word of a knight, my thoughts and yearnings concern not your fair Hildegardis. Far brighter than ever does Aslauga's radiant image shine into my heart: but now hear what I am going to relate to you.

"At the very moment when we met together in the course —oh, had I words to express it to you!—I was enwrapped, encircled, dazzled by Aslauga's golden tresses, which were waving all around me. Even my noble steed must have beheld the apparition, for I felt him start and rear under me. I saw you no more,—the world no more,—I saw only the angel-face of Aslauga close before me, smiling, blooming like a flower in a sea of sunshine which floated round her. My senses failed me. Not till you raised me from beneath my horse, did my consciousness return, and then I knew, with exceeding joy, that her own gracious pleasure had struck me down. But I felt a strange weariness, far greater than my fall alone could have caused, and I felt assured at the same time that my lady was about to send me on a far-distant mission. I hastened to repose myself in my chamber, and a deep sleep immediately fell upon me. Then came Aslauga in a dream to me, more royally adorned than ever; she placed herself at the head of my couch, and said, 'Haste to array thyself in all the splendour of thy silver armour, for thou art not the wedding-guest alone, thou art also the—'

"And before she could speak the word, my dream had melted away, and I felt a longing desire to fulfil her gracious command, and rejoiced in my heart. But in the midst of the festival, I seemed to myself more lonely than in all my life before, and I cannot cease to ponder what that unspoken word of my lady could be intended to announce."

"You are of a far loftier spirit than I am, Froda," said Edwald after a silence, "and I cannot soar with you into the sphere of your joys. But tell me, has it never awakened a deep pang within you that you serve a lady so withdrawn from you—alas! a lady, who is almost ever invisible?"

"No, Edwald, not so," answered Froda, his eyes sparkling with happiness. "For well I know that she scorns not my service; she has even deigned sometimes to appear to me. Oh, I am in truth a happy knight and minstrel!"

"And yet your silence to-day,—your troubled yearnings?"

"Not troubled, dear Edchen; only so heartfelt, so fervent in the depth of my heart,—and so strangely mysterious to myself withal. But this, with all belonging to me, springs alike from the words and commands of Aslauga. How, then, can it be otherwise than something good and fair, and tending to a high and noble aim?"

A squire, who had hastened after them, announced that the knightly bridegroom was expected for the torch-dance; and as they returned, Edwald entreated his friend to take his place in the solemn dance next to him and Hildegardis. Froda inclined his head in token of friendly assent.

The horns and hautboys had already sounded their solemn invitation; Edwald hastened to give his hand to his fair bride; and while he advanced with her to the midst of the stately hall, Froda offered his hand for the torch-dance to a noble lady who stood the nearest to him, without farther observing her, and took with her the next place to the wedded pair.

But how was it when a light began to beam from his companion, before which the torch in his left hand lost all its brightness? Hardly dared he, in sweet and trembling hope, to raise his eyes to the lady; and when at last he ventured, all his boldest wishes and longings were fulfilled.[1] Adorned with a radiant bridal crown of emeralds, Aslauga moved in solemn loveliness beside him, and beamed on him from amid the sunny light of her golden hair, blessing him with her heavenly countenance. The amazed spectators could not withdraw their eyes from the mysterious pair,—the knight in his light silver mail, with the torch raised on high in his hand, earnest and joyful, moving with a measured step, as if engaged in a ceremony of deep and myterious meaning. His lady beside him, rather floating than dancing, beaming light from her golden hair, so that

[1] See the Baron de la Motte Fouqué's *Waldemar*—

"Let none henceforward shrink from daring dreams,
For earnest hearts shall find their dreams fulfilled."

you would have thought the day was shining into the night; and when a look could reach through all the surrounding splendour to her face, rejoicing heart and sense with the unspeakably sweet smile of her eyes and lips.

Near the end of the dance, she inclined towards Froda, and whispered to him with an air of tender confidence, and with the last sound of the horns and hautboys she had disappeared.

The most curious spectator dared not question Froda about his partner. Hildegardis did not seem to have been conscious of her presence; but shortly before the end of the festival, Edwald approached his friend, and asked in a whisper, "Was it?"

"Yes, dear youth," answered Froda; "your marriage-dance has been honoured by the presence of the most exalted beauty which has been ever beheld in any land. Ah! and if I rightly understood her meaning, you will never more see me stand sighing and gazing upon the ground. But hardly dare I hope it. Now good night, dear Edchen, good night. As soon as I may, I will tell you all."

CHAPTER IX.

The light and joyous dreams of morning still played round Edwald's head, when it seemed as though a clear light encompassed him. He remembered Aslauga; but it was Froda, the golden locks of whose helmet shone now with no less sunny brightness than the flowing hair of his lady. "Ah!" thought Edwald in his dream, "how beautiful has my dear brother-in-arms become!" And Froda said to him, "I will sing something to you, Edchen; but softly, softly, so that it may not awaken Hildegardis. Listen to me.

> She glided in, bright as the day,
> There where her knight in slumber lay;

And in her lily hand was seen
A band that seemed of the moonlight sheen.
'We are one,' she sang, as about his hair
She twin'd it, and over her tresses fair.
Beneath them the world lay dark and drear:
But he felt the touch of her hand so dear,
Uplifting him far above mortals' sight,
While around him were shed her locks of light,
Till a garden fair lay about him spread—
And this was Paradise, angels said."

"Never in your life did you sing so sweetly," said the dreaming Edwald.

"That may well be, Edchen," said Froda, with a smile, and vanished.

But Edwald dreamed on and on, and many other visions passed before him, all of a pleasing kind, although he could not recall them, when, in the full light of morning, he unclosed his eyes with a smile. Froda alone, and his mysterious song, stood clear in his memory. He now knew full well that his friend was dead; but the thought gave him no pain, for he felt sure that the pure spirit of that minstrel-warrior could only find its proper joy in the gardens of Paradise, and in blissful solace with the lofty spirits of the ancient times. He glided softly from the side of the sleeping Hildegardis to the chamber of the departed. He lay upon his bed of rest, almost as beautiful as he had appeared in the dream, and his golden helmet was entwined with a wondrously-shining lock of hair. Then Edwald made a fair and shady grave in consecrated ground, summoned the chaplain of the castle, and with his assistance laid his beloved Froda therein.

He came back just as Hildegardis awoke; she beheld, with wonder and humility, his mien of chastened joy, and asked him whither he had been so early; to which he replied, with a smile, "I have just buried the corpse of my dearly-loved Froda, who, this very night, has passed away to his golden-haired mistress." Then he related the whole history of Aslauga's Knight, and lived on in subdued, unruffled happiness, though for some time he was even more silent and thoughtful than before. He was often found sitting on the grave of his friend, and singing the following song to his lute:—

Listening to celestial lays,
Bending thy unclouded gaze
On the pure and living light,
Thou art blest, Aslauga's Knight!

Send us from thy bower on high
Many an angel-melody,
Many a vision soft and bright,
Aslauga's dear and faithful Knight!

Sintram and his Companions.

LONDON:
PRINTED BY LEVEY, ROBSON, AND FRANKLYN,
Great New Street, Fetter Lane.

Alb. Durer. W. Linton sc.

SINTRAM AND HIS COMPANIONS.

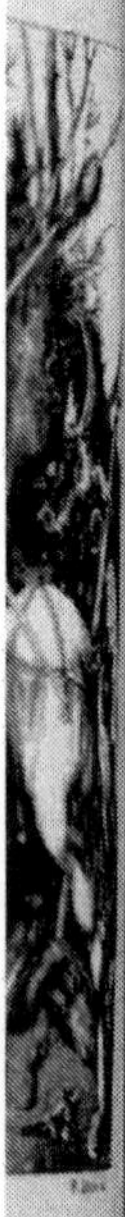

Sintram and his Companions

from the German
of
De la Motte Fouqué.

London:
James Burns

SINTRAM AND HIS COMPANIONS.

Sintram and his Companions

from the German
of
De la Motte Fouqué.

London:
James Burns

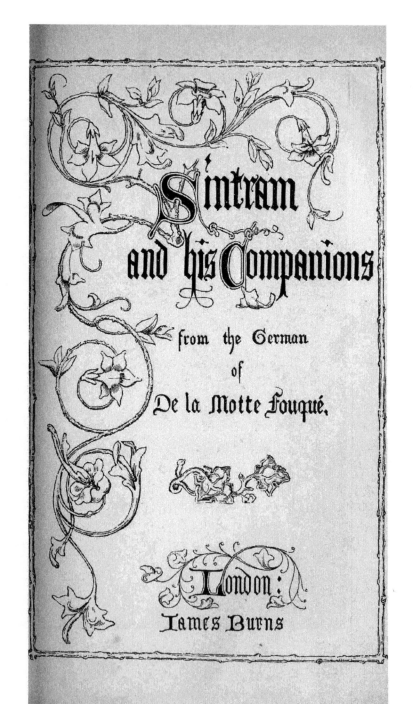

Illustrations.

DRAWN BY H. C. SELOUS.

TO THE READER.

QUESTIONS have sometimes arisen, whether a poet has taken the images of his fancy from the works of older times; or how he has come by them. The subject seems to me not without interest; and I think that, when the author can himself give a clear account of the matter, he is allowed, or rather obliged, to make it known to his readers. Hence the following narrative.

Some years ago there lay among my birthday-gifts a beautiful engraving* of Albert Dürer's:—"An armed knight, of elderly countenance, is riding on a tall horse, accompanied by his dog, through a fearful valley, where the clefts of the rocks and the roots of the trees assume horrid shapes, and poisonous plants grow upon the ground. Hideous reptiles are creeping among them. Near him rides Death upon a small lean horse; from behind, a demon-form stretches forth its claws to reach him. The horse and dog look strangely, as if bewitched by the horrors that surround them; but the knight rides quietly on his way, and bears upon the point of his lance an already impaled reptile. Far off a castle looks down upon him, with lofty friendly towers, which makes the loneliness of the valley sink still deeper into his soul."

My friend Edward Hitzig, who gave me this print, sent with it a letter, requesting that I would illustrate the allegorical figures in a ballad. It was not permitted me to do it then, nor for long afterwards; but I still carried the remembrance of the picture within me, through peace and war, till it wove and shaped itself out before me quite distinctly: but instead of a ballad, it has become a little romance, if the kind reader will accept it as such.

Written on the 5th December, 1814. FOUQUÉ.

* The frontispiece is a reduced copy of this print.

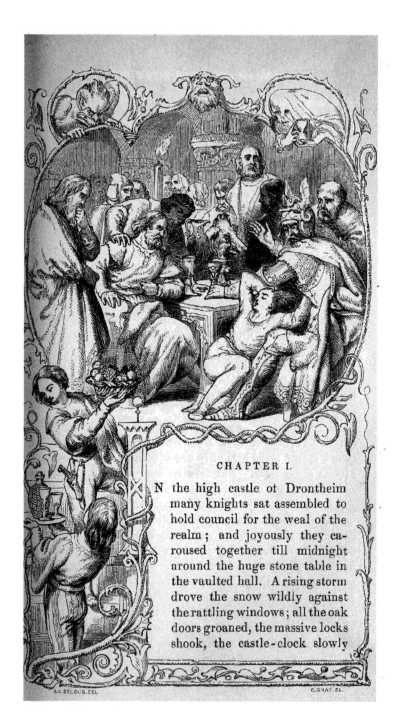

CHAPTER I.

IN the high castle ot Drontheim many knights sat assembled to hold council for the weal of the realm; and joyously they caroused together till midnight around the huge stone table in the vaulted hall. A rising storm drove the snow wildly against the rattling windows; all the oak doors groaned, the massive locks shook, the castle-clock slowly and heavily struck the hour of one. Then a boy, pale as death, with disordered hair and closed eyes, rushed into the hall, uttering a wild scream of terror. He stopped beside the richly carved seat of the mighty Biorn, clung to the glittering knight with both his hands, and shrieked in a piercing voice, "Knight and father! father and knight! Death and another are closely pursuing me!"

An awful stillness lay like ice on the whole assembly, save that the boy screamed ever the fearful words. But one of Biorn's numerous retainers, an old esquire, known by the name of Rolf the Good, advanced towards the terrified child, took him in his arms, and half chanted this prayer: "O Father, help Thy servant! I believe, and yet I cannot believe." The boy, as if in a dream, at once loosened his hold of the knight; and the good Rolf bore him from the hall unresisting, yet still shedding hot tears and murmuring confused sounds.

The lords and knights looked at one another much amazed, until the mighty Biorn said, wildly and fiercely laughing, "Marvel not at that strange boy. He is my only son; and has been thus since he was five years old: he is now twelve. I am therefore accustomed to see him so; though, at the first, I too was disquieted by it. The attack comes upon him only once in the year, and always at this same time. But forgive me for having spent so many words on my poor Sintram, and let us pass on to some worthier subject for our discourse."

Again there was silence for a while; then whisperingly and doubtfully single voices strove to renew their broken-off discourse, but without success. Two of the youngest and most joyous began a roundelay; but the storm howled and raged so wildly without, that this too was soon interrupted. And now they all sat silent and motionless in the lofty hall; the lamp flickered sadly under the vaulted roof; the whole party of knights looked like pale, lifeless images dressed up in gigantic armour.

Then arose the chaplain of the castle of Drontheim, the

only priest among the knightly throng, and said, "Dear Lord Biorn, our eyes and thoughts have all been directed to you and your son in a wonderful manner; but so it has been ordered by the providence of God. You perceive that we cannot withdraw them; and you would do well to tell us exactly what you know concerning the fearful state of the boy. Perchance the solemn tale, which I expect from you, might do good to this disturbed assembly."

Biorn cast a look of displeasure on the priest, and answered, "Sir chaplain, you have more share in the history than either you or I could desire. Excuse me, if I am unwilling to trouble these light-hearted warriors with so rueful a tale."

But the chaplain approached nearer to the knight, and said, in a firm yet very mild tone, "Dear lord, hitherto it rested with you alone to relate, or not to relate it; but now that you have so strangely hinted at the share which I have had in your son's calamity, I must positively demand that you will repeat word for word how every thing came to pass. My honour will have it so, and that will weigh with you as much as with me."

In stern compliance Biorn bowed his haughty head, and began the following narration. "This time seven years I was keeping the Christmas-feast with my assembled followers. We have many venerable old customs which have descended to us by inheritance from our great forefathers; as, for instance, that of placing a gilded boar's head on the table, and making thereon knightly vows of daring and wondrous deeds. Our chaplain here, who used then frequently to visit me, was never a friend to keeping up such traditions of the ancient heathen world. Such men as he were not much in favour in those olden times."

"My excellent predecessors," interrupted the chaplain, "belonged more to God than to the world, and with Him they were in favour. Thus they converted your ancestors; and if I can in like manner be of service to you, even your jeering will not vex me."

With looks yet darker, and a somewhat angry shudder, the knight resumed: "Yes, yes; I know all your promises and threats of an invisible Power, and how they are meant to persuade us to part more readily with whatever of this world's goods we may possess. Once, ah, truly, once I too had such! Strange!—Sometimes it seems to me as though ages had passed over since then, and as if I were alone the survivor, so fearfully is every thing changed. But now I bethink me, that the greater part of this noble company knew me in my happiness, and have seen my wife, my lovely Verena."

He pressed his hands on his eyes, and it seemed as though he wept. The storm had ceased; the soft light of the moon shone through the windows, and her beams played on his wild features. Suddenly he started up, so that his heavy armour rattled with a fearful sound, and he cried out in a thundering voice, "Shall I turn monk, as she has become a nun? No, crafty priest; your webs are too thin to catch flies of my sort."

"I have nothing to do with webs," said the chaplain. "In all openness and sincerity have I put heaven and hell before you during the space of six years; and you gave full consent to the step which the holy Verena took. But what all that has to do with your son's sufferings I know not, and I wait for your narration."

"You may wait long enough," said Biorn, with a sneer. "Sooner shall ——"

"Swear not!" said the chaplain in a loud commanding tone, and his eyes flashed almost fearfully.

"Hurra!" cried Biorn in wild affright; "hurra! Death and his companion are loose!" and he dashed madly out of the chamber and down the steps. The rough and fearful notes of his horn were heard summoning his retainers; and presently afterwards the clatter of horses' feet on the frozen court-yard gave token of their departure.

The knights retired, silent and shuddering; while the chaplain remained alone at the huge stone table, praying.

CHAPTER II.

AFTER some time the good Rolf returned with slow and soft steps, and started with surprise at finding the hall deserted. The chamber where he had been occupied in quieting and soothing the unhappy child was in so distant a part of the castle that he had heard nothing of the knight's hasty departure. The chaplain related to him all that had passed, and then said, "But my good Rolf, I much wish to ask you concerning those strange words with which you seemed to lull poor Sintram to rest. They sounded like sacred words, and no doubt they are; but I could not understand them. 'I believe, and yet I cannot believe.'"

"Reverend sir," answered Rolf, "I remember that from my earliest years no history in the Gospels has taken such hold of me as that of the child possessed with a devil, which the disciples were not able to cast out; but when our Saviour came down from the mountain where He had been transfigured, He broke the bonds wherewith the evil spirit had held the miserable child bound. I always felt as if I must have known and loved that boy, and been his play-fellow in his happy days; and when I grew older, then the distress of the father on account of his lunatic son lay heavy at my heart. It must surely have all been a foreboding of our poor young Lord Sintram, whom I love as if he were my own child; and now the words of the weeping father in the Gospel often come into my mind,—'Lord, I believe; help Thou my unbelief;' and something similar I may very likely have repeated to-day as a chant or a prayer. Reverend father, when I consider how one dreadful imprecation of the father has kept its withering hold on the son, all seems dark before me; but, God be praised! my faith and my hope remain above."

"Good Rolf," said the priest, "I cannot clearly understand what you say about the unhappy Sintram; for I do not know when and how this affliction came upon him. If no oath or solemn promise bind you to secrecy, will you make known to me all that is connected with it?"

"Most willingly," replied Rolf. "I have long desired to have an opportunity of so doing; but you have been almost always separated from us. I dare not now leave the sleeping boy any longer alone; and to-morrow, at the earliest dawn, I must take him to his father. Will you come with me, dear sir, to our poor Sintram?"

The chaplain at once took up the small lamp which Rolf had brought with him, and they set off together through the long vaulted passages. In the small distant chamber they found the poor boy fast asleep. The light of the lamp fell strangely on his very pale face. The chaplain stood gazing at him for some time, and at length said: "Certainly from his birth his features were always sharp and strongly marked, but now they are almost fearfully so for such a child; and yet no one can help having a kindly feeling towards him, whether he will or not."

"Most true, dear sir," answered Rolf. And it was evident how his whole heart rejoiced at any word which betokened affection for his beloved young lord. Thereupon he placed the lamp where its light could not disturb the boy, and seating himself close by the priest, he began to speak in the following terms:—"During that Christmas-feast of which my lord was talking to you, he and his followers discoursed much concerning the German merchants, and the best means of keeping down the increasing pride and power of the trading-towns. At length Biorn laid his impious hand on the golden boar's head, and swore to put to death without mercy every German trader whom fate, in what way soever, might bring alive into his power. The gentle Verena turned pale, and would have interposed

—but it was too late, the bloody word was uttered. And immediately afterwards, as though the great enemy of souls were determined at once to secure with fresh bonds the vassal thus devoted to him, a warder came into the hall to announce that two citizens of a trading-town in Germany, an old man and his son, had been shipwrecked on this coast, and were now without the gates, asking hospitality of the lord of the castle. The knight could not refrain from shuddering; but he thought himself bound by his rash vow and by that accursed heathenish golden boar. We, his retainers, were commanded to assemble in the castle-yard, armed with sharp spears, which were to be hurled at the defenceless strangers at the first signal made to us. For the first, and I trust the last time in my life, I said 'No' to the commands of my lord; and that I said in a loud voice, and with the heartiest determination. The Almighty, who alone knows whom He will accept, and whom He will reject, armed me with resolution and strength. And Biorn might perceive whence the refusal of his faithful old servant arose, and that it was worthy of respect. He said to me, half in anger and half in scorn: 'Go up to my wife's apartments: her attendants are running to and fro, perhaps she is ill. Go up, Rolf the Good, I say to thee, and so women shall be with women.' I thought to myself, 'Jeer on, then;' and I went silently the way that he had pointed out to me. On the stairs there met me two strange and right fearful beings, whom I had never seen before; and I know not how they got into the castle. One of them was a great, tall man, frightfully pallid and thin; the other was a dwarf-like man, with a most hideous countenance and features. Indeed, when I collected my thoughts and looked carefully at him, it appeared to me ——"

Low moanings and convulsive movements of the boy here interrupted the narrative. Rolf and the chaplain hastened to his bed-side, and perceived that his countenance wore an expression of fearful agony, and that he was struggling in vain to open his eyes. The priest made the Sign of the Cross over him, and immediately peace seemed to be restored, and his sleep again became quiet: they both returned softly to their seats.

"You see," said Rolf, "that it will not do to describe more closely those two awful beings. Suffice it to say, that they went down into the court-yard, and that I proceeded to my lady's apartments. I found the gentle Verena almost fainting with terror and overwhelming anxiety, and I hastened to restore her with some of those remedies which I was able to apply by my skill, through God's gift and the healing virtues of herbs and minerals. But scarcely had she recovered her senses, when, with that calm holy power which, as you know, is hers, she desired me to conduct her down to the court-yard, saying that she must either put a stop to the fearful doings of this night, or herself fall a sacrifice. Our way took us by the little bed of the sleeping Sintram. Alas! hot tears fell from my eyes to see how evenly his gentle breath then came and went, and how sweetly he smiled in his peaceful slumbers."

The old man put his hands to his eyes, and wept bitterly; but soon he resumed his sad story. "As we approached the lowest window of the staircase, we could hear distinctly the voice of the elder merchant; and on looking out, the light of the torches shewed me his noble features, as well as the bright youthful countenance of his son. 'I take Almighty God to witness,' cried he, 'that I had no evil thought against this house! But surely I must have fallen unawares amongst heathens; it cannot be that I am in a Christian knight's castle; and if you are indeed heathens, then kill us at once. And thou, my beloved son, be patient and of good courage; in heaven we shall learn wherefore it could not be otherwise.' I thought I could see those two fearful ones amidst the throng of retainers. The pale one had a huge curved sword in his hand, the little one held a spear notched in a strange fashion.

Verena tore open the window, and cried in silvery tones through the wild night, 'My dearest lord and husband, for the sake of your only child, have pity on those harmless men! Save them from death, and resist the temptation of the evil spirit.' The knight answered in his fierce wrath—but I cannot repeat his words. He staked his child on the desperate cast; he called Death and the Devil to see that he kept his word:—but hush! the boy is again moaning. Let me bring the dark tale quickly to a close. Biorn commanded his followers to strike, casting on them those fierce looks which have gained him the title of Biorn of the Fiery Eyes; while at the same time the two frightful strangers bestirred themselves very busily. Then Verena called out, with piercing anguish, 'Help, O God, my Saviour!' Those two dreadful figures disappeared; and the knight and his retainers, as if seized with blindness, rushed wildly one against the other, but without doing injury to themselves, or yet being able to strike the merchants, who ran so close a risk. They bowed reverently towards Verena, and with calm thanksgivings departed through the castle-gates, which at that moment had been burst open by a violent gust of wind, and now gave a free passage to any who would go forth. The lady and I were yet standing bewildered on the stairs, when I fancied I saw the two fearful forms glide close by me, but mist-like and unreal. Verena called to me: 'Rolf, did you see a tall pale man, and a little hideous one with him, pass just now up the staircase?' I flew after them; and found, alas, the poor boy in the same state in which you saw him a few hours ago. Ever since, the attack has come on him regularly at this time, and he is in all respects fearfully changed. The lady of the castle did not fail to discern the avenging hand of Heaven in this calamity; and as the knight, her husband, instead of repenting, ever became more truly Biorn of the Fiery Eyes, she resolved, in the walls of a cloister, by unremitting prayer, to obtain mercy in time and eternity for herself and her unhappy child."

Rolf was silent; and the chaplain, after some thought, said: "I now understand why, six years ago, Biorn confessed his guilt to me in general words, and consented that his wife should take the veil. Some faint compunction must then have stirred within him, and perhaps may stir him yet. At any rate it was impossible that so tender a flower as Verena could remain longer in so rough keeping. But who is there now to watch over and protect our poor Sintram?"

"The prayer of his mother," answered Rolf. "Reverend sir, when the first dawn of day appears, as it does now, and when the morning breeze whispers through the glancing window, they ever bring to my mind the soft beaming eyes of my lady, and I again seem to hear the sweet tones of her voice. The holy Verena is, next to God, our chief aid."

"And let us add our devout supplications to the Lord," said the chaplain; and he and Rolf knelt in silent and earnest prayer by the bed of the pale sufferer, who began to smile in his dreams.

CHAPTER III.

The rays of the sun shining brightly into the room awoke Sintram, and raising himself up, he looked angrily at the chaplain, and said, "So there is a priest in the castle! And yet that accursed dream continues to torment me even in his very presence. Pretty priest he must be!"

"My child," answered the chaplain in the mildest tone, "I have prayed for thee most fervently, and I shall never cease doing so—but God alone is Almighty."

"You speak very boldly to the son of the knight Biorn," cried Sintram. "'My child!' If those horrible dreams had not been again haunting me, you would make me laugh heartily."

"Young Lord Sintram," said the chaplain, "I am by no means surprised that you do not know me again; for, in truth, neither do I know you again." And his eyes filled with tears as he spoke.

The good Rolf looked sorrowfully in the boy's face, saying, "Ah, my dear young master, you are so much better than you would make people believe. Why do you that? Your memory is so good, that you must surely recollect your kind old friend the chaplain, who used formerly to be constantly at the castle, and to bring you so many gifts—bright pictures of saints, and beautiful songs?"

"I know all that very well," replied Sintram thoughtfully. "My sainted mother was alive in those days."

"Our gracious lady is still living, God be praised!" said the good Rolf.

"But she does not live for us, poor sick creatures that we are!" cried Sintram. "And why will you not call her sainted? Surely she knows nothing about my dreams?"

"Yes, she does know of them," said the chaplain; "and she prays to God for you. But take heed, and restrain that wild, haughty temper of yours. It might, indeed, come to pass that she would know nothing about your dreams, and that would be if your soul were separated from your body; and then the holy angels also would cease to know any thing of you."

Sintram fell back on his bed as if thunderstruck; and Rolf said, with a gentle sigh, "You should not speak so severely to my poor sick child, reverend sir."

The boy sat up, and with tearful eyes he turned caressingly towards the chaplain: "Let him do as he pleases, you good tender-hearted Rolf; he knows very well what he is about. Would you reprove him if I were slipping down a snowcleft, and he caught me up roughly by the hair of my head?"

The priest looked tenderly at him, and would have

spoken his holy thoughts, when Sintram suddenly sprang off the bed and asked after his father. As soon as he heard of the knight's departure, he would not remain another hour in the castle; and put aside the fears of the chaplain and the old esquire, lest a rapid journey should injure his hardly restored health, by saying to them, "Believe me, reverend sir, and dear old Rolf, if I were not subject to these hideous dreams, there would not be a bolder youth in the whole world; and even as it is, I am not so far behind the very best. Besides, till another year has passed, my dreams are at an end."

On his somewhat imperious sign Rolf brought out the horses. The boy threw himself boldly into the saddle, and taking a courteous leave of the chaplain, he dashed along the frozen valley that lay between the snow-clad mountains. He had not ridden far, in company with his old attendant, when he heard a strange indistinct sound proceeding from a neighbouring cleft in the rock; it was partly like the clapper of a small mill, but mingled with that were hollow groans and other tones of distress. Thither they turned their horses, and a wonderful sight shewed itself to them.

A tall man, deadly pale, in a pilgrim's garb, was striving with violent though unsuccessful efforts, to work his way out of the snow and to climb up the mountain; and thereby a quantity of bones, which were hanging loosely all about his garments, rattled one against the other, and caused the mysterious sound already mentioned. Rolf, much terrified, crossed himself, while the bold Sintram called out to the stranger, "What art thou doing there? Give an account of thy solitary labours."

"I live in death," replied that other one with a fearful grin.

"Whose are those bones on thy clothes?"

"They are relics, young sir."

"Art thou a pilgrim?"

"Restless, quietless, I wander up and down."

"Thou must not perish here in the snow before my eyes."

"That I will not."

"Thou must come up and sit on my horse."

"That I will." And all at once he started up out of the snow with surprising strength and agility, and sat on the horse behind Sintram, clasping him tight in his long arms. The horse, startled by the rattling of the bones, and as if seized with madness, rushed away through the most trackless passes. The boy soon found himself alone with his strange companion; for Rolf, breathless with fear, spurred on his horse in vain, and remained far behind them. From a snowy precipice the horse slid, without falling, into a narrow gorge, somewhat indeed exhausted, yet continuing to snort and foam as before, and still unmastered by the boy. Yet his headlong course being now changed into a rough irregular trot, Sintram was able to breathe more freely, and to begin the following discourse with his unknown companion.

"Draw thy garment closer around thee, thou pale man, so the bones will not rattle, and I shall be able to curb my horse."

"It would be of no avail, boy; it would be of no avail. The bones must rattle."

"Do not clasp me so tight with thy long arms, they are so cold."

"It cannot be helped, boy; it cannot be helped. Be content. For my long cold arms are not pressing yet on thy heart."

"Do not breathe on me so with thy icy breath. All my strength is departing."

"I must breathe, boy; I must breathe. But do not complain. I am not blowing thee away."

The strange dialogue here came to an end; for to Sintram's surprise he found himself on an open plain, over which the sun was shining brightly, and at no great distance before him he saw his father's castle. While he was thinking whether he might invite the unearthly pilgrim to rest there, this one put an end to his doubts by throwing himself suddenly off the horse, whose wild course was checked by the shock. Raising his forefinger, he said to the boy, "I know old Biorn of the Fiery Eyes well; perhaps but too well. Commend me to him. It will not need to tell him my name; he will recognise me at the description." So saying, the ghastly stranger turned aside into a thick fir-wood, and disappeared rattling amongst the tangled branches.

Slowly and thoughtfully Sintram rode on towards his father's castle, his horse now again quiet and altogether exhausted. He scarcely knew how much he ought to relate of his wonderful journey, and he also felt oppressed with anxiety for the good Rolf, who had remained so far behind. He found himself at the castle-gate sooner than he had expected; the drawbridge was lowered, the doors were thrown open; an attendant led the youth into the great hall, where Biorn was sitting all alone at a huge table, with many flagons and glasses before him, and suits of armour ranged on either side of him. It was his daily custom, by way of company, to have the armour of his ancestors, with closed vizors, placed all round the table at which he sat. The father and son began conversing as follows:

"Where is Rolf?"

"I do not know, father; he left me in the mountains."

"I will have Rolf shot, if he cannot take better care than that of my only child."

"Then, father, you will have your only child shot at the same time, for without Rolf I cannot live; and if even one single dart is aimed at him, I will be there to receive it, and to shield his true and faithful heart."

"So!—Then Rolf shall not be shot; but he shall be driven from the castle."

"In that case, father, you will see me go away also;

and I will give myself up to serve him in forests, in mountains, in caves."

"So!—Well, then, Rolf must remain here."

"That is just what I think, father."

"Were you riding quite alone?"

"No, father; but with a strange pilgrim. He said that he knew you very well—perhaps too well." And thereupon Sintram began to relate and to describe all that had passed with the pale man.

"I know him also very well," said Biorn. "He is half crazed and half wise, as we sometimes are astonished at seeing that people can be. But do thou, my boy, go to rest after thy wild journey. I give you my word that Rolf shall be kindly received if he arrive here; and that if he do not come soon, he shall be sought for in the mountains."

"I trust to your word, father," said Sintram, half humble, half proud; and he did after the command of the grim lord of the castle.

CHAPTER IV.

Towards evening Sintram awoke. He saw the good Rolf sitting at his bedside, and looked up in the old man's kind face with a smile of unusually innocent brightness. But soon again his dark brows were knit, and he asked, "How did my father receive you, Rolf? Did he say a harsh word to you?"

"No, my dear young lord, he did not; indeed he did not speak to me at all. At first he looked very wrathful; but he checked himself, and ordered a servant to bring me food and wine to refresh me, and afterwards to take me to your room."

"He might have kept his word better. But he is my father, and I must not judge him too hardly. I will now go down to the evening meal." So saying, he sprang up and threw on his furred mantle.

But Rolf stopped him, and said, entreatingly: "My dear young master, you would do better to take your meal to-day alone here in your own apartment; for there is a guest with your father, in whose company I should be very sorry to see you. If you will remain here, I wiil entertain you with pleasant tales and songs."

"There is nothing in the world which I should like better, dear Rolf," answered Sintram; "but it does not befit me to shun any man. Tell me, whom should I find with my father?"

"Alas!" said the old man, "you have already found him in the mountain. Formerly, when I used to ride about the country with Biorn, we often met with him, but I was forbidden to tell you any thing about him; and this is the first time that he has ever come to the castle."

"The crazy pilgrim!" replied Sintram; and he stood awhile in deep thought, as if considering the matter. At last, rousing himself, he said: "Dear old friend, I would most willingly stay here this evening all alone with you and your stories and songs, and all the pilgrims in the world should not entice me from this quiet room. But one thing must be considered. I feel a kind of dread of that pale, tall man; and by such fears no knight's son can ever suffer himself to be overcome. So be not angry, dear Rolf, if I determine to go and look that strange palmer in the face." And he shut the door of the chamber behind him, and with firm and echoing steps proceeded to the hall.

The pilgrim and the knight were sitting opposite to each other at the great table, on which many lights were burning; and it was fearful, amongst all the lifeless armour, to see those two tall grim men move, and eat, and drink.

As the pilgrim looked up on the boy's entrance, Biorn said: "You know him already: he is my only child, and your fellow-traveller this morning."

The palmer fixed an earnest look on Sintram, and answered, shaking his head, "I know not what you mean."

Then the boy burst forth, impatiently, "It must be confessed that you deal very unfairly by us! You say that you know my father but too much, and now it seems that you know me altogether too little. Look me in the face: who allowed you to ride on his horse, and in return had his good steed driven almost wild? Speak, if you can!"

Biorn smiled, shaking his head, but well pleased, as was his wont, with his son's wild behaviour; while the pilgrim shuddered as if terrified and overcome by some fearful irresistible power. At length, with a trembling voice, he said these words: "Yes, yes, my dear young lord, you are surely quite right; you are perfectly right in every thing which you may please to assert."

Then the lord of the castle laughed aloud, and said: "Why, thou strange pilgrim, what is become of all thy wonderfully fine speeches and warnings now? Has the boy all at once struck thee dumb and powerless? Beware, thou prophet-messenger, beware!"

But the palmer cast a fearful look on Biorn, which seemed to quench the light of his fiery eyes, and said solemnly, in a thundering voice, "Between me and thee, old man, the case stands quite otherwise. We have nothing to reproach each other with. And now suffer me to sing a song to you on the lute." He stretched out his hand, and took down from the wall a forgotten and half-strung lute, which was hanging there; and, with surprising skill and rapidity, having put it in a state fit for use, he struck some chords, and raised this song to the low melancholy tones of the instrument:

"The flow'ret was mine own, mine own,
But I have lost its fragrance rare,
And knightly name and freedom fair,
Through sin, through sin alone.

The flow'ret was thine own, thine own,
Why cast away what thou didst win?
Thou knight no more, but slave of sin,
Thou'rt fearfully alone!"

"Have a care!" shouted he at the close in a pealing voice, as he pulled the strings so mightily that they all broke with a clanging wail, and a cloud of dust rose from the old lute, which spread round him like a mist.

Sintram had been watching him narrowly whilst he was singing, and more and more did he feel convinced that it was impossible that this man and his fellow-traveller of the morning could be one and the same. Nay, the doubt rose to certainty, when the stranger again looked round at him with the same timid, anxious air, and with many excuses and low reverences hung the lute in its old place, and then ran out of the hall as if bewildered with terror, in strange contrast with the proud and stately bearing which he had shewn to Biorn.

The eyes of the boy were now directed to his father, and he saw that he had sunk back senseless in his seat, as if struck by a blow. Sintram's cries called Rolf and other attendants into the hall; and only by great labour did their united efforts awake the lord of the castle. His looks were still wild and disordered; but he allowed himself to be taken to rest, quiet and yielding.

CHAPTER V.

An illness followed this sudden attack; and during the course of it the stout old knight, in the midst of his delirious ravings, did not cease to affirm confidently that he must and should recover. He laughed proudly when his fever-fits came on, and rebuked them for daring to attack him so needlessly. Then he murmured to himself, "That was not the right one yet; there must still be another one out in the cold mountains."

Always at such words Sintram involuntarily shuddered; they seemed to strengthen his notion that he who had ridden with him, and he who had sat at table in the castle, were two quite distinct persons; and he knew not why, but this thought was inexpressibly awful to him.

Biorn recovered, and appeared to have entirely forgotten his adventure with the palmer. He hunted in the mountains; he carried on his usual wild warfare with his neighbours; and Sintram, as he grew up, became his almost constant companion; whereby each year a fearful strength of body and spirit was unfolded in the youth. Every one trembled at the sight of his sharp pallid features, his dark rolling eyes, his tall, muscular, and somewhat lean form; and yet no one hated him—not even those whom he distressed or injured in his wildest humours. This might arise in part out of regard to old Rolf, who seldom left him for long, and who always held a softening influence over him; but also many of those who had known the Lady Verena while she still lived in the world, affirmed that a faint reflection of her heavenly expression floated over the very unlike features of her son, and that by this their hearts were won.

Once, just at the beginning of spring, Biorn and his son were hunting in the neighbourhood of the sea-coast, over a tract of country which did not belong to them; drawn thither less by the love of sport than by the wish of bidding defiance to a chieftain whom they detested, and thus exciting a feud. At that season of the year, when his winter dreams had just passed off, Sintram was always unusually fierce and disposed for warlike adventures. And this day he was enraged at the chieftain for not coming in arms from his castle to hinder their hunting; and he cursed, in the wildest words, his tame patience and love of peace. Just then one of his wild young companions rushed towards him, shouting joyfully: "Be content, my dear young lord! I will wager that all is coming about as we and you wish; for as I was pursuing a wounded deer down to the sea-shore, I saw a sail and a vessel filled with armed men making for the shore. Doubtless your enemy purposes to fall upon you from the coast."

Joyfully and secretly Sintram called all his followers together, being resolved this time to take the combat on himself alone, and then to rejoin his father, and astonish him with the sight of captured foes and other tokens of victory.

The hunters, thoroughly acquainted with every cliff and rock on the coast, hid themselves round the landing-place; and soon the strange vessel hove nearer with swelling sails, till at length it came to anchor, and its crew began to disembark in unsuspicious security. At the head of them appeared a knight of high degree, in blue steel armour richly inlaid with gold. His head was bare, for he carried his costly golden helmet hanging on his left arm. He looked royally around him; and his countenance, which dark brown locks shaded, was pleasant to behold; and a well-trimmed moustache fringed his mouth, from which, as he smiled, gleamed forth two rows of pearl-white teeth.

A feeling came across Sintram that he must already have seen this knight somewhere; and he stood motionless for a few moments. But suddenly he raised his hand, to make the agreed signal of attack. In vain did the good Rolf, who had just succeeded in getting up to him, whisper in his ear that these could not be the foes whom he had taken them for, but that they were unknown, and certainly high and noble strangers.

"Let them be who they may," replied the wild youth, "they have enticed me here to wait, and they shall pay the penalty of thus fooling me. Say not another word, if you value your life." And immediately he gave the signal, a thick shower of javelins followed from all sides, and the Norwegian warriors rushed forth with flashing swords.

They found their foes as brave, or somewhat braver, than they could have desired. More fell on the side of those who made than of those who received the assault; and the strangers appeared to understand surprisingly the Norwegian manner of fighting. The knight in steel armour had not in his haste put on his helmet; but it seemed as if he in no wise needed such protection, for his good sword afforded him sufficient defence even against the spears and darts which were incessantly hurled at him, as with rapid skill he received them on the shining blade, and dashed them far away, shivered into fragments.

Sintram could not at the first onset penetrate to where this shining hero was standing, as all his followers, eager after such a noble prey, thronged closely round him; but now the way was cleared enough for him to spring towards the brave stranger, shouting a war-cry, and brandishing his sword above his head.

"Gabrielle!" cried the knight, as he dexterously parried the heavy blow which was descending, and with one powerful sword-thrust he laid the youth prostrate on the ground; then placing his knee on Sintram's breast, he drew forth a flashing dagger, and held it before his eyes as he lay astonished. All at once the men-at-arms stood round like walls. Sintram felt that no hope remained for him. He determined to die as it became a bold warrior; and, without giving one sign of emotion, he looked on the fatal weapon with a steady gaze.

As he lay with his eyes cast upwards, he fancied that there appeared suddenly from heaven a wondrously beautiful female form in a bright attire of blue and gold. "Our ancestors told truly of the Valkyrias," murmured he. "Strike, then, thou unknown conqueror."

But with this the knight did not comply, neither was it a Valkyria who had so suddenly appeared, but the beautiful wife of the stranger, who, having advanced to the high edge of the vessel, had thus met the upraised look of Sintram.

"Folko," cried she, in the softest tone, "thou knight without reproach! I know that thou sparest the vanquished."

The knight sprang up, and with courtly grace stretched out his hand to the conquered youth, saying, "Thank the noble lady of Montfaucon for your life and liberty. But if you are so totally devoid of all goodness as to wish to resume the combat, here am I; let it be yours to begin."

Sintram sank, deeply ashamed, on his knees, and wept; for he had often heard speak of the high renown of the French knight Folko of Montfaucon, who was related to his father's house, and of the grace and beauty of his gentle lady Gabrielle.

CHAPTER VI.

The lord of Montfaucon looked with astonishment at his strange foe; and as he gazed on him more and more, recollections arose in his mind of that northern race from whom he was descended, and with whom he had always maintained friendly relations. A golden bear's claw, with which Sintram's cloak was fastened, at length made all clear to him.

"Have you not," said he, "a valiant and far-famed kinsman, called the Sea-king Arinbiorn, who carries on his helmet golden vulture-wings? And is not your father the knight Biorn? For surely the bear's claw on your mantle must be the cognisance of your house."

Sintram assented to all this, in deep and humble shame.

The knight of Montfaucon raised him from the ground, and said gravely, yet gently, "We are, then, of kin the one to the other; but I could never have believed that any one of our noble house would attack a peaceful man without provocation, and that, too, without giving warning."

"Slay me at once," answered Sintram, "if indeed I am worthy to die by so noble hands. I can no longer endure the light of day."

"Because you have been overcome?" asked Montfaucon.

Sintram shook his head.

"Or is it, rather, because you have committed an unknightly action?"

The glow of shame that overspread the youth's countenance said yes to this.

"But you should not on that account wish to die," continued Montfaucon. "You should rather wish to live, that you may prove your repentance, and make your name illustrious by many noble deeds; for you are endowed with a bold spirit and with strength of limb, and also with the eagle-glance of a chieftain. I should have made you a knight this very hour, if you had borne yourself as bravely in a good cause, as you have just now in a bad. See to it, that I may do it soon. You may yet become a vessel of high honour."

A joyous sound of shawms and silver rebecks interrupted his discourse. The lady Gabrielle, bright as the morning, had now come down from the ship, surrounded by her maidens; and, instructed in a few words by Folko who was his late foe, she took the combat as some mere trial of arms, saying, "You must not be cast down, noble youth, because my wedded lord has won the prize; for be it known to you, that in the whole world there is but one knight who can boast of not having been overcome by the Baron of Montfaucon. And who can say," continued she, sportively, "whether even that would have happened, had he not set himself to win back the magic ring from me, his lady-love, destined to him, as well by the choice of my own heart as by the will of Heaven!"

Folko, smiling, bent his head over the snow-white hand of his lady; and then bade the youth conduct them to his father's castle.

Rolf took upon himself to see to the disembarking of

the horses and valuables of the strangers, filled with joy at the thought that an angel in woman's form had appeared to soften his beloved young master, and perhaps even to free him from that early curse.

Sintram sent messengers in all directions to seek for his father, and to announce to him the arrival of his noble guests. They therefore found the old knight in his castle, with every thing prepared for their reception. Gabrielle could not enter the vast, dark-looking building without a slight shudder, which was increased when she saw the rolling fiery eyes of its lord; even the pale, dark-haired Sintram seemed to her very fearful; and she sighed to herself, "Oh! what an awful abode have you brought me to visit, my knight! Would that we were once again in my sunny Gascony, or in your knightly Normandy!"

But the grave yet courteous reception, the deep respect paid to her grace and beauty, and to the high fame of Folko, helped to re-assure her; and soon her bird-like pleasure in novelties was awakened through the strange significant appearances of this new world. And besides, it could only be for a passing moment that any womanly fears found a place in her breast when her lord was near at hand, for well did she know what effectual protection that brave Baron was ever ready to afford to all those who were dear to him, or committed to his charge.

Soon afterwards Rolf passed through the great hall in which Biorn and his guests were seated, conducting their attendants, who had charge of the baggage, to their rooms. Gabrielle caught sight of her favourite lute, and desired a page to bring it to her, that she might see if the precious instrument had been injured by the sea-voyage. As she bent over it with earnest attention, and her taper fingers ran up and down the strings, a smile, like the dawn of spring, passed over the dark countenances of Biorn and his son; and both said, with an involuntary sigh, "Ah! if you would but play on that lute, and sing to it! It would be but too beautiful!" The lady looked up at them, well pleased, and smiling her assent, she began this song:—

"Songs and flowers are returning,
  And radiant skies of May,
Earth her choicest gifts is yielding,
  But one is past away.

The spring that clothes with tend'rest green
  Each grove and sunny plain,
Shines not for my forsaken heart,
  Brings not my joys again.

Warble not so, thou nightingale,
  Upon thy blooming spray,
Thy sweetness now will burst my heart,
  I cannot bear thy lay.

For flowers and birds are come again,
  And breezes mild of May,
But treasured hopes and golden hours
  Are lost to me for aye.!"

The two Norwegians sat plunged in melancholy thought; but especially Sintram's eyes began to brighten with a milder expression, his cheeks glowed, every feature softened, till those who looked at him could have fancied they saw a glorified spirit. The good Rolf, who had stood listening to the song, rejoiced thereat from his heart, and devoutly raised his hands in pious gratitude to heaven. But Gabrielle's astonishment suffered her not to take her eyes from Sintram. At last she said to him, "I should much like to know what has so struck you in that little song. It is merely a simple lay of the spring, full of the images which that sweet season never fails to call up in the minds of my countrymen."

"But is your home really so lovely, so wondrously rich in song?" cried the enraptured Sintram. "Then I am no longer surprised at your heavenly beauty, at the power which you exercise over my hard, wayward heart! For a paradise of song must surely send such angelic messengers through the ruder parts of the world." And so saying, he fell on his knees before the lady in an attitude of deep humility. Folko looked on all the while with an approving smile, whilst Gabrielle, in much embarrassment, seemed hardly to know how to treat the half-wild, half-tamed young stranger. After some hesitation, however, she held out her fair hand to him, and said as she gently raised him: "Surely one who listens with such delight to music must himself know how to awaken its strains. Take my lute, and let us hear a graceful inspired song."

But Sintram drew back, and would not take the instrument; and he said, "Heaven forbid that my rough untutored hand should touch those delicate strings! For even were I to begin with some soft strains, yet before long the wild spirit which dwells in me would break out, and there would be an end of the form and sound of the beautiful instrument. No, no; suffer me rather to fetch my own huge harp, strung with bears' sinews set in brass, for in truth I do feel myself inspired to play and sing."

Gabrielle murmured a half-frightened assent; and Sintram having quickly brought his harp, began to strike it loudly, and to sing these words with a voice no less powerful:

"Sir knight, sir knight, oh! whither away
With thy snow-white sail on the foaming spray?"
Sing heigh, sing ho, for that land of flowers!

"Too long have I trod upon ice and snow;
I seek the bowers where roses blow."
Sing heigh, sing ho, for that land of flowers!

He steer'd on his course by night and day
Till he cast his anchor in Naples Bay.
Sing heigh, sing ho, for that land of flowers!

There wander'd a lady upon the strand,
Her fair hair bound with a golden band.
Sing heigh, sing ho, for that land of flowers!

"Hail to thee! hail to thee! lady bright,
Mine own shalt thou be ere morning light."
Sing heigh, sing ho, for that land of flowers!

"Not so, sir knight," the lady replied,
"For you speak to the margrave's chosen bride."
Sing heigh, sing ho, for that land of flowers!

"Your lover may come with his shield and spear,
And the victor shall win thee, lady dear!"
Sing heigh, sing ho, for that land of flowers!

"Nay, seek for another bride, I pray;
Most fair are the maidens of Naples Bay."
Sing heigh, sing ho, for that land of flowers!

"No, lady; for thee my heart doth burn,
And the world cannot now my purpose turn."
Sing heigh, sing ho, for that land of flowers!

Then came the young margrave, bold and brave;
But low was he laid in a grassy grave.
Sing heigh, sing ho, for that land of flowers!

And then the fierce Northman joyously cried,
"Now shall I possess lands, castle, and bride!"
Sing heigh, sing ho, for that land of flowers!

Sintram's song was ended, but his eyes glared wildly, and the vibrations of the harp-strings still resounded in a marvellous manner. Biorn's attitude was again erect; he stroked his long beard and rattled his sword, as if in great delight at what he had just heard. Much shuddered Gabrielle before the wild song and these strange forms, but only till she cast a glance on the Lord of Montfaucon, who sat there smiling in all his hero strength, unmoved, while the rough uproar passed by him like an autumnal storm.

CHAPTER VII.

SOME weeks after this, in the twilight of evening, Sintram, very disturbed, came down to the castle-garden. Although the presence of Gabrielle never failed to soothe and calm him, yet if she left the apartment for even a few instants, the fearful wildness of his spirit seemed to return with renewed strength. So even now, after having long and kindly read legends of the olden times to his father Biorn, she had retired to her chamber. The tones of her lute could be distinctly heard in the garden below; but the sounds only drove the bewildered youth more impetuously through the shades of the ancient elms. Stooping suddenly to avoid some over-hanging branches, he unexpectedly came upon something against which he had almost struck, and which, at first sight, he took for a small bear standing on its hind legs, with a long and strangely crooked horn on its head. He drew back in surprise and fear. It addressed him in a grating man's voice; "Well, my brave young knight, whence come you? whither go you? wherefore so terrified?" And then first he saw that he had before him a little old man so wrapped up in a rough garment of fur, that scarcely one of his features was visible, and wearing in his cap a strange-looking long feather.

"But whence come *you?* and whither go *you?*" returned the angry Sintram. "For of you such questions should be asked. What have you to do in our domains, you hideous little being!"

"Well, well," sneered the other one, "I am thinking that I am quite big enough as I am—one cannot always be a giant. And as to the rest, why should you find fault that I go here hunting for snails? Surely snails do not belong to the game which your high mightinesses consider that you alone have a right to follow! Now, on the other hand, I know how to prepare from them an excellent high-flavoured drink; and I have taken enough for to-day:

marvellous fat little beasts, with wise faces like a man's, and long twisted horns on their heads. Would you like to see them? Look here!"

And then he began to unfasten and fumble about his fur garment; but Sintram, filled with disgust and horror, said, "Psha! I detest such animals! Be quiet, and tell me at once who and what you yourself are."

"Are you so bent upon knowing my name?" replied the little man. "Let it content you that I am master of all secret knowledge, and well versed in the most intricate depths of ancient history. Ah! my young sir, if you would only hear them! But you are afraid of me."

"Afraid of you!" cried Sintram, with a wild laugh.

"Many a better man than you has been so before now," muttered the little Master; "but they did not like being told of it any more than you do."

"To prove that you are mistaken," said Sintram, "I will remain here with you till the moon stands high in the heavens. But you must tell me one of your stories the while."

The little man, much pleased, nodded his head; and as they paced together up and down a retired elm-walk, he began discoursing as follows:—

"Many hundred years ago a young knight, called Paris of Troy, lived in that sunny land of the south where are found the sweetest songs, the brightest flowers, and the most beautiful ladies. You know a song that tells of that fair land, do you not, young sir? 'Sing heigh, sing ho, for that land of flowers.'" Sintram bowed his head in assent, and sighed deeply. "Now," resumed the little Master, "it happened that Paris led that kind of life which is not uncommon in those countries, and of which their poets often sing—he would pass whole months together in the garb of a peasant, piping in the woods and mountains, and pasturing his flocks. Here one day three beautiful sorceresses appeared to him, disputing about a golden apple; and from him they sought to know which of them was the most beautiful, since to her the golden fruit was to be awarded. The first knew how to give thrones, and sceptres, and crowns; the second could give wisdom and knowledge; and the third could prepare philtres and love-charms which could not fail of securing the affections of the fairest of women. Each one in turn proffered her choicest gifts to the young shepherd, in order that, tempted by them, he might adjudge the apple to her. But as fair women charmed him more than anything else in the world, he said that the third was the most beautiful —her name was Venus. The two others departed in great displeasure; but Venus bid him put on his knightly armour and his helmet adorned with waving feathers, and then she led him to a famous city called Sparta, where ruled the noble duke Menelaus. His young duchess Helen was the loveliest woman on earth, and the sorceress offered her to Paris in return for the golden apple. He was most ready to have her, and wished for nothing better; but he asked how he was to gain possession of her."

"Paris must have been a sorry knight," interrupted Sintram. "Such things are easily settled. The husband is challenged to a single combat, and he that is victorious carries off the wife."

"But duke Menelaus was the host of the young knight," said the narrator.

"Listen to me, little Master," cried Sintram; "he might have asked the sorceress for some other beautiful woman, and then have mounted his horse, or weighed anchor, and departed."

"Yes, yes; it is very easy to say so," replied the old man. "But if you only knew how bewitchingly lovely this duchess Helen was, no room was left for change." And then he began a glowing description of the charms of this wondrously beautiful woman, but likening the image to Gabrielle so closely, feature for feature, that Sintram, tottering, was forced to lean against a tree. The little Master stood opposite to him grinning, and asked, "Well now, could you have advised that poor knight Paris to fly from her?"

"Tell me at once what happened next," stammered Sintram.

"The sorceress acted honourably towards Paris," continued the old man. "She declared to him that if he would carry away the lovely duchess to his own city Troy, he might do so, and thus cause the ruin of his whole house and of his country; but that during ten years he would be able to defend himself in Troy, and rejoice in the sweet love of Helen."

"And he accepted those terms, or he was a fool!" cried the youth.

"To be sure he accepted them," whispered the little Master. "I would have done so in his place! And do you know, young sir, the look of things then was just as they are happening to-day. The newly risen moon, partly veiled by clouds, was shining dimly through the thick branches of the trees in the silence of evening. Leaning against an old tree, as you now are doing, stood the young enamoured knight Paris, and at his side the enchantress Venus, but so disguised and transformed, that she did not look much more beautiful than I do. And by the silvery light of the moon, the form of the beautiful beloved one was seen sweeping by alone amidst the whispering boughs." He was silent; and like as in the mirror of his deluding words, Gabrielle just then actually herself appeared, musing as she walked alone down the alley of elms.

"Man,—fearful Master,—by what name shall I call you? To what would you drive me?" muttered the trembling Sintram.

"Thou knowest thy father's strong stone castle on the Moon-rocks!" replied the old man. "The castellan and the garrison are true and devoted to thee. It could stand a ten years' siege; and the little gate which leads to the hills is open, as was that of the citadel of Sparta for Paris."

And, in fact, the youth saw through a gate, left open

he knew not how, the dim, distant mountains glittering in the moonlight. "And if he did not accept, he was a fool," said the little Master, with a grin, echoing Sintram's former words.

At that moment Gabrielle stood close by him. She was within reach of his grasp, had he made the least movement; and a moonbeam, suddenly breaking forth, transfigured, as it were, her heavenly beauty. The youth had already bent forward—

"My Lord and God, I pray,
Turn from his heart away
This world's turmoil;
And call him to Thy light,
Be it through sorrow's night,
Through pain or toil."

These words were sung by old Rolf at that very time, as he lingered on the still margin of the castle fish-pond, where he prayed alone to Heaven, full of foreboding care. They reached Sintram's ear; he stood as if spell-bound, and made the Sign of the Cross. Immediately the little Master fled away, jumping uncouthly on one leg, through the gates, and shutting them after him with a yell.

Gabrielle shuddered, terrified at the wild noise. Sintram approached her softly, and said, offering his arm to her: "Suffer me to lead you back to the castle. The night in these northern regions is often wild and fearful."

CHAPTER VIII.

THEY found the two knights drinking wine within. Folko was relating stories in his usual mild and cheerful manner, and Biorn was listening with a moody air, but yet as if, against his will, the dark cloud might pass away before that bright and gentle courtesy. Gabrielle saluted the baron with a smile, and signed to him to continue his discourse, as she took her place near the knight Biorn, full of watchful kindness. Sintram stood by the hearth, abstracted and melancholy; and the embers, as he stirred them, cast a strange glow over his pallid features.

"And of all the German trading towns," continued Montfaucon, "the largest and richest is Hamburgh. In Normandy we willingly see their merchants land on our coasts, and those excellent people never fail to prove themselves our friends when we seek their advice and assistance. When I first visited Hamburgh, every honour and respect was paid to me. I found its inhabitants engaged in a war with a neighbouring count, and immediately I used my sword for them, vigorously and successfully."

"Your sword! your knightly sword!" interrupted Biorn; and the old wonted fire flashed from his eyes. "Against a knight, and for shopkeepers!"

"Sir knight," replied Folko, calmly, "the barons of Montfaucon have ever used their swords as they chose, without the interference of another; and as I have received this good custom, so do I wish to hand it on. If you agree not to this, so speak it freely out. But I forbid every rude word against the men of Hamburgh, since I have declared them to be my friends."

Biorn cast down his haughty eyes, and their fire faded away. In a low voice he said, "Proceed, noble baron. You are right, and I am wrong."

Then Folko stretched out his hand to him across the table, and resumed his narration: "Amongst all my beloved Hamburghers the dearest to me are two men of marvellous experience—a father and son. What have they not seen and done in the remotest corners of the earth, and instituted in their native town! Praise be to God, my life cannot be called unfruitful; but, compared with the wise Gotthard Lenz and his stout-hearted son Rudlieb, I look upon myself as an esquire who has perhaps been some few times to tourneys, and, besides that, has never hunted out of his own forests. They have converted, subdued, gladdened, dark men whom I know not how to name; and the wealth which they have brought back with them has all been devoted to the common weal, as if fit for no other purpose. On their return from their long and perilous sea-voyages, they hasten to an hospital which has been founded by them, and where they undertake the part of overseers, and of careful and patient nurses. Then they proceed to select the most fitting spots whereon to erect new towers and fortresses for the defence of their beloved country. Next they repair to the houses where strangers and travellers receive hospitality at their cost; and at last they return to their own abode, to entertain their guests, rich and noble like kings, and simple and unconstrained like shepherds. Many a tale of their wondrous adventures serves to enliven these sumptuous feasts. Amongst others, I remember to have heard my friends relate one at which my hair stood on end. Possibly I may gain some more complete information on the subject from you. It appears that several years ago, just about the time of the Christmas festival, Gotthard and Rudlieb were shipwrecked on the coast of Norway, during a violent winter tempest. They could never exactly ascertain the situation of the rocks on which their vessel stranded; but so much is certain, that very near the sea-shore stood a huge castle, to which the father and son betook themselves, seeking for that assistance and shelter which Christian people are ever willing to afford each other in case of need. They went alone, leaving their followers to watch the injured ship. The castle-gates were thrown open, and they thought all was well. But on a sudden the court-yard was filled with armed men, who with one accord aimed their sharp iron-pointed spears at the defenceless strangers; whose dignified remonstrances and mild entreaties were only heard in sullen silence or with scornful jeerings. After a while a knight came down the stairs, with fire-flashing eyes. They hardly knew whether

to think they saw a spectre, or a wild heathen; he gave a signal, and the fatal spears closed around them. At that instant the soft tones of a woman's voice fell on their ear, calling on the Saviour's holy name for aid; at the sound, the spectres in the court-yard rushed madly one against the other, the gates burst open, and Gotthard and Rudlieb fled away, catching a glimpse as they went of an angelic woman who appeared at one of the windows of the castle. They made every exertion to get their ship again afloat, choosing to trust themselves to the sea rather than to that barbarous coast; and at last, after manifold dangers, they landed in Denmark. They say that some heathen must have owned the cruel castle; but I hold it to be some ruined fortress, deserted by men, in which hellish spectres were wont to hold their nightly meetings. What heathen could be found so demon-like as to offer death to shipwrecked strangers, instead of refreshment and shelter?"

Biorn gazed fixedly on the ground, as though he were turned into stone; but Sintram came towards the table, and said, "Father, let us seek out this godless abode, and lay it level with the dust. I cannot tell how, but somehow I feel quite sure that the accursed deed of which we have just heard is alone the cause of my frightful dreams."

Enraged at his son, Biorn rose up, and would perhaps again have uttered some dreadful words; but heaven decreed otherwise, for just at that moment the pealing notes of a trumpet were heard, which drowned the angry tones of his voice, the great doors opened slowly, and a herald entered the hall. He bowed reverently, and then said, "I am sent by Jarl Eric the Aged. He returned two days ago from his expedition to the Grecian seas. His wish had been to take vengeance on the island which is called Chios, where fifty years ago his father was slain by the soldiers of the emperor. But your kinsman, the sea-king Arinbiorn, who was lying there at anchor, tried to pacify him. To this Jarl Eric would not listen; so the sea-king said next that he would never suffer Chios to be laid waste, because it was an island where the lays of an old Greek bard, called Homer, were excellently sung, and where moreover a very choice wine was made. Words proving of no avail, a combat ensued; in which Arinbiorn had so much the advantage that Jarl Eric lost two of his ships, and only with difficulty escaped in one which had already sustained great damage. Eric the Aged has now resolved to take revenge on some of the sea-king's race, since Arinbiorn himself is seldom on the spot. Will you, Biorn of the Fiery Eyes, at once pay as large a penalty in cattle, and money, and goods, as it may please the Jarl to demand? Or will you prepare to meet him with an armed force at Niflung's Heath seven days hence?"

Biorn bowed his head quietly, and replied in a mild tone, "Seven days hence at Niflung's Heath." He then offered to the herald a golden goblet full of rich wine, and added, "Drink that, and then carry off with thee the cup which thou hast emptied."

"The Baron of Montfaucon likewise sends greeting to thy chieftain, Jarl Eric," interposed Folko; "and engages to be also at Niflung's Heath, as the hereditary friend of the sea-king, and also as the kinsman and guest of Biorn of the Fiery Eyes."

The herald was seen to tremble at the name of Montfaucon; he bowed very low, cast an anxious, reverential look at the baron, and left the hall.

Gabrielle looked on her knight, smiling lovingly and securely, for she well knew his victorious prowess; and she only asked, "Where shall I remain, whilst you go forth to battle, Folko?"

"I had hoped," answered Biorn, "that you would be well contented to stay in this castle, lovely lady; I leave my son to guard you and attend on you."

Gabrielle hesitated an instant; and Sintram, who had resumed his position near the fire, muttered to himself as he fixed his eyes on the bright flames which were flashing up, "Yes, yes, so it will probably happen. I can fancy that duke Menelaus had just left Sparta on some warlike expedition, when the young knight Paris met the lovely Helen that evening in the garden."

But Gabrielle, shuddering, although she knew not why, said quickly, "Without you, Folko? And must I forego the joy of seeing you fight? or the honour of tending you, should you chance to receive a wound?"

Folko bowed, gracefully thanking his lady, and replied, "Come with your knight, since such is your pleasure, and be to him a bright guiding star. It is a good old northern custom that ladies should be present at knightly combats, and no true warrior of the north will fail to respect the place whence beams the light of their eyes. Unless, indeed," continued he with an inquiring look at Biorn, "unless Jarl Eric is not worthy of his forefather?"

"A man of honour," said Biorn confidently.

"Then array yourself, my fairest love," said the delighted Folko; "array yourself, and come forth with us to the battle-field to behold and judge our deeds."

"Come forth with us to the battle," echoed Sintram in a sudden transport of joy.

And they all dispersed in calm cheerfulness; Sintram betaking himself again to the wood, while the others retired to rest.

CHAPTER IX.

It was a wild dreary tract of country that, which bore the name of Niflung's Heath. According to tradition, the young Niflung, son of Hogni, the last of his race, had there ended darkly a sad and unsuccessful life. Many ancient grave-stones were still standing round about; and in the few oak-trees scattered here and there over the plain, huge eagles had built their nests. The beating of their heavy wings as they fought together, and their wild screams, were heard far off in more thickly peopled regions; and at the sound children would tremble in their cradles, and old men quake with fear as they slumbered over the blazing hearth.

As the seventh night, the last before the day of combat, was just beginning, two large armies were seen descending from the hills in opposite directions: that which came from the west was commanded by Eric the Aged, that from the east by Biorn of the Fiery Eyes. They appeared thus early in compliance with the custom which required that adversaries should always present themselves at the appointed field of battle before the time named, in order to prove that they rather sought than dreaded the fight. Folko forthwith pitched on the most convenient spot the tent of blue samite fringed with gold, which he carried with him to shelter his gentle lady; whilst Sintram, in the character of herald, rode over to Jarl Eric to announce to him that the beauteous Gabrielle of Montfaucon was present in the army of the knight Biorn, and would the next morning be present as a judge of the combat.

Jarl Eric bowed low on receiving this pleasing message; and ordered his bards to strike up a lay, the words of which ran as follows:—

"Warriors bold of Eric's band,
Gird your glittering armour on,
Stand beneath to-morrow's sun,
In your might.
Fairest dame that ever gladden'd
Our wild shores with beauty's vision,
May thy bright eyes o'er our combat,
Judge the right!

Tidings of yon noble stranger
Long ago have reach'd our ears,
Wafted upon southern breezes,
O'er the wave.
Now midst yonder hostile ranks,
In his warlike pride he meets us,
Folko comes! Fight, men of Eric,
True and brave!"

These wondrous tones floated over the plain, and reached the tent of Gabrielle. It was no new thing to her to hear her knight's fame celebrated on all sides; but now that she listened to his praises bursting forth in the stillness of night from the mouth of his enemies, she could scarce refrain from kneeling at the feet of the mighty chieftain. But he with courteous tenderness held her up, and pressing his lips fervently on her soft hand, he said, "My deeds, O lovely lady, belong to thee, and not to me!"

Now the night had passed away, and the east was glowing; and on Niflung's Heath there was waving, and resounding, and glowing too. Knights put on their rattling armour, war-horses began to neigh, the morning draught went round in gold and silver goblets, while war-songs and the clang of harps resounded in the midst. A joyous march was heard in Biorn's camp, as Montfaucon, with his troops and retainers, clad in bright steel armour, conducted their lady up to a neighbouring hill, where she would be safe from the spears which would soon be flying in all directions, and whence she could look freely over the battle-field. The morning sun, as it were in homage, played over her beauty; and as she came in view of the camp of Jarl Eric, his soldiers lowered their weapons, whilst the chieftains bent low the crests of their huge helmets. Two of Montfaucon's pages remained in attendance on Gabrielle; for so noble a service not unwillingly bridling their love of fighting. Both armies passed in front of her, saluting her and singing as they went; they then placed themselves in array, and the fight began.

The spears flew from the hands of the stout northern warriors, rattling against the broad shields under which they sheltered themselves, or sometimes clattering as they met in the air; at intervals, on one side or the other, a man was struck, and fell silent in his blood. Then the Knight of Montfaucon advanced with his troop of Norman horsemen—even as he dashed past, he did not fail to lower his shining sword to salute Gabrielle; and then with an exulting war-cry, which burst from many a voice, they charged the left wing of the enemy. Eric's foot-soldiers, kneeling firmly, received them with fixed javelins—many a noble horse fell wounded to death, and in falling brought his rider with him to the ground; others again crushed their foes under them in their death-fall. Folko rushed through—he and his war-steed unwounded—followed by a troop of chosen knights. Already were they falling into disorder—already were Biorn's warriors giving shouts of victory—when a troop of horse, headed by Jarl Eric himself, advanced against the valiant baron; and whilst his Normans, hastily assembled, assisted him in repelling this new attack, the enemy's infantry were gradually forming themselves into a thick mass, which rolled on and on. All these movements seemed caused by a warrior whose loud piercing shout was heard in the midst. And scarcely were the troops formed into this strange array, when suddenly they spread themselves out on all sides, carrying every thing before them with the irresistible force of the burning torrent from Hecla.

Biorn's soldiers, who had thought to enclose their enemies, lost courage and gave way before this wondrous onset. The knight himself in vain attempted to stem the tide of fugitives, and with difficulty escaped being carried away by it.

Sintram stood looking on this scene of confusion with mute indignation; friends and foes passed by him, all equally avoiding him, and dreading to come in contact with one whose aspect was so fearful; nay, almost unearthly, in his motionless rage. He aimed no blow either to right or left; his powerful battle-axe rested in his hand; but his eyes flashed fire, and seemed to be piercing the enemy's ranks through and through, as if he would find out who it was that had conjured up this sudden warlike spirit. He succeeded. A small man clothed in strange-looking armour, with large golden horns on his helmet, and a long vizor advancing in front of it, was leaning on a two-edged curved spear, and seemed to be looking with derision at the flight of Biorn's troops as they were pursued by their victorious foes. "That is he," cried Sintram; "he who will drive us from the field before the eyes of Gabrielle!" And with the swiftness of an arrow he flew towards him with a wild shout. The combat was fierce, but not of long duration. To the wondrous dexterity of his adversary, Sintram opposed his far superior size; and he dealt so fearful a blow on the horned helmet, that a stream of blood rushed forth, the small man fell as if stunned, and after some frightful convulsive movements, his limbs appeared to stiffen in death.

His fall gave the signal for that of all Eric's army. Even those who had not seen him fall, suddenly lost their courage and eagerness for the battle, and retreated with uncertain steps, or ran in wild affright on the spears of their enemies. At the same time Montfaucon was dispersing Jarl Eric's cavalry, after a desperate conflict—had hurled their chief from the saddle, and taken him prisoner with his own hand. Biorn of the Fiery Eyes stood victorious in the middle of the field of battle. The day was won.

CHAPTER X.

In sight of both armies, with glowing cheeks and looks of modest humility, Sintram was conducted by the brave baron up the hill where Gabrielle stood in all the lustre of her beauty. Both warriors bent the knee before her, and Folko said, solemnly, "Lady, this valiant youth of a noble race has deserved the reward of this day's victory. I pray you let him receive it from your fair hand."

Gabrielle bowed courteously, took off her scarf of blue and gold, and fastened to it a bright sword, which a page brought to her on a cushion of cloth of silver. She then, with a smile, presented the noble gift to Sintram, who was bending forward to receive it, when suddenly Gabrielle drew back, and turning to Folko, said, "Noble baron, should not he on whom I bestow a scarf and sword be first admitted into the order of knighthood?" Light as a feather, Folko sprang up, and bowing low before his lady, gave the youth the accolade with solemn earnestness. Then Gabrielle buckled on his sword, saying, "For the honour of God and the service of virtuous ladies, young knight. I saw you fight, I saw you conquer, and my earnest prayers followed you. Fight and conquer often again, as you have done this day, that the beams of your renown may shine over my far-distant country." And at a sign from Folko, she offered her tender lips for the new knight to kiss. Thrilling all over, and full of a holy joy, Sintram arose in deep silence, and hot tears streamed down his softened countenance, whilst the shout and the trumpets of the assembled troops greeted the youth with stunning applause. Old Rolf stood silently on one side, and as he looked in the mild beaming eyes of his foster-child, he calmly and piously returned thanks:

"The strife at length hath found its end,
Rich blessings now shall heaven send!
The evil foe is slain!"

Biorn and Jarl Eric had the while been talking together eagerly, but not unkindly. The conqueror now led his vanquished enemy up the hill and presented him to the baron and Gabrielle, saying, "Instead of two enemies you now see two sworn allies; and I request you, my beloved guests and kinsfolk, to receive him graciously as one who henceforward belongs to us."

"He was so always," added Eric, smiling; "I sought, indeed, revenge; but I have now had enough of defeats both by sea and land. Yet I thank heaven that neither in the Grecian seas, to the sea-king, nor on Niflung's Heath, to you, have I yielded ingloriously."

The lord of Montfaucon assented cordially, and heartily and solemnly was reconciliation made. Then Jarl Eric addressed Gabrielle with so noble a grace, that with a smile of wonder she gazed on the gigantic grey hero, and gave him her beautiful hand to kiss.

Meanwhile Sintram was speaking earnestly to his good Rolf; and at length he was heard to say, "But before all, be sure that you bury that wonderfully brave knight whom my battle-axe smote. Choose out the greenest hill for his resting-place, and the loftiest oak to shade his grave. Also, I wish you to open his vizor and to examine his countenance carefully, that so, though mortally smitten, we may not bury him alive; and moreover, that you may be able to describe to me him to whom I owe the noblest prize of victory."

Rolf bowed readily, and went.

"Our young knight is speaking there of one amongst the slain of whom I should like to hear more," said Folko, turning to Jarl Eric. "Who, dear Jarl, was that wonderful chieftain who led on your troops so skilfully, and who at last fell under Sintram's powerful battle-axe?"

"You ask me more than I know how to answer," replied Jarl Eric. "About three nights ago this stranger made his appearance amongst us. I was sitting with my chieftains and warriors round the hearth, forging our armour, and singing the while. Suddenly, above the din of our hammering and our singing, we heard so loud a noise that it silenced us in a moment, and we sat motionless as if we had been turned into stone. Before long the sound was repeated; and at last we made out that it must be caused by some person blowing a huge horn outside the castle, seeking for admittance. I went down myself to the gate, and as I passed through the court-yard all my dogs were so terrified by the extraordinary noise as to be howling and crouching in their kennels instead of barking. I chid them, and called to them, but even the fiercest would not follow me. Then, thought I, I must shew you the way to set to work; so I grasped my sword firmly, I set my torch on the ground close beside me, and I let the gates fly open without further delay. For I well knew that it would be no easy matter for any one to come in against my will. A loud laugh greeted me, and I heard these words, 'Well, well, what mighty preparations are these before one small man can find the shelter he seeks!' And in truth I did feel myself redden with shame when I saw the small stranger standing opposite to me quite alone. I called to him to come in at once, and offered my hand to him; but he still shewed some displeasure, and would not give me his in return. As he went up, however, he became more friendly —he shewed me the golden horn on which he sounded that blast, and which he carried screwed on his helmet, as well as another exactly like it. When he was sitting with us in the hall, he behaved in a very strange manner—sometimes he was merry, sometimes cross; by turns courteous and rude in his demeanour, without any one being able to see a motive for such constant changes. I longed to know where he came from; but how could I ask my guest such a question? He told us as much as this, that he was starved with cold in our country, and that his own was much warmer. Also he appeared well acquainted with the city of Constantinople, and related fearful stories of how brothers, uncles, and nephews, nay, even fathers and sons, thrust each other from the throne, blinded, cut out tongues, and murdered. At length he said his own name —it sounded harmonious, like a Greek name, but none of us could remember it. Before long he displayed his skill as an armourer. He understood marvellously well how to handle the red-hot iron, and how to form it into more murderous weapons than any I had ever before seen. I would not suffer him to go on making them, for I was resolved to meet you in the field with equal arms, and such as we are all used to in our northern countries. Then he laughed, and said he thought it would be quite possible to be victorious without them, by skilful movements and the like; if only I would entrust the command of my infantry to him, I was sure of victory. Then I thought that he who makes arms well must also wield them well—yet I required some proof of his powers. Ye lords, he came off victorious in trials of strength such as you can hardly imagine; and although the fame of young Sintram, as a bold and brave warrior, is spread far and wide, yet I can scarce believe that he could slay such an one as my Greek ally."

He would have continued speaking, but the good Rolf came hastily back with a few followers, the whole party so ghastly pale, that all eyes were involuntarily fixed on them, and looked anxiously to hear what tidings they brought. Rolf stood still, silent and trembling.

"Take courage, my old friend!" cried Sintram. "Whatever thou mayest have to tell is truth and light from thy faithful mouth."

"My dear master," began the old man, "be not angry, but as to burying that strange warrior whom you slew, it is a thing impossible. Would that we had never opened that wide hideous vizor! For so horrible a countenance grinned at us from underneath it, so distorted by death, and with so hellish an expression, that we hardly kept our senses. We could not by any possibility have touched him. I would rather be sent to kill wolves and bears in the desert, and look on whilst fierce birds of prey feast on their carcasses."

All present shuddered, and were silent for a time, till Sintram nerved himself to say, "Dear good old man, why use such wild words as I never till now heard thee utter?

But tell me, Jarl Eric, did your ally appear altogether so awful while he was yet alive?"

"Not as far as I know," answered Jarl Eric, looking inquiringly at his companions, who were standing around. They said the same thing; but on further questioning, it appeared that neither the chieftain, nor the knights, nor the soldiers, could say exactly what the stranger was like.

"We must then find it out for ourselves, and bury the corpse," said Sintram; and he signed to the assembled party to follow him. All did so except the lord of Montfaucon, whom the whispered entreaty of Gabrielle kept at her side. He lost nothing thereby. For though Niflung's Heath was searched from one end to the other many times, yet the body of the unknown warrior was no longer to be found.

CHAPTER XI.

THE joyful calm which came over Sintram on this day appeared to be more than a passing gleam. If too, at times, a thought of the knight Paris and Helen would inflame his heart with bolder and wilder wishes, it needed but one look at his scarf and sword, and the stream of his inner life glided again clear as a mirror, and serene within. "What can any man wish for more than has been already bestowed on me?" would he say to himself at such times, in still delight. And thus it went on for a long while.

The beautiful northern autumn had already begun to redden the leaves of the oaks and elms round the castle, when one day it chanced that Sintram was sitting in company with Folko and Gabrielle in almost the very same spot in the garden where he had before met that mysterious being whom, without knowing why, he had named the Little Master. But on this day how different did every thing appear! The sun was sinking slowly over the sea, the mist of an autumnal evening was rising from the fields and meadows around, towards the hill on which stood the huge castle. Gabrielle, placing her lute in Sintram's hands, said to him, "Dear friend, so mild and gentle as you now are, I may well dare to entrust to you my tender little darling. Let me again hear you sing that lay of the land of flowers; for I am sure that it will now sound much sweeter than when you accompanied it with the vibrations of your fearful harp."

The young knight bowed as he prepared to obey the lady's commands. With a grace and softness hitherto unwonted, the tones resounded from his lips, and the wild song appeared to transform itself, and to bloom into a garden of the blessed. Tears stood in Gabrielle's eyes; and Sintram, as he gazed on the pearly brightness, poured forth tones of yet richer sweetness. When the last notes were sounded, Gabrielle's angelic voice was heard to echo them; and as she repeated

"Sing heigh, sing ho, for that land of flowers,"

Sintram put down the lute, and sighed with a thankful glance towards the stars, now rising in the heavens. Then Gabrielle, turning towards her lord, murmured these words: "Oh, how long have we been far away from our own shining castles and bright gardens! Oh! for that land of the sweetest flowers!"

Sintram could scarce believe that he heard aright, so suddenly did he feel himself as if shut out from paradise. But his last hope vanished before the courteous assurances of Folko, that he would endeavour to fulfil his lady's wishes the very next week, and that their ship was lying off the shore ready to put to sea. She thanked him with a kiss imprinted softly on his forehead; and leaning on his arm, she bent her steps, singing and smiling, towards the castle.

Sintram, troubled in mind, as though turned into stone, remained behind forgotten. At length, when night was now in the sky, he started up wildly, ran up and down the garden, as if all his former madness had again taken possession of him; and then rushed out and wandered upon the wild moonlit hills. There he dashed his sword against the trees and bushes, so that on all sides was heard a sound of crashing and falling. The birds of night flew about him screeching in wild alarm; and the deer, startled by the noise, sprang away and took refuge in the thickest coverts.

On a sudden old Rolf appeared, returning home from a visit to the chaplain of Drontheim, to whom he had been relating, with tears of joy, how Sintram was softened by the presence of the angel Gabrielle, yea, almost healed, and how he dared to hope that the evil dreams had yielded. And now the sword, as it whizzed round the furious youth, had well nigh wounded the good old man. He stopped short, and clasping his hands, he said, with a deep sigh, "Alas, Sintram! my foster child, darling of my heart, what has come over thee, thus fearfully stirring thee to rage?"

The youth stood awhile as if spell-bound; he looked in his old friend's face with a fixed and melancholy gaze, and his eyes became dim, like expiring watch-fires seen through a thick cloud of mist. At length he sighed forth these words, almost inaudibly: "Good Rolf, good Rolf, depart from me! thy garden of heaven is no home for me; and if sometimes a light breeze blow open its golden gates, so that I can look in and see the flowery meadow-land where the dear angels dwell, then straightway between them and me come the cold north wind and the icy storm, and the sounding doors fly together, and I remain without, lonely, in endless winter."

"Beloved young knight, oh, listen to me—listen to the good angel within you! Do you not bear in your hand that very sword with which the pure lady girded you? does not her scarf wave over your raging breast? Do you not recollect how you used to say, that no man could wish for more than had fallen to you?"

"Yes, Rolf, I have said that," replied Sintram, sinking on the mossy turf, bitterly weeping. Tears also ran over the old man's white beard. Before long the youth stood again erect, his tears ceased to flow, his looks were fearful, cold, and grim; and he said, "You see, Rolf, I have passed blessed peaceful days, and I thought that the powers of evil would never again have dominion over me. So, perchance, it might have been, as day would ever be did the Sun ever stand in the sky. But ask the poor benighted Earth, wherefore she looks so dark! Bid her again smile as she was wont to do! Old man, she cannot smile: and now that the gentle compassionate Moon has disappeared behind the clouds with her holy funeral veil, she cannot even weep. And in this hour of darkness, all that is wild and mad wakes up. So, stop me not, I tell thee, stop me not! Hurrah, behind, behind the pale Moon!" His voice changed to a hoarse murmur at these last words, stormlike. He tore away from the trembling old man, and rushed through the forest. Rolf knelt down and prayed, and wept silently.

CHAPTER XII.

Where the sea-beach was wildest, and the cliffs most steep and rugged, and close by the remains of three shattered oaks, haply marking where, in heathen times, human victims had been sacrificed, now stood Sintram, leaning, as if exhausted, on his drawn sword, and gazing intently on the dancing waves. The Moon had again shone forth; and as her pale beams fell on his motionless figure through the quivering branches of the trees, he might have been taken for some fearful idol-image. Suddenly some one on the left half raised himself out of the high withered grass, uttered a faint groan, and again lay down. Then between the two companions began this strange talk:

"Thou that movest thyself so strangely in the grass, dost thou belong to the living or to the dead?"

"As one may take it. I am dead to heaven and joy —I live for hell and anguish."

"Methinks that I have heard thee before."

"Oh, yes."

"Art thou a troubled spirit? and was thy life-blood poured out here of old in sacrifice to idols?"

"I am a troubled spirit; but no man ever has, or ever can, shed my blood. I have been cast down—oh, into a frightful abyss!"

"And didst thou there break thy neck?"

"I live,—and shall live longer than thou."

"Almost thou seemest to me the crazy pilgrim with the dead men's bones."

"I am not he, though often we are companions,—ay, walk together right near and friendly. But to you be it said, he thinks me mad. If sometimes I urge him, and say to him, 'Take!' then he hesitates, and points upwards towards the stars. And again, if I say, 'Take not!' then, to a certainty, he seizes on it in some awkward manner, and so he spoils my best joys and pleasures. But, in spite of this, we remain in some measure brothers in arms, and, indeed, all but kinsmen."

"Give me hold of thy hand, and let me help thee to get up."

"Ho, ho! my active young sir, that might bring you no good. Yet, in fact, you have already helped to raise me. Give heed awhile."

Wilder and ever wilder were the strugglings on the ground; thick clouds hurried over the moon and the stars, on a long unknown wild journey; and Sintram's thoughts grew no less wild and stormy, while far and near an awful howling could be heard amidst the trees and the grass. At length the mysterious being arose from the ground. As if with a fearful curiosity, the moon, through a rent in the clouds, cast a beam upon Sintram's companion, and made clear to the shuddering youth that the little Master stood by him.

"Avaunt!" cried he, "I will listen no more to thy evil stories about the knight Paris: they would end by driving me quite mad."

"My stories about Paris are not needed for that!" grinned the little Master. "It is enough that the Helen of thy heart should be journeying towards Montfaucon. Believe me, madness has thee already, head and heart. Or wouldest thou that she should remain? For that, however, thou must be more courteous to me than thou art now."

Therewith he raised his voice towards the sea, as if fiercely rebuking it, so that Sintram could not but shudder and tremble before the dwarf. But he checked himself, and, grasping his sword-hilt with both hands, he said, contemptuously: "Thou and Gabrielle! what acquaintance hast thou with Gabrielle?"

"Not much," was the reply. And the little Master might be seen to quake with fear and rage as he continued: "I cannot well bear the name of thy Helen; do not din it in my ears ten times in a breath. But if the tempest should increase? If the waves should swell, and roll on till they form a foaming ring round the whole coast of Norway? The voyage to Montfaucon must in that case be altogether given up, and thy Helen would remain here, at least through the long, long, dark winter."

"If! if!" replied Sintram, with scorn. "Is the sea thy bond-slave? Are the storms thy fellow-workmen?"

"They are rebels, accursed rebels," muttered the little Master in his red beard. "Thou must lend me thy aid, sir knight, if I am to subdue them; but thou hast not the heart for it."

"Boaster, evil boaster!" answered the youth; "what dost thou ask of me?"

"Not much, sir knight; nothing at all for one who has strength and ardour of soul. Thou needest only look at the sea steadily and keenly for one half-hour, without ever ceasing to wish with all thy might that it should foam and rage and swell, and never again rest till winter has laid its icy hold upon your mountains. Then winter is enough to hinder Duke Menelaus from his voyage to Montfaucon. And now give me a lock of your black hair, which is blowing so wildly about your head, like ravens' or vultures' wings."

The youth drew his sharp dagger, madly cut off a lock of his hair, threw it to the strange being, and now gazed, as he desired, powerfully wishing, on the waves of the sea. And softly, quite softly, did the waters stir themselves, as one whispers in troubled dreams who would gladly rest and cannot. Sintram was on the point of giving up, when in the moonbeams a ship appeared, with white-swelling sails, towards the south. Anguish came over him, that Gabrielle would soon thus quickly sail away; he wished again with all his power, and fixed his eyes intently on the watery abyss. "Sintram," a voice might have said to him—"ah, Sintram, art thou indeed the same who so lately wert gazing on the moistened heaven of the eyes of Gabrielle?"

And now the waves heaved more mightily, and the howling tempest swept over the ocean; the breakers, white with foam, became visible in the moonlight. Then the little Master threw the lock of Sintram's hair up towards the clouds, and, as it was blown to and fro by the blast of wind, the storm burst in all its fury, so that sea and sky were covered with one thick cloud, and far off might be heard the cries of distress from many a sinking vessel.

But the crazy pilgrim with the dead men's bones rose up in the midst of the waves, close to the shore, gigantic, tall, fearfully rocking; the boat in which he stood was hidden from sight, so mightily raged the waves round about it.

"Thou must save him, little Master—thou must certainly save him," cried Sintram's voice, angrily entreating, through the roaring of the winds and waves. But the dwarf replied, with a laugh: "Be quite at rest for him; he will be able to save himself. The waves can do him no harm. Seest thou? They are only begging of him, and therefore they jump up so boldly round him; and he gives them bountiful alms—very bountiful, that I can assure thee."

In fact, as it seemed, the pilgrim threw some bones into the sea, and passed scatheless on his way. Sintram felt his blood run cold with horror, and he rushed wildly towards the castle. His companion had either fled or vanished away.

CHAPTER XIII.

In the castle, Biorn and Gabrielle and Folko of Montfaucon were sitting round the great stone table, from which, since the arrival of his noble guests, those suits of armour had been removed, formerly the established companions of the lord of the castle, and placed altogether in a heap in the adjoining room. At this time, while the storm was beating so furiously against doors and windows, it seemed as if the ancient armour were also stirring in the next room, and Gabrielle several times half rose from her seat in great alarm, fixing her eyes on the small iron door, as though she expected to see an armed spectre issue therefrom, bending with his mighty helmet through the low vaulted doorway.

The knight Biorn smiled grimly, and said, as if he had guessed her thoughts: "Oh, he will never again come out thence; I have put an end to that for ever."

His guests stared at him doubtingly; and with a strange air of unconcern, as though the storm had awakened all the fierceness of his soul, he began the following history:

"I was once a happy man myself; I could smile, as you do, and I could rejoice in the morning as you do; that was before the hypocritical chaplain had so bewildered the wise mind of my lovely wife with his canting talk, that she went into a cloister, and left me alone with our wild boy. That was not fair usage from the fair Verena. Well, so it was, that in the first days of her dawning beauty, before I knew her, many knights sought her hand, amongst whom was Sir Weigand the Slender; and towards him the gentle maiden shewed herself the most favourably inclined. Her parents were well aware that Weigand's rank and station were little below their own, and that his early fame as a warrior without reproach stood high; so that before long Verena and he were accounted as affianced. It happened one day that they were walking together in the orchard, when a shepherd was driving his flock up the mountain beyond. The maiden saw a little snow-white lamb frolicking gaily, and longed for it. Weigand vaults over the railings, overtakes the shepherd, and offers him two gold bracelets for the lamb. But the shepherd will not part with it, and scarcely listens to the knight, going quietly the while up the mountain-side, with Weigand close upon him. At last Weigand loses patience. He threatens; and the shepherd, sturdy and proud like all of his race in our northern land, threatens in return. Suddenly Weigand's sword resounds upon his head,—the stroke should have fallen flat, but who can control a fiery horse or a drawn sword? The bleeding shepherd, with a cloven skull, falls down the precipice; his frightened flock bleats on the mountain. Only the little lamb runs in its terror to the orchard, pushes itself through the garden-rails, and lies at Verena's feet, as if asking for help, all red with his master's blood. She took it up in her arms, and from that moment never suffered Weigand the Slender to appear again before her face. She continued to cherish the little lamb, and seemed to take pleasure in nothing else in the world, and became pale and turned towards heaven, as the lilies are. She would soon have taken the veil, but just then I came to aid her father in a bloody war, and rescued him from his enemies. The old man represented this to her, and, softly smiling, she gave me her lovely hand. His grief would not suffer the unhappy Weigand to remain in his own country. It drove him forth as a pilgrim to Asia, whence our forefathers came, and there he did wonderful deeds, both of valour and self-abasement. Truly, my heart was strangely weak when I heard him spoken of at that time. After some years he returned; and wished to build a church or monastery on that mountain towards the west, whence the walls of my castle are distinctly seen. It was said that he wished to become a priest there, but it fell out otherwise. For some pirates had sailed from the southern seas, and, hearing of the building of this monastery, their chief thought to find much gold belonging to the lord of the castle and to the master builders, or else, if he surprised and carried them off, to extort from them a mighty ransom. He did not yet know northern courage and northern weapons; but he soon gained that knowledge. Having landed in the creek under the black rocks, he made his way through a by-path up to the building, surrounded it, and thought in himself that the affair was now ended. Ha! then out rushed Weigand and his builders, and fell upon them with swords and hatchets and hammers. The heathens fled away to their ships, with Weigand behind to take vengeance on them. In passing by our castle he caught a sight of Verena on the terrace, and, for the first time during so many years, she bestowed a courteous and kind salutation on the glowing victor. At that moment a dagger, hurled by one of the pirates in the midst of his hasty flight, struck Weigand's uncovered head, and he fell to the ground bleeding and insensible. We completed the rout of the heathens: then I had the wounded knight brought into the castle; and my pale Verena glowed as lilies in the light of the morning sun, and Weigand opened his eyes with a smile when he was brought near her. He refused to be taken into any room but the small one close to this where the armour is now placed; for he said that he felt as if it were a cell like that which he hoped soon to inhabit in his quiet cloister. All was done after his wish: my sweet Verena nursed him, and he appeared at first to be on the straightest road to recovery; but his head continued weak and liable to be confused by the slightest emotion, his walk was rather a falling than a walking, and his cheeks were colourless. We could not let him go. When we were sitting here together in the evening, he used always to come tottering into the hall through the low doorway; and my heart was sad and wrathful too, when the soft eyes of Verena beamed so sweetly on him, and a glow like that of the evening sky hovered over her lily cheeks. But I bore it, and I could have borne it to the end of our lives,—when, alas! Verena went into a cloister!"

His head fell so heavily on his folded hands, that the stone table seemed to groan beneath it, and he remained a long while motionless as a corpse. When he again raised himself up, his eyes glared fearfully as he looked round the hall, and he said to Folko: "Your beloved Hamburghers, Gotthard Lentz, and Rudlieb his son, they have much to answer for! Who bid them come and be shipwrecked so close to my castle?"

Folko cast a piercing look on him, and a fearful inquiry was on the point of escaping his lips, but another look at the trembling Gabrielle made him silent, at least for the present moment, and the knight Biorn continued his narrative.

"Verena was with her nuns, I was left alone, and my despair had driven me throughout the day through forest and brook and mountain. In the twilight I returned to my deserted castle, and scarcely was I in the hall, when the little door creaked, and Weigand, who had slept through all, crept towards me and asked: 'Where can Verena be?' Then I became as mad, and howled to him, 'She is gone mad, and so am I, and you also, and now we are all mad!' Merciful heaven, the wound on his head burst open, and a dark stream flowed over his face—ah! how different from the redness when Verena met him at the castle-gate; and he rushed forth, raving mad, into the wilderness without, and ever since has wandered all around as a crazy pilgrim."

He was silent, and so were Folko and Gabrielle, all three pale and cold like images of the dead. At length the fearful narrator added in a low voice, and as if he were quite exhausted: "He has visited me since that time, but he will never again come through the little door. Have I not established peace and order in my castle?"

CHAPTER XIV.

SINTRAM had not returned home, when those of the castle betook themselves to rest in deep bewilderment. No one thought of him, for every heart was filled with strange forebodings, and with uncertain cares. Even the heroic breast of the knight of Montfaucon heaved in doubt.

Old Rolf still remained without, weeping in the forest, heedless of the storm which beat on his unprotected head, while he waited for his young master. But he had gone a very different way; and when the morning dawned, he entered the castle from the opposite side.

Gabrielle's slumbers had been sweet during the whole night. It had seemed to her that angels with golden wings had blown away the wild histories of the evening before, and had wafted to her the bright flowers, the sparkling sea, and the green hills of her own home. She smiled, and drew her breath calmly and softly, whilst the magical tempest raged and howled through the forests, and continued to battle with the troubled sea. But in truth when she awoke in the morning, and heard still the rattling of the windows, and saw the clouds, as if dissolved in mist and steam, still hiding the face of the heavens, she could have wept for anxiety and sadness, especially when she heard from her maidens that Folko had already left their apartment clad in full armour as if prepared for a combat. At the same time she heard the sound of the heavy tread of armed men in the echoing halls, and, on inquiring, found that the knight of Montfaucon had assembled all his retainers to be in readiness to protect their lady.

Wrapped in a cloak of ermine, she stood trembling like a tender flower just sprung up out of the snow, tottering beneath a winter's storm. Then Sir Folko entered the room, in all his shining armour, and peacefully carrying his golden helmet with the long shadowy plumes in his hand. He saluted Gabrielle with cheerful serenity, and at a sign from him, her attendants retired, while the men-at-arms without were heard quietly dispersing.

"Lady," said he, as he took his seat beside her, on a couch to which he led her, already re-assured by his presence; "lady, will you forgive your knight for having left you to endure some moments of anxiety; but honour and stern justice called him. Now all is set in order, quietly and peacefully; dismiss your fears and every thought that has troubled you, as things which are no more."

"But you and Biorn?" asked Gabrielle.

"On the word of a knight," replied he, "all is well there." And thereupon he began to talk over indifferent subjects with his usual ease and wit; but Gabrielle, bending towards him, said with deep emotion:

"O Folko, my knight, the flower of my life, my protector and my dearest hope on earth, tell me all, if thou mayst. But if a promise binds thee, it is different. Thou knowest that I am of the race of Portamour, and I would ask nothing from my knight which could cast even a breath of suspicion on his spotless shield."

Folko thought gravely for one instant; then looking at her with a bright smile, he said: "It is not that, Gabrielle;

but canst thou bear what I have to disclose? Wilt thou not sink down under it, as a slender fir gives way under a mass of snow?"

She raised herself somewhat proudly, and said: "I have already reminded thee of the name of my father's house. Let me now add, that I am the wedded wife of the Baron of Montfaucon."

"Then so let it be," replied Folko solemnly; "and if that must come forth openly which should ever have remained hidden in the darkness which belongs to such deeds of wickedness, at least let it come forth less fearfully with a sudden flash, Know then, Gabrielle, that the wicked knight who would have slain my friends Gotthard and Rudlieb is none other than our kinsman and host, Biorn of the Fiery Eyes."

Gabrielle shuddered and covered her eyes with her fair hands; but at the end of a moment she looked up with a bewildered air, and said: "I have heard wrong surely, although it is true that yesterday evening such a thought struck me. For did not you say awhile ago that all was settled and at peace between you and Biorn? Between the brave baron and such a man after such a crime?"

"You heard aright," answered Folko, looking with fond delight on the delicate yet high-minded lady. "This morning with the earliest dawn I went to him and challenged him to a mortal combat in the neighbouring valley, if he were the man whose castle had well nigh become an altar of sacrifice to Gotthard and Rudlieb. He was already completely armed, and merely saying, 'I am he,' he followed me to the forest. But when we stood alone at the place of combat, he flung away his shield down a giddy precipice, then his sword was hurled after it, and next with gigantic strength he tore off his coat of mail, and said, 'Now fall on, thou minister of vengeance; for I am a heavy sinner, and I dare not fight with thee.' How could I then attack him? A strange truce was agreed on between us. He is half as my vassal; and yet I solemnly forgave him in my own name and in that of my friends. He was contrite, and yet no tear was in his eye, no gentle word on his lips. He is only kept under by the power with which I am endued by having right on my side, and it is on that tenure that Biorn is my vassal. I know not, lady, whether you can bear to see us together on these terms; if not, I will ask for hospitality in some other castle; there are none in Norway which would not receive us joyfully and honourably, and this wild autumnal storm may put off our voyage for many a day. Only this I think, that if we depart directly and in such a manner, the heart of this savage man will break."

"Where my noble lord remains, there I also remain joyfully under his protection," replied Gabrielle; and again her heart glowed with rapture at the greatness of her knight.

CHAPTER XV.

THE noble lady had just unbuckled her knight's armour with her own fair hands,—on the field of battle alone were pages or esquires bidden handle Montfaucon's armour,—and now she was throwing over his shoulders his mantle of blue velvet embroidered with gold, when the door opened gently, and Sintram entered the room, humbly greeting them. Gabrielle received him kindly, as she was wont, but suddenly turning pale, she looked away and said:

"O Sintram, what has happened to you? And how can one single night have so fearfully altered you?"

Sintram stood still, thunderstruck, and feeling as if he himself did not know what had befallen him. Then Folko took him by the hand, led him towards a bright polished shield, and said very earnestly, "Look here at yourself, young knight!"

At the first glance Sintram drew back horrified. He

fancied that he saw the little Master before him with that single upright feather sticking out of his cap; but he at length perceived that the mirror was only shewing him his own image and none other, and that his own wild dagger had given him this strange and spectre-like aspect, as he could not deny to himself.

"Who has done that to you?" asked Folko, yet more grave and solemn. "And what terror makes your disordered hair stand on end?"

Sintram knew not what to answer. He felt as if a judgment were coming on him, and a shameful degrading from his knightly rank. Suddenly Folko drew him away from the shield, and taking him towards the rattling window, he asked: "Whence comes this tempest?"

Still Sintram kept silence. His limbs began to tremble under him; and Gabrielle, pale and terrified, whispered, "O Folko, my knight, what has happened? Oh, tell me; are we come into an enchanted castle?"

"The land of our northern ancestors," replied Folko with solemnity, "is full of mysterious knowledge. But we may not, for all that, call its people enchanters; still this youth has cause to watch himself narrowly; he whom the evil one has touched by so much as one hair of his head . . . ."

Sintram heard no more; with a deep groan he staggered out of the room. As he left it, he met old Rolf, still almost benumbed by the cold and storms of the night. Now, in his joy at again seeing his young master, he did not remark his altered appearance; but as he accompanied him to his sleeping-room he said, "Witches and spirits of the tempest must have taken up their abode on the sea-shore. I am certain that such wild storms never arise without some devilish arts."

Sintram fell into a fainting-fit, from which Rolf could with difficulty recover him sufficiently to appear in the great hall at the mid-day hour. But before he went down, he caused a shield to be brought, saw himself therein, and cut close round, in grief and horror, the rest of his long black hair, so that he made himself look almost like a monk; and thus he joined the others already assembled round the table. They all looked at him with surprise; but old Biorn rose up and said fiercely, "Are you going to betake yourself to a cloister, as well as the fair lady your mother?"

A commanding look from the Baron of Montfaucon checked any farther outbreak; and as if in apology, Biorn added, with a forced smile, "I was only thinking if any accident had befallen him, like Absolom's, and if he had been obliged to save himself from being strangled by parting with all his hair."

"You should not jest with holy things," answered the baron severely, and all were silent. No sooner was the repast ended, than Folko and Gabrielle, with a grave and courteous salutation, retired to their apartments.

CHAPTER XVI.

LIFE in the castle took from this time quite another form. Those two bright beings, Folko and Gabrielle, spent most part of the day in their apartments, and when they shewed themselves, it was with quiet dignity and grave silence, while Biorn and Sintram stood before them in humble fear. Nevertheless, Biorn could not bear the thought of his guests seeking shelter in any other knight's abode. When Folko once spoke of it, something like a tear stood in the wild man's eye. His head sank, and he said softly, "As you please; but I feel that if you go, I shall run among the rocks for days."

And thus they all remained together; for the storm continued to rage with such increasing fury over the sea, that no sea voyage could be thought of, and the oldest man in Norway could not call to mind such an autumn. The priests examined all the Runic books, the bards looked through their lays and tales, and yet they could find no record of the like. Biorn and Sintram braved the tempest; but during the few hours in which Folko and Gabrielle shewed themselves, the father and son were always in the castle, as if respectfully waiting upon them; the rest of the day—nay, often through whole nights, they rushed through the forests and over the rocks in pursuit of bears. Folko the while called up all the brightness of his fancy, all his courtly grace, in order to make Gabrielle forget that she was living in this wild castle, and that the long, hard northern winter was setting in, which would ice them in for many a month. Sometimes he would relate bright tales; then he would play the liveliest airs to induce Gabrielle to lead a dance with her attendants; then, again, handing his lute to one of the women, he would himself take a part in the dance, well knowing to express thereby after some new fashion his devotion to his lady. Another time he would have the spacious halls of the castle prepared for his armed retainers to go through their warlike exercises, and Gabrielle always adjudged the reward to the conqueror. Folko often joined the circle of combatants; yet so that he only met their attacks, defending himself, but depriving no one of the prize. The Norwegians, who stood around as spectators, used to compare him to the demi-god Baldur, one of the heroes of their old traditions, who was wont to let the darts of his companions be all hurled against him, conscious that he was invulnerable, and of his own indwelling strength.

At the close of one of these martial exercises, old Rolf advanced towards Folko, and beckoning him with an humble look, said softly, "They call you the beautiful, mighty Baldur,—and they are right. But even the beautiful, mighty Baldur did not escape death. Take heed to yourself." Folko looked at him wondering. "Not that I know of any treachery," continued the old man; "or that I can even foresee the likelihood of any. God keep a Norwegian from such a fear. But when you stand before me in all the brightness of your glory, the fleetingness of every thing earthly weighs down my mind, and I cannot refrain from saying, 'Take heed, noble baron! oh, take heed! Even the most beautiful glory comes to an end.'"

"Those are wise and pious thoughts," replied Folko calmly, "and I will treasure them in a pure heart."

The good Rolf was often with Folko and Gabrielle, and made a connecting link between the two widely differing parties in the castle. For how could he have ever forsaken his own Sintram! Only in the wild hunting expeditions through the howling storms and tempests he no longer was able to follow his young lord.

At length the icy reign of winter began in all its glory. On this account a return to Normandy was impossible, and therefore the magical storm was lulled. The hills and valleys shone brilliantly in their white attire of snow, and Folko used sometimes, with skates on his feet, to draw his lady in a light sledge over the glittering frozen lakes and streams. On the other hand, the bear-hunts of the lord of the castle and his son took a still more desperate and to them joyous course.

About this time,—when Christmas was drawing near, and Sintram was seeking to overpower his dread of the awful dreams by the most daring expeditions,—about this time, Folko and Gabrielle stood together on one of the terraces of the castle. The evening was mild; the snow-clad fields were glowing in the red light of the setting sun; from below there were heard men's voices singing songs of ancient heroic times, while they worked in the armourer's forge. At last the songs died away, the beating of hammers ceased, and, without the speakers being seen, or there being any possibility of distinguishing them by their voices, the following discourse arose:—

"Who is the bravest amongst all those whose race derives its origin from our renowned land?"

"It is Folko of Montfaucon."

"Rightly said; but tell me, is there any thing from which even this bold baron draws back?"

"In truth there is one thing,—and we who have never left Norway face it quite willingly and joyfully."

"And that is ——?"

"A bear-hunt in winter, over trackless plains of snow, down frightful ice-covered precipices."

"Truly thou answerest aright, my comrade. He who knows not how to fasten our skates on his feet, how to turn in them to the right or left at a moment's warning, he may be a valiant knight in other respects, but he had better keep away from our hunting parties, and remain with his timid wife in her apartments." At which the speakers were heard to laugh well pleased, and then to betake themselves again to their armourers' work.

Folko stood long buried in thought. A glow beyond that of the evening sky reddened his cheek. Gabrielle also remained silent, considering she knew not what. At last she took courage, and embracing her beloved, she said: "To-morrow thou wilt go forth to hunt the bear, wilt thou not? and thou wilt bring the spoils of the chase to thy lady?"

The knight gave a joyful sign of assent; and the rest of the evening was spent in dances and music.

CHAPTER XVII.

"See, my noble lord," said Sintram the next morning, when Folko had expressed his wish of going out with him, "these skates of ours give such wings to our course, that we go down the mountain-side swiftly as the wind; and even in going up again we are too quick for any one to be able to pursue us, and on the plains no horse can keep up with us; and yet they can only be worn with safety by those who are well practised. It seems as though some strange spirit dwelt in them, which is fearfully dangerous to any that have not learnt the management of them in their childhood."

Folko answered somewhat proudly: "Do you suppose that this is the first time that I have been amongst your mountains? Years ago I have joined in this sport, and, thank heaven, there is no knightly exercise which does not speedily become familiar to me."

Sintram did not venture to make any further objections, and still less did old Biorn. They both felt relieved when they saw with what skill and ease Folko buckled the skates on his feet, without suffering any one to assist him. This day they hunted up the mountain in pursuit of a fierce bear which had often before escaped from them. Before long it was necessary that they should separate, and Sintram offered himself as companion to Folko, who, touched by the humble manner of the youth, and his devotion to him, forgot all that had latterly seemed mysterious in the pale altered being before him, and agreed heartily. As now they continued to climb higher and higher up the mountain, and saw from many a giddy height the rocks and crags below them looking like a vast expanse of sea suddenly turned into ice whilst tossed by a violent tempest, the noble Montfaucon drew his breath more freely. He poured forth war-songs and love-songs in the clear mountain air, and the startled echoes repeated from rock to rock the lays of his Frankish home. He sprang lightly from one precipice to another, using strongly and safely his staff for support, and turning now to the right, now to the left, as the fancy seized him; so that Sintram was fain to exchange his former anxiety for a wondering admiration, and the hunters, whose eyes had never been taken off the baron, burst forth with loud applause, proclaiming far and wide the fresh glory of their guest.

The good fortune which usually accompanied Folko's deeds of arms seemed still unwilling to leave him. After a short search, he and Sintram found distinct traces of the savage animal, and with beating hearts they followed the track so swiftly, that even a winged enemy would have been unable to escape from them. But the creature whom they sought did not attempt a flight—he lay sulkily in a cavern near the top of a steep precipitous rock, infuriated by the shouts of the hunters, and only waiting in his lazy fury for some one to be bold enough to climb up to his retreat, that he might tear him to pieces. Folko and Sintram had now reached the foot of this rock, the rest of the hunters being dispersed over the far-extending plain. The track led the two companions up the rock, and they set about climbing on the opposite sides of it, that they might be the more sure of not missing their prey. Folko reached the lonely topmost point first, and cast his eyes around. A wide, boundless tract of country, covered with untrodden snow, was spread before him, melting in the distance into the lowering clouds of the gloomy evening sky. He almost thought that he must have missed the traces of the fearful beast; when close beside him from a cleft in the rock issued a long growl, and a huge black bear appeared on the snow, standing on its hind legs, and with glaring eyes it advanced towards the baron. Sintram the while was struggling in vain to make his way up the rock against the masses of snow continually slipping down.

Joyful at a combat so long untried as almost to be new, Folko of Montfaucon levelled his hunting spear, and awaited the attack of the wild beast. He suffered it to approach so near that its fearful claws were almost upon him; then he made a thrust, and the spear-head was buried deep in the bear's breast. But the furious beast still pressed on with a fierce growl, kept up on its hind legs by the cross-iron of the spear, and the knight was forced to plant his feet deep in the earth to resist the savage assault; and ever close before him the grim and bloody face of the bear, and close in his ear its deep savage growl, wrung forth partly by the agony of death, partly by thirst for blood. At length the bear's resistance grew weaker, and the dark blood streamed freely upon the snow; he tottered; and one powerful thrust hurled him backwards over the edge of the precipice. At the same instant, Sintram stood by the Baron of Montfaucon. Folko said, drawing a deep breath: "But I have not yet the prize in my hands, and have it I must, since fortune has given me a claim to it. Look, one of my skates seems to be out of order. Thinkest thou, Sintram, that it holds enough to slide down to the foot of the precipice?"

"Let me go instead," said Sintram. "I will bring you the head and the claws of the bear."

"A true knight," replied Folko with some displeasure, "never does a knightly deed by halves. What I ask is, whether my skate will still hold?"

As Sintram bent down to look, and was on the point of saying "No!" he suddenly heard a voice close to him, saying, "Why, yes, to be sure; there is no doubt about it."

Folko thought that Sintram had spoken, and slid down with the swiftness of an arrow, whilst his companion looked up in great surprise. The hated form of the little Master met his eyes. As he was going to address him with angry words, he heard the sound of the baron's fearful fall, and he stood still in silent horror. There was a breathless silence also in the abyss below.

"Now, why dost thou delay?" said the little Master, after a pause. "He is dashed to pieces. Go back to the castle, and take the fair Helen to thyself."

Sintram shuddered. Then his hateful companion began to praise Gabrielle's charms in so glowing, deceiving words, that the heart of the youth swelled with emotions he had never before known. He only thought of him who was now lying at the foot of the rock as of an obstacle removed between him and heaven: he turned towards the castle.

But a cry was heard below: "Help! help! my comrade! I am yet alive, but I am sorely wounded."

Sintram's will was changed, and he called to the baron, "I am coming."

But the little Master said, "Nothing can be done to help Duke Menelaus; and the fair Helen knows it already. She is only waiting for Knight Paris to comfort her." And with detestable craft he wove in that tale with what was actually happening, bringing in the most highly wrought praises of the lovely Gabrielle; and alas! the dazzled youth yielded to him, and fled! Again he heard far off the baron's voice calling to him, "Knight Sintram, Knight Sintram, thou on whom I bestowed the holy order, haste to me and help me! The she-bear and her whelps will be upon me, and I cannot use my right arm! Knight Sintram, Knight Sintram, haste to help me!"

His cries were overpowered by the furious speed with which the two were carried along on their skates, and by the evil words of the little Master, who was mocking at the late proud bearing of Duke Menelaus towards the poor Sintram. At last he shouted, "Good luck to you, she-bear! good luck to your whelps! There is a glorious meal for you! Now you will feed upon the fear of Heathendom, him at whose name the Moorish brides weep, the mighty Baron of Montfaucon. Never again, O dainty knight, will you shout at the head of your troops, 'Mountjoy St. Denys!'" But scarce had this holy name passed the lips of the little Master, than he set up a howl of anguish, writhing himself with horrible contortions, and wringing his hands, and ended by disappearing in a storm of snow which then arose.

Sintram planted his staff firmly in the ground, and stopped. How strangely did the wide expanse of snow, the distant mountains rising above it, and the dark green fir-woods—how strangely did they all look at him in cold reproachful silence! He felt as if he must sink under the weight of his sorrow and his guilt. The bell of a distant hermitage came floating sadly over the plain. With a burst of tears he exclaimed, as the darkness grew thicker round him, "My mother! my mother! I had once a beloved tender mother, and she said I was a good child!" A ray of comfort came to him as if brought on an angel's wing; perhaps Montfaucon was not yet dead! and he flew like lightning along the path, back to the steep rock. When he got to the fearful place, he stooped and looked anxiously down the precipice. The moon, just risen in full majesty, helped him. The knight of Montfaucon, pale and bleeding, was half kneeling against the rock; his right arm, crushed in his fall, hung powerless at his side; it was plain that he could not draw his good sword out of the scabbard. But nevertheless he was keeping the bear and her young ones at bay by his bold threatening looks, so that they only crept round him, growling angrily; every moment ready for a fierce attack, but as often driven back affrighted at the majestic air by which he conquered even when defenceless.

"Oh! what a hero would there have perished!" groaned Sintram, "and through whose guilt?" In an instant his spear flew with so true an aim that the bear fell weltering in her blood; the young ones ran away howling.

The baron looked up with surprise. His countenance beamed as the light of the moon fell upon it, grave and stern, yet mild, like some angelic vision. "Come down!" he beckoned; and Sintram slid down the side of the precipice, full of anxious haste. He was going to attend to the wounded man, but Folko said, "First cut off the head and claws of the bear which I slew. I promised to bring the spoils of the chase to my lovely Gabrielle. Then come to me, and bind up my wounds. My right arm is broken." Sintram obeyed the baron's commands. When the tokens of victory had been secured, and the broken arm bound up, Folko desired the youth to help him back to the castle.

"O heavens!" said Sintram in a low voice, "if I dared to look in your face! or only knew how to come near you!"

"Thou wert indeed going on in an evil course," said Montfaucon gravely; "but how could we, any of us, stand before God, did not repentance help us! At any rate, thou hast now saved my life, and let that thought cheer thy heart."

The youth with tenderness and strength supported the baron's left arm, and they both went their way silently in the moonlight.

CHAPTER XVIII.

Sounds of wailing were heard from the castle as they approached; the chapel was solemnly lighted up; within it knelt Gabrielle, lamenting for the death of the knight of Montfaucon.

But how quickly was all changed, when the noble baron, pale indeed, and bleeding, yet having escaped all mortal danger, stood smiling at the entrance of the holy building, and said, in a low, gentle voice, "Look up, Gabrielle, and be not affrighted; for, by the honour of my race, thy knight still lives." Oh! with what joy did Gabrielle's eyes sparkle, as she turned to her knight, and then raised them again to heaven, still streaming, but from the deep source of thankful joy! With the help of two pages, Folko knelt down beside her, and they both sanctified their happiness with a silent prayer.

When they left the chapel, the wounded knight being tenderly supported by his lady, Sintram was standing without in the darkness, himself as gloomy as the night, and, like a bird of the night, shunning the sight of men. Yet he came trembling forward into the torch-light, laid the bear's head and claws at the feet of Gabrielle, and said, "The noble Folko of Montfaucon presents the spoils of to-day's chase to his lady."

The Norwegians burst forth with shouts of joyful surprise at the stranger knight, who in the very first hunting expedition had slain the most fearful and dangerous beast of their mountains.

Then Folko looked around with a smile as he said, "And now none of you must jeer at me, if I stay at home for a short time with my timid wife."

Those who the day before had talked together in the armourer's forge came out from the crowd, and bowing low, they replied, "Noble baron, who could have thought that there was no knightly exercise in the whole world in the which you would not shew yourself far above all other men?"

"The pupil of old Sir Hugh may be somewhat trusted," answered Folko kindly. "But now, you bold northern warriors, bestow some praises also on my deliverer, who saved me from the claws of the she-bear, when I was leaning against the rock wounded by my fall."

He pointed to Sintram, and the general shout was again raised; and old Rolf, with tears of joy in his eyes, bent his head over his foster-son's hand. But Sintram drew back shuddering.

"Did you but know," said he, "whom you see before you, all your spears would be aimed at my heart; and perhaps that would be the best thing for me. But I spare the honour of my father and of his race, and for this time I will not confess. Only this much must you know, noble warriors ——"

"Young man," interrupted Folko with a reproving look, "already again so wild and fierce? I desire that thou wilt hold thy peace about thy dreaming fancies."

Sintram was silenced for a moment; but hardly had Folko begun smilingly to move towards the steps of the castle, than he cried out, "Oh, no, no, noble wounded knight, stay yet awhile; I will serve thee in every thing that thy heart can desire; but herein I cannot serve thee. Brave warriors, you must and shall know so much as this: I am no longer worthy to live under the same roof with the noble Baron of Montfaucon and his angelic wife Gabrielle. And you, my aged father, good night; long not for me. I intend to live in the stone fortress on the Rocks of the Moon, till a change of some kind come over me."

There was that in his way of speaking against which no one dared to set himself, not even Folko.

The wild Biorn bowed his head humbly, and said, "Do according to thy pleasure, my poor son; for I fear that thou art right."

Then Sintram walked solemnly and silently through the castle-gate, followed by the good Rolf. Gabrielle led her exhausted lord up to their apartments.

CHAPTER XIX.

THAT was a mournful journey on which the youth and his aged foster-father went towards the Rocks of the Moon, through the wild tangled paths of the snow-clad valleys. Rolf from time to time sang some verses of hymns, in which comfort and peace were promised to the penitent sinner, and Sintram thanked him for them with looks of grateful sadness. Neither of them spoke a word else.

At length, when the dawn of day was approaching, Sintram broke silence by saying, "Who are those two sitting yonder by the frozen stream—a tall man and a little one? Their own wild hearts must have driven them also forth into the wilderness. Rolf, dost thou know them? The sight of them makes me shudder."

"Sir," answered the old man, "your disturbed mind deceives you. There stands a lofty fir-tree, and the old weather-beaten stump of an oak, half-covered with snow, which gives them a somewhat strange appearance. There are no men sitting yonder."

"But, Rolf, look there! look again carefully! Now they move, they whisper together."

"Sir, the morning breeze moves the branches, and whistles in the sharp pine-leaves and in the yellow oak-leaves, and rustles the crisp snow."

"Rolf, now they are both coming towards us. Now they are standing before us, quite close."

"Sir, it is we who get nearer to them as we walk on, and the setting moon throws such long giant-like shadows over the plain."

"Good evening!" said a hollow voice; and Sintram

knew it was the crazy pilgrim, near to whom stood the malignant little Master, looking more hideous than ever.

"You are right, sir knight," whispered Rolf, as he drew back behind Sintram, and made the sign of the cross on his breast and his forehead.

The bewildered youth, however, advanced towards the two figures, and said, "You have always taken wonderful pleasure in being my companions. What do you expect will come of it? And do you choose to go now with me to the stone fortress? There I will tend thee, poor pale pilgrim; and as to thee, frightful Master, most evil dwarf, I will make thee shorter by the head, to reward thee for thy deeds yesterday."

"That would be a fine thing," sneered the little Master; "and perhaps thou imaginest that thou wouldst be doing a great service to the whole world? And, indeed, who knows? Something might be gained by it! Only, poor wretch, thou canst not do it."

The pilgrim meantime was waving his pale head to and fro thoughtfully, saying, "I believe truly, that thou wouldst willingly have me, and I would go to thee willingly, but I may not yet. Have patience awhile; thou wilt yet surely see me come, but at a distant time; and first we must again visit thy father together, and then also thou wilt learn to call me by my right name, my poor friend."

"Beware of disappointing me again!" said the little Master to the pilgrim in a threatening voice; but he, pointing with his long, shrivelled hand towards the sun, which was just now rising, said, "Stop either that sun or me, if thou canst!"

Then the first rays fell on the snow, and little Master ran, muttering, down a precipice; but the pilgrim walked on in the bright beams, calmly and with great solemnity, towards a neighbouring castle on the mountain. It was not long before its chapel-bell was heard tolling for the dead.

"For heaven's sake," whispered the good Rolf to his knight—"for heaven's sake, Sir Sintram, what kind of companions have you here? One of them cannot bear the light of God's blessed sun, and the other has no sooner set foot in a dwelling than tidings of death wail after his track. Could he have been a murderer?"

"I do not think that," said Sintram. "He seemed to me the best of the two. But it is a strange wilfulness of his not to come with me. Did I not invite him kindly? I believe that he can sing well, and he should have sung to me some gentle lullaby. Since my mother has lived in a cloister, no one sings lullabies to me any more."

At this tender recollection his eyes were bedewed with tears. But he did not himself know what he had said besides, for there was wildness and confusion in his spirit. They arrived at the Rocks of the Moon, and mounted up to the stone fortress. The castellan, an old, gloomy man, the more devoted to the young knight from his dark melancholy and wild deeds, hastened to lower the drawbridge. Greetings were exchanged in silence, and in silence did Sintram enter, and those joyless gates closed with a crash behind the future recluse.

CHAPTER XX.

Yes truly, a recluse, or at least something like it, did poor Sintram now become! For towards the time of the approaching Christmas festival his fearful dreams came over him, and seized him so fiercely, that all the esquires and servants fled with shrieks out of the castle, and would never venture back again. No one remained with him except Rolf and the old castellan. After a while, indeed, Sintram became calm, but he went about looking so pallid and still, that he might have been taken for a wandering corpse. No comforting of the good Rolf, no devout soothing lays, were of any avail; and the castellan, with his fierce, scarred features, his head almost entirely bald from a huge sword-cut, his stubborn silence, seemed like a yet darker shadow of the miserable knight. Rolf often thought of going to summon the holy chaplain of Drontheim; but how could he have left his lord alone with the gloomy castellan, a man who at all times raised in him a secret horror? Biorn had long had this wild strange warrior in his service, and honoured him on account of his unshaken fidelity and his fearless courage, though neither the knight nor any one else knew whence the castellan came, nor, indeed, exactly who he was. Very few people knew by what name to call him; but that was the more needless, since he never entered into discourse with any one. He was the castellan of the stone fortress on the Rocks of the Moon, and nothing more.

Rolf committed his deep heartfelt cares to the merciful God, trusting that He would soon come to his aid; and the merciful God did not fail him. For on Christmas-eve the bell at the drawbridge sounded, and Rolf, looking over the battlements, saw the chaplain of Drontheim standing there, with a companion, indeed, that surprised him,—for close beside him appeared the crazy pilgrim, and the dead men's bones on his dark mantle shone very strangely in the glimmering starlight: but the sight of the chaplain filled the good Rolf too full of joy to leave room for any doubt in his mind; for, thought he, whoever comes with *him* cannot but be welcome! And so he let them both in with respectful haste, and ushered them up to the hall, where Sintram, pale and with a fixed look, was sitting under the light of one flickering lamp. Rolf was obliged to support and assist the crazy pilgrim up the stairs, for he was quite benumbed with cold.

"I bring you a greeting from your mother," said the chaplain as he came in; and immediately a sweet smile passed over the young knight's countenance, and its deadly pallidness gave place to a bright soft glow.

"O heaven!" murmured he, "does then my mother yet live, and does she care to know any thing about me?"

"She is endowed with a wonderful presentiment of the future," replied the chaplain; "and all that you ought either to do or to leave undone is faithfully mirrored in various ways in her mind, during a half-waking trance. Now she knows of your deep sorrow; and she sends me, the father-confessor of her convent, to comfort you, but at the same time to warn you; for, as she affirms, and as I am also inclined to think, many strange and heavy trials lie before you."

Sintram bowed himself towards the chaplain with his arms crossed over his breast, and said, with a gentle smile, "Much have I been favoured—more, a thousand times more, than I could have dared to hope in my best hours—by this greeting from my mother, and your visit, reverend sir; and all after falling more fearfully low that I had ever fallen before. The mercy of the Lord is great; and how heavy soever may be the weight and punishment which He may send, I trust, with His grace, to be able to bear it."

Just then the door opened, and the castellan came in with a torch in his hand, the red glare of which made his face look the colour of blood. He cast a terrified glance at the crazy pilgrim, who had just sunk back in a swoon, and was supported on his seat and tended by Rolf; then he stared with astonishment at the chaplain, and at last murmured, "A strange meeting! I believe that the hour for confession and reconciliation is now arrived."

"I believe so too," replied the priest, who had heard his low whisper; "this seems to be truly a day rich in grace and peace. That poor man yonder, whom I found half frozen by the way, would make a full confession to me at once, before he followed me to a place of shelter. Do as he has done, my dark-browed warrior, and delay not your good purpose for one instant."

Thereupon he left the room with the willing castellan, but he turned back to say, "Sir Knight, and your esquire! take good care the while of my sick charge."

Sintram and Rolf did according to the chaplain's desire: and when at length their cordials made the pilgrim open his eyes once again, the young knight said to him, with a friendly smile, "Seest thou? thou art come to visit me after all. Why didst thou refuse me when, a few nights ago, I asked thee so earnestly to come? Perhaps I may have spoken wildly and hastily. Did that scare thee away?"

A sudden expression of fear came over the pilgrim's countenance; but soon he again looked up at Sintram with an air of gentle humility, saying, "O my dear, dear lord, I am most entirely devoted to you—only never speak to me of former passages between you and me. I am terrified whenever you do it. For, my lord, either I am mad and have forgotten all that is past, or that Being has met you in the wood, whom I look upon as my very powerful twin-brother."

Sintram laid his hand gently on the pilgrim's mouth, as he answered, "Say nothing more about that matter: I most willingly promise to be silent."

Neither he nor old Rolf could understand what appeared to them so awful in the whole matter; but both shuddered.

After a short pause, the pilgrim said, "I would rather sing you a song—a soft, comforting song. Have you not a lute here?"

Rolf fetched one; and the pilgrim, half-raising himself on the couch, sang the following words:

"When death is coming near,
When thy heart shrinks in fear
And thy limbs fail,
Then raise thy hands and pray
To Him who smoothes thy way
Through the dark vale.

Seest thou the eastern dawn,
Hear'st thou in the red morn
    The angel's song?
Oh, lift thy drooping head,
Thou who in gloom and dread
    Hast lain so long.

Death comes to set thee free;
Oh, meet him cheerily
    As thy true friend,
And all thy fears shall cease,
And in eternal peace
    Thy penance end."

"Amen," said Sintram and Rolf, folding their hands; and whilst the last chords of the lute still resounded, the chaplain and the castellan came slowly and gently into the room. "I bring a precious Christmas gift," said the priest. "After many sad years, hope of reconciliation and peace of conscience are returning to a noble, disturbed mind. This concerns thee, beloved pilgrim; and do thou, my Sintram, with a joyful trust in God, take encouragement and example from it."

"More than twenty years ago," began the castellan, at a sign from the chaplain—"more than twenty years ago I was a bold shepherd, driving my flock up the mountains. A young knight followed me, whom they called Weigand the Slender. He wanted to buy of me my favourite little lamb for his fair bride, and offered me much red gold for it. I sturdily refused. Overbold youth boiled up in us both. A stroke of his sword hurled me senseless down the precipice."

"Not killed?" asked the pilgrim in a scarce audible voice.

"I am no ghost," replied the castellan, somewhat morosely; and then, after an earnest look from the priest, he continued, more humbly: "I recovered slowly and in solitude, with the help of remedies which were easily found by me, a shepherd, in our productive valleys. When I came back into the world, no man knew me, with my scarred face, and my now bald head. I heard a report going through the country, that on account of this deed of his, Sir Weigand the Slender had been rejected by his fair betrothed Verena, and how he had pined away, and she had wished to retire into a convent, but her father had persuaded her to marry the great knight Biorn. Then there came a fearful thirst for vengeance into my heart, and I disowned my name, and my kindred, and my home, and entered the service of the mighty Biorn, as a strange wild man, in order that Weigand the Slender should always remain a murderer, and that I might feed on his anguish. So have I fed upon it for all these long years; I have fed frightfully upon his self-imposed banishment, upon his cheerless return home, upon his madness. But to-day—" and hot tears gushed from his eyes—" but to-day God has broken the hardness of my heart; and, dear Sir Weigand, look upon yourself no more as a murderer, and say that you will forgive me, and pray for him who has done you so fearful an injury, and —"

Sobs choked his words. He fell at the feet of the pilgrim, who with tears of joy pressed him to his heart, in token of forgiveness.

CHAPTER XXI.

THE joy of this hour passed from its first overpowering brightness to the calm, thoughtful aspect of daily life; and Weigand, now restored to health, laid aside the mantle with dead men's bones, saying: " I had chosen for my penance to carry these fearful remains about with me, with the thought that some of them might have belonged to him whom I have murdered. Therefore I sought for them round about, in the deep beds of the mountain-torrents, and in the high nests of the eagles and vultures. And while I was searching, I sometimes—could it have been only an illusion?—seemed to meet a being who was very like myself, but far, far more powerful, and yet still paler and more haggard."

An imploring look from Sintram stopped the flow of his words. With a gentle smile, Weigand bowed towards him, and said: "You know now all the deep, unutterably deep, sorrow which preyed upon me. My fear of you, and my yearning love for you, are no longer an enigma to your kind heart. For, dear youth, though you may be like your fearful father, you have also the kind, gentle heart of your mother; and its reflection brightens your pallid, stern features, like the glow of a morning sky, which lights up ice-covered mountains and snowy valleys with the soft radiance of joy. But, alas! how long you have lived alone amidst your fellow-creatures! And how long since you have seen your mother, my dearly loved Sintram!"

"I feel, too, as though a spring were gushing up in the barren wilderness," replied the youth; "and I should perchance be altogether restored, could I but keep you long with me, and weep with you, dear lord. But I have that within me which says that you will very soon be taken from me."

"I believe, indeed," said the pilgrim, "that my late song was very nearly my last, and that it contained a prediction full soon to be accomplished in me. But, as the soul of man is always like the thirsty ground, the more blessings God has bestowed on us, the more earnestly do we look out for new ones; so would I crave for one more before, as I hope, my blessed end. Yet, indeed, it cannot be granted me," added he, with a faltering voice; "for I feel myself too utterly unworthy of so high a gift."

"But it will be granted!" said the chaplain, joyfully. "'He that humbleth himself shall be exalted;' and I fear not to take one purified from murder to receive a farewell from the holy and forgiving countenance of Verena."

The pilgrim stretched both his hands up towards heaven, and an unspoken thanksgiving poured from his beaming eyes, and brightened the smile that played on his lips.

Sintram looked sorrowfully on the ground, and sighed gently to himself: "Alas! who would dare accompany?"

"My poor, good Sintram," said the chaplain, in a tone of the softest kindness, "I understand thee well; but the time is not yet come. The powers of evil will again raise up their wrathful heads within thee, and Verena must check both her own and thy longing desires, until all is pure in thy spirit as in hers. Comfort thyself with the thought that God looks mercifully upon thee, and that the joy so earnestly sought for will come—if not here, most assuredly beyond the grave."

But the pilgrim, as though awaking out of a trance, rose mightily from his seat, and said: "Do you please to come forth with me, reverend chaplain? Before the sun appears in the heavens, we could reach the convent-gates, and I should not be far from heaven."

In vain did the chaplain and Rolf remind him of his weakness: he smiled, and said that there could be no words about it; and he girded himself, and tuned the lute which he had asked leave to take with him. His decided manner overcame all opposition, almost without words; and the chaplain had already prepared himself for the journey, when the pilgrim looked with much emotion at Sintram, who, oppressed with a strange weariness, had sunk, half asleep, on a couch, and said: "Wait a moment. I know that he wants me to give him a soft lullaby." The pleased smile of the youth seemed to say, Yes; and the pilgrim, touching the strings with a light hand, sang these words:

"Sleep peacefully, dear boy;
Thy mother sends the song
That whispers round thy couch,
To lull thee all night long.

In silence and afar
  For thee she ever prays,
And longs once more in fondness
  Upon thy face to gaze.

And when thy waking cometh,
  Then in thy every deed,
In all that may betide thee,
  Unto her words give heed.
Oh, listen for her voice,
  If it be yea or nay;
And though temptation meet thee,
  Thou shalt not miss the way.

If thou canst listen rightly,
  And nobly onward go,
Then pure and gentle breezes
  Around thy cheeks shall blow.
Then on thy peaceful journey
  Her blessing thou shalt feel,
And though from thee divided,
  Her presence o'er thee steal

O safest, sweetest comfort!
  O blest and living light!
That, strong in heaven's power,
  All terrors puts to flight!
Rest quietly, sweet child,
  And may the gentle numbers
Thy mother sends to thee
  Waft peace unto thy slumbers."

Sintram fell into a deep sleep, smiling, and breathing softly. Rolf and the castellan remained by his bed, whilst the two travellers pursued their way in the quiet starlight.

CHAPTER XXII.

The dawn had almost appeared, when Rolf, who had been asleep, was awakened by low singing; and as he looked round, he perceived, with surprise, that the sounds came from the lips of the castellan, who said, as if in explanation, "So does Sir Weigand sing at the convent-gates, and they are kindly opened to him." Upon which, old Rolf fell asleep again, uncertain whether what had passed had been a dream or a reality. After a while the bright sunshine awoke him again; and when he rose up, he saw the countenance of the castellan wonderfully illuminated by the red morning rays; and altogether those features, once so fearful, were shining with a soft, nay almost child-like mildness. The mysterious man seemed to be the while listening to the motionless air, as if he were hearing a most pleasant discourse or lofty music; and as Rolf was about to speak, he made him a sign of entreaty to remain quiet, and continued in his eager listening attitude.

At length he sank slowly and contentedly back in his seat, whispering, "God be praised! She has granted his last prayer; he will be laid in the burial-ground of the convent, and now he has forgiven me in the depths of his heart. I can assure you that he finds a peaceful end."

Rolf did not dare ask a question, or awake his lord; he felt as if one already departed had spoken to him.

The castellan long remained still, always smiling brightly. At last he raised himself a little, again listened, and said, "It is over. The sound of the bells is very sweet. We have overcome. Oh, how soft and easy does the good God make it to us!" And so it came to pass. He stretched himself back as if weary, and his soul was freed from his care-worn body.

Rolf now gently awoke his young knight, and pointed to the smiling dead. And Sintram smiled too; he and his good esquire fell on their knees, and prayed to God for the departed spirit. Then they rose up, and bore the cold body to the vaulted hall, and watched by it with holy candles until the return of the chaplain. That the pilgrim would not come back again, they very well knew.

Accordingly towards mid-day the chaplain returned alone. He could scarcely do more than confirm what was already known to them. He only added a comforting and hopeful greeting from Sintram's mother to her son, and told that the blissful Weigand had fallen asleep like a tired child, whilst Verena, with calm tenderness, held a crucifix before him.

"And in eternal peace our penance end!"

sang Sintram, gently to himself; and they prepared a last resting-place for the now so peaceful castellan, and laid him therein with all the due solemn rites.

The chaplain was obliged soon afterwards to depart; but bidding Sintram farewell, he again said kindly to him, "Thy dear mother assuredly knows how gentle and calm and good thou art now!"

CHAPTER XXIII.

In the castle of Sir Biorn of the Fiery Eyes, Christmas-eve had not passed so brightly and happily; but yet, there too all had gone visibly according to God's will.

Folko, at the entreaty of the lord of the castle, had allowed Gabrielle to support him into the hall; and the three now sat at the round stone table, whereon a sumptuous meal was laid. On either side there were long tables, at which sat the retainers of both knights in full armour, according to the custom of the north. Torches and lamps lighted the lofty hall with an almost dazzling brightness.

Midnight had now begun its solemn reign, and Gabrielle softly reminded her wounded knight to withdraw. Biorn heard her, and said: "You are right, fair lady; our knight needs rest. Only let us first keep up one more old honourable custom."

And at his sign four attendants brought in with pomp a great boar's head, which looked as if cut out of solid gold, and placed it in the middle of the stone table. Biorn's retainers rose with reverence, and took off their helmets; Biorn himself did the same.

"What means this?" asked Folko very gravely.

"What thy forefathers and mine have done on every Yule feast," answered Biorn. "We are going to make vows on the boar's head, and then pass the goblet round to their fulfilment."

"We no longer keep what our ancestors called the Yule feast," said Folko; "we are good Christians, and we keep holy Christmas-tide."

"To do the one, and not to leave the other undone," answered Biorn. "I hold my ancestors too dear to forget their knightly customs. Those who think otherwise may act according to their wisdom, but that shall not hinder me. I swear by the golden boar's head ——." And he stretched out his hand, to lay it solemnly upon it.

But Folko called out, "In the name of our holy Saviour, forbear. Where I am, and still have breath and will, none shall celebrate undisturbed the rites of the wild heathens."

Biorn of the Fiery Eyes glared angrily at him. The men of the two barons separated from each other, with a hollow sound of rattling armour, and ranged themselves in two bodies on either side of the hall, each behind its leader. Already here and there helmets were fastened and visors closed.

"Bethink thee yet what thou art doing," said Biorn. "I was about to vow an eternal union with the house of Montfaucon, nay, even to bind myself to do it grateful homage; but if thou disturb me in the customs which have come to me from my forefathers, look to thy safety and the safety of all that is dear to thee. My wrath no longer knows any bounds."

Folko made a sign to the pale Gabrielle to retire behind his followers, saying to her, "Be of good cheer, my noble wife, weaker Christians have braved, for the sake of God and of His holy Church, greater dangers than now seem to threaten us. Believe me, the Lord of Montfaucon is not so easily ensnared."

Gabrielle obeyed, something comforted by Folko's fearless smile, but this smile inflamed yet more the fury of Biorn. He again stretched out his hand towards the boar's head, as if about to make some dreadful vow, when Folko snatched a gauntlet of Biorn's off the table, with

which he, with his unwounded left arm, struck so powerful a blow on the gilt idol, that it fell crashing to the ground, shivered to pieces. Biorn and his followers stood as if turned to stone. But soon swords were grasped by armed hands, shields were taken down from the walls, and an angry, threatening murmur sounded through the hall.

At a sign from Folko, a battle-axe was brought him by one of his faithful retainers; he swung it high in air with his powerful left hand, and stood looking like an avenging angel as he spoke these words through the tumult with awful calmness: "What seek ye, O deluded Northmen? What wouldst thou, sinful lord? Ye are indeed become heathens; and I hope to shew you, by my readiness for battle, that it is not in my right arm alone that God has put strength for victory. But if ye can yet hear, listen to my words. Biorn, on this same accursed, and now, by God's help, shivered boar's head, thou didst lay thy hand when thou didst swear to sacrifice any inhabitants of the German towns that should fall into thy power. And Gotthard Lentz came, and Rudlieb came, driven on these shores by the storm. What didst thou then do, O savage Biorn? What did ye do at his bidding, ye who were keeping the Yule feast with him? Try your fortune on me. The Lord will be with me, as He was with those holy men. To arms, and—" (he turned to his warriors) "let our battle-cry be Gotthard and Rudlieb!"

Then Biorn let drop his drawn sword, then his followers paused, and none among the Norwegians dared lift his eyes from the ground. By degrees, they one by one began to disappear from the hall; and at last Biorn stood quite alone opposite to the baron and his followers. He seemed hardly aware that he had been deserted, but he fell on his knees, stretched out his shining sword, pointed to the broken boar's head, and said, "Do with me as you have done with that; I deserve no better. I ask but one favour, only one; do not disgrace me, noble baron, by seeking shelter in another castle of Norway."

"I fear you not," answered Folko, after some thought; "and, as far as may be, I freely forgive you." Then he drew the sign of the cross over the wild form of Biorn, and left the hall with Gabrielle. The retainers of the house of Montfaucon followed him proudly and silently.

The hard spirit of the fierce lord of the castle was now quite broken, and he watched with increased humility every look of Folko and Gabrielle. But they withdrew more and more into the happy solitude of their own apartments, where they enjoyed, in the midst of the sharp winter, a bright spring-tide of happiness. The wounded condition of Folko did not hinder the evening delights of songs and music and poetry—but rather a new charm was added to them when the tall, handsome knight leant on the arm of his delicate lady, and they thus, changing as it were their deportment and duties, walked slowly through the torch-lit halls, scattering their kindly greetings like flowers among the crowds of men and women.

All this time little or nothing was heard of poor Sintram. The last wild outbreak of his father had increased the terror with which Gabrielle remembered the self-accusations of the youth; and the more resolutely Folko kept silence, the more did she bode some dreadful mystery. Indeed, a secret shudder came over the knight when he thought on the pale, dark-haired youth. Sintram's repentance had bordered on settled despair; no one knew even what he was doing in the fortress of evil-report on the Rocks of the Moon. Strange rumours were brought by the retainers who had fled from it, that the evil spirit had obtained complete power over Sintram, that no man could stay with him, and that the fidelity of the dark mysterious castellan had cost him his life.

Folko could hardly drive away the fearful suspicion that the lonely young knight was become a wicked magician.

And perhaps, indeed, evil spirits did flit about the banished Sintram, but it was without his calling them up. In his dreams he often saw the wicked enchantress Venus, in her golden chariot drawn by winged cats, pass over the battlements of the stone fortress, and heard her say, mocking him, "Foolish Sintram, foolish Sintram! hadst thou but obeyed the little Master! Thou wouldst now be in Helen's arms, and the Rocks of the Moon would be called the Rocks of Love, and the stone fortress would be the garden of roses. Thou wouldst have lost thy pale face and dark hair,—for thou art only enchanted, dear youth,—and thine eyes would have beamed more softly, and thy cheeks bloomed more freshly, and thy hair would have been more golden than was that of Prince Paris when men wondered at his beauty. Oh, how Helen would have loved thee!" Then she shewed him in a mirror, how, as a marvellously beautiful knight, he knelt before Gabrielle, who sank into his arms blushing as the morning. When he awoke from such dreams, he would seize eagerly the sword and scarf given him by his lady,—as a shipwrecked man seizes the plank which is to save him; and while the hot tears fell on them, he would murmur to himself, "There was, indeed, one hour in my sad life when I was worthy and happy."

Once he sprang up at midnight after one of these dreams, but this time with more thrilling horror; for it had seemed to him that the features of the enchantress Venus had changed towards the end of her speech, as she looked down upon him with marvellous scorn, and she appeared to him as the hideous little Master. The youth had no better means of calming his distracted mind than to throw the sword and scarf of Gabrielle over his shoulders, and to hasten forth under the solemn starry canopy of the wintry sky. He walked in deep thought backwards and forwards under the leafless oaks and the snow-laden firs which grew on the high ramparts.

Then he heard a sorrowful cry of distress sound from the moat; it was as if some one were attempting to sing, but was stopped by inward grief. Sintram exclaimed, "Who's there?" and all was still. When he was silent, and again began his walk, the frightful groanings and moanings were heard afresh, as if they came from a dying person. Sintram overcame the horror which seemed to hold him back, and began in silence to climb down into the deep dry moat which was cut in the rock. He was soon so low down that he could no longer see the stars shining; beneath him moved a shrouded form; and sliding with involuntary haste down the steep descent, he stood near the groaning figure; it ceased its lamentations, and began to laugh like a maniac from beneath its long, folded, female garments.

"Oh, ho, my comrade! oh, ho, my comrade! wert thou going a little too fast? Well, well, it is all right; and see now, thou standest no higher than I, my pious, valiant youth! Take it patiently,—take it patiently!"

"What dost thou want with me? Why dost thou laugh? why dost thou weep?" asked Sintram impatiently.

"I might ask thee the same questions," answered the dark figure, "and thou wouldst be less able to answer me than I to answer thee. Why dost thou laugh? why dost thou weep?—Poor creature! But I will shew thee a remarkable thing in thy fortress, of which thou knowest nothing. Give heed!"

And the shrouded figure began to scratch and scrape at the stones till a little iron door opened, and shewed a long passage which led into the deep darkness.

"Wilt thou come with me?" whispered the strange being: "it is the shortest way to thy father's castle. In half an hour we shall come out of this passage, and we shall be in thy beauteous lady's apartment. Duke Menelaus shall lie in a magic sleep,—leave that to me,—and then thou wilt take the slight, delicate form in thine arms, and bring her to the Rocks of the Moon; so thou wilt win back all that seemed lost by thy former wavering."

Sintram trembled visibly, fearfully shaken to and fro by the fever of passion and the stings of conscience. But at last, pressing the sword and scarf to his heart, he cried out, "Oh! that fairest, most glorious hour of my life! If I lose all other joys, I will hold fast that brightest hour!"

"A bright, glorious hour!" said the figure from under its veil, like an evil echo. "Dost thou know whom thou then conqueredst? A good old friend, who only shewed himself so sturdy to give thee the glory of overcoming him. Wilt thou convince thyself? Wilt thou look?"

The dark garments of the little figure flew open, and the dwarf warrior in strange armour, the gold horns on his helmet, and the curved spear in his hand, the very same whom Sintram thought he had slain on Niflung's Heath, now stood before him and laughed: "Thou seest, my youth, every thing in the wide world is but dreams and froth; wherefore hold fast the dream which delights thee, and sip up the froth which refreshes thee! Hasten to that underground passage, it leads up to thy angel Helen. Or wouldst thou first know thy friend yet better?"

His visor opened, and the hateful face of the little Master glared upon the knight. Sintram asked, as if in a dream, "Art thou also that wicked enchantress Venus?"

"Something like her," answered the little Master, laughing, "or rather she is something like me. And if thou wilt only get disenchanted, and recover the beauty of Prince Paris,—then, O Prince Paris," and his voice changed to an alluring song, "then, O Prince Paris, I shall be fair like thee!"

At this moment the good Rolf appeared above on the rampart; a consecrated taper in his lantern shone down into the moat, as he sought for the missing young knight. "In God's name, Sir Sintram," he called out, "what has the spectre of him whom you slew on Niflung's Heath, and whom I never could bury, to do with you?"

"Seest thou well? hearest thou well?" whispered the little Master, and drew back into the darkness of the underground passage. "The wise man up there knows me well. There was nothing in thy heroic feat. Come, take the joys of life while thou mayst."

But Sintram sprang back, with a strong effort, into the circle of light made by the shining of the taper from above, and cried out, "Depart from me, unquiet spirit! I know well that I bear a name on me in which thou canst have no part."

Little Master rushed in fear and rage into the passage, and, yelling, shut the iron door behind him. It seemed as if he could still be heard groaning and roaring.

Sintram climbed up the wall of the moat, and made a sign to his foster-father not to speak to him: he only said, "One of my best joys, yes, the very best, has been taken from me; but, by God's help, I am not yet lost."

In the earliest light of the following morning, he and Rolf stopped up the entrance to the perilous passage with huge blocks of stone.

CHAPTER XXIV.

The long northern winter was at last ended, the fresh green leaves rustled merrily in the woods, patches of soft moss twinkled amongst the rocks, the valleys grew green, the brooks sparkled, the snow melted from all but the highest mountain-tops, and the bark which was ready to carry away Folko and Gabrielle danced on the sunny waves of the sea. The baron, now quite recovered, and strong and fresh as though his health had sustained no injury, stood one morning on the shore with his fair lady; and, full of glee at the prospect of returning to their home, the noble pair looked on well pleased at their attendants who were busied in lading the ship.

Then said one of them in the midst of a confused sound of talking: "But what has appeared to me the most fearful and the most strange thing in this northern land is the stone fortress on the Rocks of the Moon: I have never, indeed, been inside it, but when I used to see it in our huntings, towering above the tall fir-trees, there came a tightness over my breast, as if something unearthly were dwelling in it. And a few weeks ago, when the snow was yet lying hard in the valleys, I came unawares quite close upon the strange building. The young knight Sintram was walking alone on the ramparts as twilight came on, like the spirit of a departed knight, and he drew from the lute which he carried such soft, melancholy tones, and he sighed so deeply and sorrowfully . . . ."

The voice of the speaker was drowned in the noise of the crowd, and as he also just then reached the ship with his package hastily fastened up, Folko and Gabrielle could not hear the rest of his speech. But the fair lady looked on her knight with eyes dim with tears, and sighed: "Is it not behind those mountains that the Rocks of the Moon lie? The unhappy Sintram makes me sad at heart."

"I understand thee, sweet gracious lady, and the pure

compassion of thy heart," replied Folko; instantly ordering his swift-footed steed to be brought. He placed his noble lady under the charge of his retainers, and leaping into the saddle, he hastened, followed by the grateful smiles of Gabrielle, along the valley towards the stone fortress.

Sintram was seated near the drawbridge, touching the strings of the lute, and shedding some tears on the golden chords, almost as Montfaucon's esquire had described him. Suddenly a cloudy shadow passed over him, and he looked up, expecting to see a flight of cranes in the air; but the sky was clear and blue. While the young knight was still wondering, a long bright spear fell at his feet from a battlement of the armory-turret.

"Take it up,—make good use of it! thy foe is near at hand! Near also is the downfal of thy dearest happiness." Thus he heard it distinctly whispered in his ear; and it seemed to him that he saw the shadow of the little Master glide close by him to a neighbouring cleft in the rock. But at the same time also, a tall, gigantic, haggard figure passed along the valley, in some measure like the departed pilgrim, only much, very much larger, and he raised his long bony arm fearfully threatening, then disappeared in an ancient tomb.

At the very same instant Sir Folko of Montfaucon came swiftly as the wind up the Rocks of the Moon, and he must have seen something of those strange apparitions, for as he stopped close behind Sintram, he looked rather pale, and asked low and earnestly; "Sir knight, who are those two with whom you were just now holding converse here?"

"The good God knows," answered Sintram; "I know them not." "If the good God does but know!" cried Montfaucon: "but I fear me that He knows very little more of you or your deeds."

"You speak strangely harsh words," said Sintram. "Yet ever since that evening of misery,—alas! and even long before,—I must bear with all that comes from you. Dear sir, you may believe me, I know not those fearful companions; I call them not, and I know not what terrible curse binds them to my footsteps. The merciful God, as I would hope, is mindful of me the while,—as a faithful shepherd does not forget even the worst and most widely-straying of his flock, but calls after it with an anxious voice in the gloomy wilderness."

Then the anger of the baron was quite melted. Two bright tears stood in his eyes, and he said: "No, assuredly, God has not forgotten thee; only do thou not forget thy gracious God. I did not come to rebuke thee—I came to bless thee in Gabrielle's name and in my own. The Lord preserve thee, the Lord guide thee, the Lord lift thee up! And, Sintram, on the far-off shores of Normandy I shall bear thee in mind, and I shall hear how thou strugglest against the curse which weighs down thy unhappy life; and if thou ever shake it off, and stand as a noble conqueror over Sin and Death, then thou shalt receive from me a token of love and reward, more precious than either thou or I can understand at this moment."

The words flowed prophetically from the baron's lips; he himself was only half-conscious of what he said. With a kind salutation he turned his noble steed, and again flew down the valley towards the sea-shore.

"Fool, fool! thrice a fool!" whispered the angry voice of the little Master in Sintram's ear. But old Rolf was singing his morning hymn in clear tones within the castle, and the last lines were these:—

"Whom worldlings scorn,
Who lives forlorn,
On God's own word doth rest;
With heavenly light
His path is bright,
His lot among the blest."

Then a holy joy took possession of Sintram's heart, and he looked around him yet more gladly than in the hour when Gabrielle gave him the scarf and sword, and Folko dubbed him knight.

CHAPTER XXV.

THE baron and his lovely lady were sailing across the broad sea with favouring gales of spring, nay the coast of Normandy had already appeared above the waves; but still was Biorn of the Fiery Eyes sitting gloomy and speechless in his castle. He had taken no leave of his guests. There was more of proud fear of Montfaucon than of reverential love for him in his soul, especially since the adventure with the boar's head; and the thought was bitter to his haughty spirit, that the great baron, the flower and glory of their whole race, should have come in peace to visit him, and should now be departing in displeasure, in stern reproachful displeasure. He had constantly before his mind, and it never failed to bring fresh pangs, the remembrance of how all had came to pass, and how all might have gone otherwise; and he was always fancying he could hear the songs in which after generations would recount this voyage of the great Folko, and the worthlessness of the savage Biorn. At length, full of fierce anger, he cast away the fetters of his troubled spirit, he burst out of the castle with all his horsemen, and began to carry on a warfare more fearful and more lawless than any in which he had yet been engaged.

Sintram heard the sound of his father's war-horn; and committing the stone fortress to old Rolf, he sprang forth ready armed for the combat. But the flames of the cottages and farms on the mountains rose up before him, and shewed him, written as if in characters of fire, what kind of war his father was waging. Yet he went on towards the spot where the army was mustered, but only to offer his mediation, affirming that he would not lay his hand on his good sword in so abhorred a service, even though the stone fortress, and his father's castle besides, should fall before the vengeance of their enemies. Biorn hurled the spear which he held in his hand against his son with mad fury. The deadly weapon whizzed past him: Sintram remained standing with his vizor raised, he did not move one limb in his defence, when he said: "Father, do what you will; but I join not in your godless warfare."

Biorn of the Fiery Eyes laughed scornfully: "It seems I am always to have a spy over me here; my son succeeds to the dainty French knight!" But nevertheless he came to himself, accepted Sintram's mediation, made amends for the injuries he had done, and returned gloomily to his castle. Sintram went back to the Rocks of the Moon.

Such occurrences were frequent after that time. It went so far that Sintram came to be looked upon as the protector of all those whom his father pursued with relentless fury; but nevertheless sometimes his own wildness would carry the young knight away to accompany his fierce father in his fearful deeds. Then Biorn used to laugh with horrible pleasure, and to say: "See there, my son, how the flames we have lighted blaze up from the villages, as the blood spouts up from the wounds our swords have made! It is plain to me, however much thou mayst pretend to the contrary, that thou art, and wilt ever remain, my true and beloved heir!"

After thus fearfully erring, Sintram could find no comfort but in hastening to the chaplain of Drontheim, and confessing to him his misery and his sins. The chaplain would freely absolve him, after due penance and repentance, and again raise up the broken-hearted youth; but would often say: "Oh, how nearly hadst thou reached thy last trial, and gained the victory, and looked on Verena's countenance, and atoned for all! Now thou hast thrown thyself back for years. Think, my son, on the shortness of man's life; if thou art always falling back anew, how wilt thou ever gain the summit on this side the grave?"

Years came and went, and Biorn's hair was white as snow, and the youth Sintram had reached the middle-age. Old Rolf was now scarcely able to leave the stone fortress; and sometimes he said: "I feel it a burden that my life should yet be prolonged; but also there is much comfort in it, for I still think the good God has in store for me here below some great happiness; and it must be something in which you are concerned, my beloved Sir Sintram, for what else in the whole world could rejoice me?"

But all remained as it was, and Sintram's fearful dreams at Christmas-time each year rather increased than diminished in horror. Again the holy season was drawing near, and the mind of the sorely afflicted knight was more troubled than ever before. Sometimes, if he had been reckoning up the nights till it should come, a cold sweat would stand on his forehead, while he said, "Mark my words, dear old foster-father, this time something most awfully decisive lies before me."

One evening he felt an overwhelming anxiety about his father. It seemed to him that the Prince of Darkness was going up to Biorn's castle; and in vain did Rolf remind him that the snow was lying deep in the valleys, in vain did he suggest that the knight might be overtaken by his frightful dreams in the lonely mountains during the night-time. "Nothing can be worse to me than remaining here would be," replied Sintram.

He took his horse from the stable and rode forth in the gathering darkness. The noble steed slipped and stumbled and fell in the trackless ways, but his rider always raised him up, and urged him only more swiftly and eagerly towards the object which he longed and yet dreaded to reach. Nevertheless he might never have arrived at it, had not his faithful hound Skovmark kept with him. The dog sought out the lost track for his beloved master, and invited him into it with joyous barkings, and warned him by his howls against precipices and treacherous ice under the snow. Thus they arrived about midnight at Biorn's castle. The windows of the hall shone opposite to them with a brilliant light, as though some great feast were kept there, and confused sounds, as of singing, met their ears. Sintram gave his horse hastily to some retainers in the court-yard, and ran up the steps, whilst Skovmark stayed by the well-known horse.

A good esquire came towards Sintram within the castle, and said, "God be praised, my dear master, that you are come; for surely nothing good is going on above. But take heed to yourself also, and be not deluded. Your father has a guest with him,—and, as I think, a hateful one."

Sintram shuddered as he threw open the doors. A little man in the dress of a miner was sitting with his back towards him. The armour had been for some time past again ranged round the stone table, so that only two places were left empty. The seat opposite the door had been taken by Biorn of the Fiery Eyes; and the dazzling light of the torches fell upon his features with so red a flare, that he perfectly enacted that fearful surname.

"Father, whom have you here with you?" cried Sintram; and his suspicions rose to certainty as the miner turned round, and the detestable face of the little Master grinned from under his dark hood.

"Yes, just see, my fair son," said the wild Biorn; "thou hast not been here for a long while,—and so to-night this jolly comrade has paid me a visit, and thy place has been taken. But throw one of the suits of armour out of the way, and put a seat for thyself instead of it,—and come and drink with us, and be merry."

"Yes, do so, Sir Sintram," said the little Master, with a laugh. "Nothing worse could come of it than that the broken pieces of armour might clatter somewhat strangely together, or at most that the disturbed spirit of him to whom the suit belonged might look over your shoulder; but he would not drink up any of our wine—ghosts have nothing to do with that. So now fall to!"

Biorn joined in the laughter of the hideous stranger with wild mirth; and while Sintram was mustering up his whole strength not to lose his senses at so terrible words, and was fixing a calm steady look on the little Master's face, the old man cried out, "Why dost thou look at him so? Does it seem to thee as though thou sawest thyself in a mirror? Now that you are together, I do not see it so much; but a while ago I thought that you were like enough to each other to be mistaken."

"God forbid!" said Sintram, walking up close to the fearful apparition: "I command thee, detestable stranger, to depart from this castle, in right of my authority as my father's heir,—as a consecrated knight and as a spirit!"

Biorn seemed as if he wished to oppose himself to this command with all his savage might. The little Master muttered to himself, "Thou art not by any means the master in this house, pious knight; thou hast never lighted a fire on this hearth." Then Sintram drew the sword which Gabrielle had given him, held the cross of the hilt before the eyes of his evil guest, and said, calmly, but with a powerful voice, "Worship, or fly!" And he fled, the frightful stranger,—he fled with such lightning speed, that it could scarcely be seen whether he had sprung through the window or the door. But in going he overthrew some of the armour, the tapers went out, and it seemed that the pale blue flame which lighted up the hall in a marvellous manner gave a fulfilment to the little Master's former words; and that the spirits of those to whom the armour had belonged were leaning over the table, grinning fearfully.

Both the father and the son were filled with horror; but each chose an opposite way to save himself. Biorn wished to have his hateful guest back again; and the power of his will was seen when the little Master's step resounded anew on the stairs, and his brown shrivelled hand shook the lock of the door. On the other hand, Sintram ceased not to say within himself, "We are lost, if he come back! We are lost to all eternity, if he come back!" And he fell on his knees, and prayed fervently from his troubled heart to Father, Son, and Holy Ghost. Then the little Master left the door, and again Biorn willed him to return, and again Sintram's prayers drove him away. So went on this strife of wills throughout the long night; and howling whirlwinds raged the while around the castle, till all the household thought the end of the world was come. At length the dawn of morning appeared through the windows of the hall,—the fury of the storm was lulled,—Biorn sank back powerless in slumber on his seat,—peace and hope came to the inmates of the castle,—and Sintram, pale and exhausted, went out to breathe the dewy air of the mild winter's morning before the castle-gates.

CHAPTER XXVI.

THE faithful Skovmark followed his master, caressing him; and when Sintram fell asleep on a stone-seat in the wall, he lay at his feet, keeping watchful guard. Suddenly he pricked up his ears, looked round with delight, and bounded joyfully down the mountain. Just afterwards the chaplain of Drontheim appeared amongst the rocks, and the good beast went up to him as if to greet him, and then again ran back to the knight to announce the welcome visitor.

Sintram opened his eyes, as a child whose Christmas-gifts have been placed at his bed-side. For the chaplain smiled at him as he had never yet seen him smile. There was in it a token of victory and blessing, or at least of the near approach of both. "Thou hast done much yesterday, very much," said the holy priest; and his hands were joined, and his eyes full of bright tears. "I praise God for thee, my noble knight. Verena knows all, and she too praises God for thee. I do indeed now dare hope that the time will soon come when thou mayst appear before her. But Sintram, Sir Sintram, there is need of haste; for the old man above requires speedy aid, and thou hast still a heavy—as I hope the last—yet a most heavy trial to undergo for his sake. Arm thyself, my knight, arm thyself even with bodily weapons. In truth, this time only spiritual armour is needed, but it always befits a knight, as well as a monk, to wear in decisive moments the entire solemn garb of his station. If it so please thee, we will go directly to Drontheim together. Thou must return thence to-night. Such is a part of the hidden decree, which has been dimly unfolded to Verena's foresight. Here there is yet much that is wild and distracting, and thou hast great need to-day of calm preparation."

With humble joy Sintram bowed his assent, and called for his horse and for a suit of armour. "Only," added he, "let not any of that armour be brought which was last night overthrown in the hall!"

His orders were quickly obeyed. The arms which were fetched, adorned with fine engraved work, the simple helmet, formed rather like that of an esquire than a knight, the lance of almost gigantic size, which belonged to the suit—on all these the chaplain gazed in deep thought and with melancholy emotion. At last, when Sintram, with the help of his esquires, was well nigh equipped, the holy priest spoke:

"Wonderful providence of God! See, dear Sintram, this armour and this spear were formerly those of Sir Weigand the Slender, and with them he did many mighty deeds. When he was tended by your mother in the castle, and when even your father still shewed himself kind towards him, he asked, as a favour, that his armour and his lance should be allowed to hang in Biorn's armory—Weigand himself, as you well know, intended to build a cloister and to live there as a monk—and he put his old esquire's helmet with it, instead of another, because he was yet wearing that one when he first saw the fair Verena's angelic face. How wondrously does it now come to pass, that these very arms, which have so long been laid aside, should be brought to you for the decisive hour of your life! To me, as far as my short-sighted human wisdom can tell,—to me it seems truly a very solemn token, but one full of high and glorious promise."

Sintram stood now in complete array, composed and stately, and, from his tall slender figure, might have been taken for a youth, had not the deep lines of care which furrowed his countenance shewn him to be advanced in years.

"Who has placed boughs on the head of my warhorse?" asked Sintram of the esquires, with displeasure. "I am not a conqueror, nor a wedding-guest. And besides, there are no boughs now but those red and yellow crackling oak-leaves, dull and dead like the season itself."

"Sir Knight, I know not myself," answered an esquire; "but it seemed to me that it must be so."

"Let it be," said the chaplain. "I feel that this also comes as a token full of meaning from the right source."

Then the knight threw himself into his saddle; the priest went beside him; and they both rode slowly and silently towards Drontheim. The faithful dog followed his master. When the lofty castle of Drontheim appeared in sight, a gentle smile spread itself over Sintram's countenance, like sunshine over a wintry valley.

"God has done great things for me," said he. "I once rushed from here, a fearfully wild boy; I now come back a penitent man. I trust that it will yet go well with my poor troubled life."

The chaplain assented kindly, and soon afterwards the travellers passed under the echoing vaulted gateway into the castle-yard. At a sign from the priest, the retainers approached with respectful haste, and took charge of the horse; then he and Sintram went through long winding passages and up many steps to the remote chamber which the chaplain had chosen for himself; far away from the noise of men, and near to the clouds and the stars. There the two passed a quiet day in devout prayer, and earnest reading of Holy Scripture.

When the evening began to close in, the chaplain arose and said: "And now, my knight, get ready thy horse, and mount and ride back again to thy father's castle. A toilsome way lies before thee, and I dare not go with you. But I can and will call upon the Lord for you all through the long fearful night. O beloved instrument of the Most High, thou wilt yet not be lost!"

Thrilling with strange forebodings, but nevertheless strong and vigorous in spirit, Sintram did according to the holy man's desire. The sun set as the knight approached a long valley, strangely shut in by rocks, through which lay the road to his father's castle.

CHAPTER XXVII.

Before entering the rocky pass, the knight, with a prayer and thanksgiving, looked back once more at the castle of Drontheim. There it was, so vast and quiet and peaceful; the bright windows of the chaplain's high chamber yet lighted up by the last gleam of the sun, which had already disappeared. In front of Sintram was the gloomy valley, as if his grave. Then there came towards him some one riding on a small horse; and Skovmark, who had gone up to the stranger as if to find out who he was, now ran back with his tail between his legs and his ears put back, howling and whining, and crept, terrified, under his master's war-horse. But even the noble steed appeared to have forgotten his once so fearless and warlike ardour. He trembled violently, and when the knight would have turned him towards the stranger, he reared and snorted and plunged, and began to throw himself backwards. It was only with difficulty that Sintram's strength and horsemanship got the better of him; and he was all white with foam when Sintram came up to the unknown traveller.

"You have cowardly beasts with you," said the latter, in a low, smothered voice.

Sintram was unable, in the ever-increasing darkness, rightly to distinguish what kind of being he saw before him; only a very pallid face, which at first he had thought was covered with freshly fallen snow, met his eyes from amidst the long, hanging garments. It seemed that the stranger carried a small box wrapped up; his little horse, as if wearied out, bent his head down towards the ground, whereby a bell, which hung from the wretched torn bridle under his neck, was made to give a strange sound. After a short silence, Sintram replied: "Noble steeds avoid those of a worse race, because they are ashamed of them; and the boldest dogs are attacked by a secret terror at sight of forms to which they are not accustomed. I have no cowardly beasts with me."

"Good, sir knight; then ride with me through the valley."

"I am going through the valley, but I want no companions."

"But perhaps I want one. Do you not see that I am unarmed? And at this season, at this hour, there are frightful, unearthly beasts about."

Just then, as though to confirm the awful words of the stranger, a thing swung itself down from one of the nearest trees, covered with hoar-frost,—no one could say if it were a snake or a lizard,—it curled and twisted itself, and appeared about to slide down upon the knight or his companion. Sintram levelled his spear, and pierced the creature through. But, with the most hideous contortions, it fixed itself firmly on the spear-head; and in vain did the knight endeavour to rub it off against the rocks or the trees. Then he let his spear rest upon his right shoulder, with the point behind him, so that the horrible beast no longer met his sight; and he said, with good courage, to the stranger, "It does seem, indeed, that I could help you, and I am not forbidden to have an unknown stranger in my company; so let us push on bravely into the valley!"

"Help!" so resounded the solemn answer; "not help. I perhaps may help thee. But God have mercy upon thee if the time should ever come when I could no longer help thee. Then thou wouldst be lost, and I should become very frightful to thee. But we will go through the valley—I have thy knightly word for it. Come!"

They rode forward; Sintram's horse still shewing signs of fear, the faithful dog still whining; but both obedient to their master's will. The knight was calm and stedfast. The snow had slipped down from the smooth rocks, and by the light of the rising moon could be seen various strange twisted shapes on their sides, some looking like snakes, and some like human faces; but they were only formed by the veins in the rock and the half-bare roots of trees, which had planted themselves in that desert place with capricious firmness. High above and at a great distance, the castle of Drontheim, as if to take leave, appeared again through an opening in the rocks. The knight then looked keenly at his companion, and he almost felt as if Weigand the Slender were riding beside him.

"In God's name," cried he, "art thou not the shade of that departed knight who suffered and died for Verena?"

"I have not suffered, I have not died; but ye suffer, and ye die, poor mortals!" murmured the stranger. "I am not Weigand. I am that other, who was so like him, and whom thou hast also met before now in the wood."

Sintram strove to free himself from the terror which came over him at these words. He looked at his horse; it appeared to him entirely altered. The dry, many-coloured oak-leaves on its head were waving like the flames around a sacrifice, in the uncertain moonlight. He looked down again, to see after his faithful Skovmark. Fear had likewise most wondrously changed him. On the ground in the middle of the road were lying dead men's bones, and hideous lizards were crawling about; and, in defiance of the wintry season, poisonous mushrooms were growing up all around.

"Can this be still my horse on which I am riding?" said the knight to himself, in a low voice; "and can that trembling beast which runs at my side be my dog?"

Then some one called after him, in a yelling voice, "Stop! stop! Take me also with you!"

Looking round, Sintram perceived a small, frightful figure with horns, and a face partly like a wild boar and partly like a bear, walking along on its hind-legs, which were those of a horse; and in its hand was a strange, hideous weapon, shaped like a hook or a sickle. It was the being who had been wont to trouble him in his dreams; and, alas! it was also the wretched little Master himself, who, laughing wildly, stretched out a long claw towards the knight.

The bewildered Sintram murmured, "I must have fallen asleep; and now my dreams are coming over me!"

"Thou art awake," replied the rider of the little horse, "but thou knowest me also in thy dreams. For, behold! I am Death." And his garments fell from him, and there appeared a mouldering skeleton, its ghastly head crowned with serpents; that which he had kept hidden under his mantle was an hour-glass with the sand almost run out. Death held it towards the knight in his fleshless hand. The bell at the neck of the little horse gave forth a solemn sound. It was a passing bell.

"Lord, into Thy hands I commend my spirit!" prayed Sintram; and full of earnest devotion he rode after Death, who beckoned him on.

"He has thee not yet! He has thee not yet!" screamed the fearful fiend. "Give thyself up to me rather. In one instant,—for swift are thy thoughts, swift is my might,—in one instant thou shalt be in Normandy. Helen yet blooms in beauty as when she departed hence, and this very night she would be thine." And once again he began his unholy praises of Gabrielle's loveliness, and Sintram's heart glowed like wild-fire in his weak breast.

Death said nothing more, but raised the hour-glass in his right hand yet higher and higher; and as the sand now ran out more quickly, a soft light streamed from the glass over Sintram's countenance, and then it seemed to him as if eternity in all its calm majesty were rising before him, and a world of confusion dragging him back with a deadly grasp.

"I command thee, wild form that followest me," cried he, "I command thee, in the name of our Lord Jesus Christ, to cease from thy seducing words, and to call thyself by that name by which thou art recorded in Holy Writ!"

A name, more fearful than a thunderclap, burst despairingly from the lips of the Tempter, and he disappeared.

"He will return no more," said Death in a kindly tone.

"And now I am become wholly thine, my stern companion?"

"Not yet, my Sintram. I shall not come to thee till many, many years are past. But thou must not forget me the while."

"I will keep the thought of thee steadily before my soul, thou fearful yet wholesome monitor, thou awful yet loving guide!"

"Oh! I can truly appear very gentle."

And so it proved indeed. His form became more softly defined in the increasing gleam of light which shone from the hour-glass; the features, which had been awful in their sternness, wore a gentle smile; the crown of serpents became a bright palm-wreath; instead of the horse appeared a white misty cloud in the moonlight; and the bell gave forth sounds as of sweet lullabies. Sintram thought he could hear these words amidst them:

"The world and Satan are o'ercome,
Before thee gleams eternal light,
Warrior, who hast won the strife:
Save from darkest shades of night
Him before whose aged eyes
All my terrors soon shall rise."

The knight well knew that his father was meant; and he urged on his noble steed, which now obeyed his master willingly and gladly, and the faithful dog also again ran beside him fearlessly. Death had disappeared; but in front of Sintram there floated a bright morning-cloud, which continued visible after the sun had risen clear and warm in the bright winter sky.

CHAPTER XXVIII.

"He is dead! the horrors of that fearful stormy night have killed him!" Thus said, about this time, some of Biorn's retainers, who had not been able to bring him back to his senses since the morning of the day before: they had made a couch of wolf and bear skins for him in the great hall, in the midst of the armour which still lay scattered around. One of the esquires said with a low sigh: "The Lord have mercy on his poor wild soul!"

Just then the warder blew his horn from his tower, and a trooper came into the room with a look of surprise. "A knight is coming hither," said he; "a wonderful knight. I could have taken him for our Lord Sintram—but a bright, bright morning cloud floats so close before him, and throws over him such clear light, that one could fancy red flowers were showered down upon him. Besides, his horse has a wreath of red leaves on his head, which was never a custom of the son of our dead lord."

"Just such a one," replied another, "I wove for him yesterday. He was not pleased with it at first, but afterwards he let it remain."

"But why didst thou that?"

"It seemed to me as if I heard a voice singing again and again in my ear: 'Victory! victory! the noblest victory! The knight rides forth to victory!' And then I saw a branch of our oldest oak-tree stretched towards me, which had kept on almost all its red and yellow leaves in spite of the snow. So I did according to what I had heard sung; and I plucked some of the leaves, and wove a triumphal wreath for the noble war-horse. At the same time Skovmark,—you know that the faithful beast had always a great dislike to Biorn, and therefore had gone to the stable with the horse,—Skovmark jumped upon me, fawning, and seemed pleased, as if he wanted to thank me for my work; and such noble animals understand well about good prognostics."

They heard the sound of Sintram's spurs on the stone steps, and Skovmark's joyous bark. At that instant the supposed corpse of old Biorn sat up, looked around with rolling, staring eyes, and asked of the terrified retainers in a hollow voice, "Who comes there, ye people? who comes there? I know it is my son. But who comes with him? The answer to that bears the sword of decision in its mouth. For see, good people, Gotthard and Rudlieb have prayed much for me; yet if the little Master come with him, I am lost in spite of them."

"Thou art not lost, my beloved father!" Sintram's kind voice was heard to say, as he softly opened the door, and the bright red morning cloud floated in with him.

Biorn joined his hands, cast a look of thankfulness up to heaven, and said, smiling, "Yes, praised be God! it is the right companion! It is sweet gentle death!" And then he made a sign to his son to approach, saying, "Come here, my deliverer; come, blessed of the Lord, that I may relate to thee all that has passed within me."

As Sintram now sat close by his father's couch, all who were in the room perceived a remarkable and striking change. For old Biorn, whose whole countenance, and not his eyes alone, had been wont to have a fiery aspect, was now quite pale, almost like white marble; while, on the other hand, the cheeks of the once deadly-pale Sintram glowed with a bright bloom like that of early youth. It was caused by the morning cloud which still shone upon him, whose presence in the room was rather felt than seen; but it produced a gentle thrill in every heart.

"See, my son," began the old man, softly and mildly, "I have lain for a long time in a death-like sleep, and have known nothing of what was going on around me; but within,—ah! within, I have known but too much! I thought that my soul would be destroyed by the eternal anguish; and yet again I felt, with much greater horror, that my soul was eternal like that anguish. Beloved son, thy cheeks that glowed so brightly are beginning to grow pale at my words. I refrain from more. But let me relate to you something more cheering. Far, far away, I could see a bright lofty church, where Gotthard and Rudlieb Lenz were kneeling and praying for me. Gotthard had grown very old, and looked almost like one of our mountains covered with snow, on which the sun, in the lovely evening hours, is shining; and Rudlieb was also an elderly man, but very vigorous and very strong; and they both, with all their strength and vigour, were calling upon God to aid me, their enemy. Then I heard a voice like that of an angel, saying; 'His son does the most for him! He must this night wrestle with death and with the fallen one! His victory will be victory, and his defeat will be defeat, for the old man and himself.' Thereupon I awoke; and I knew that all depended upon whom thou wouldst bring with thee. Thou hast conquered. Next to God, the praise be to thee!"

"Gotthard and Rudlieb have helped much," replied Sintram; "and, beloved father, so have the fervent prayers of the chaplain of Drontheim. I felt, when struggling with temptation and deadly fear, how the heavenly breath of holy men floated round me and aided me."

"I am-most willing to believe that, my noble son, and every thing thou sayest to me," answered the old man; and at the same moment the chaplain also coming in, Biorn stretched out his hand towards him with a smile of peace and joy. And now all seemed to be surrounded with a bright circle of unity and blessedness. "But see," said old Biorn, "how the faithful Skovmark jumps upon me now, and tries to caress me. It is not long since he used always to howl with terror when he saw me."

"My dear lord," said the chaplain, "there is a spirit dwelling in good beasts, though dreamy and unconscious."

As the day wore on, the stillness in the hall increased. The last hour of the aged knight was drawing near, but he met it calmly and fearlessly. The chaplain and Sintram prayed beside his couch. The retainers knelt devoutly around. At length the dying man said: "Is that the prayer-bell in Verena's cloister?" Sintram's looks said yea; while warm tears fell on the colourless cheeks of his father. A gleam shone in the old man's eyes, the morning cloud stood close over him, and then the gleam, the morning cloud, and life with them, departed from him.

CHAPTER XXIX.

A FEW days afterwards Sintram stood in the parlour of the convent, and waited with a beating heart for his mother to appear. He had seen her for the last time when, a slumbering child, he had been awakened by her warm farewell kisses, and then had fallen asleep again, to wonder in his dreams what his mother had wanted with him, and to seek her in vain the next morning in the castle and in the garden. The chaplain was now at his side, rejoicing in the chastened rapture of the knight, whose fierce spirit had been softened, on whose cheeks a light reflection of that solemn morning cloud yet lingered.

The inner doors opened. In her white veil, stately and noble, the Lady Verena came forward, and with a heavenly smile she beckoned her son to approach the grating. There could be no thought here of any passionate outbreak, whether of sorrow or of joy.* The holy peace

* "In whose sweet presence sorrow dares not lower,
Nor expectation rise
Too high for earth."

Christian Year.

which had its abode within these walls would have found its way to a heart less tried and less purified than that which beat in Sintram's bosom. Shedding some placid tears, the son knelt before his mother, kissed her flowing garments through the grating, and felt as if in paradise, where every wish and every care is hushed. "Beloved mother," said he, "let me become a holy man, as thou art a holy woman. Then I will betake myself to the cloister yonder; and perhaps I might one day be deemed worthy to be thy confessor, if illness or the weakness of old age should keep the good chaplain within the castle of Drontheim."

"That would be a sweet, quietly-happy life, my good child," replied the Lady Verena; "but such is not thy vocation. Thou must remain a bold, powerful knight, and thou must spend the long life, which is almost always granted to us children of the north, in succouring the weak, in keeping down the lawless, and in yet another more bright and honourable employment which I hitherto rather honour than know."

"God's will be done!" said the knight, and he rose up full of self-devotion and firmness.

"That is my good son," said the Lady Verena. "Ah! how many sweet calm joys spring up for us! See already is our longing desire of meeting again satisfied, and thou wilt never more be so entirely estranged from me. Every week on this day thou wilt come back to me, and thou wilt relate what glorious deeds thou hast done, and take back with thee my advice and my blessing."

"Am I not once more a good and happy child!" cried Sintram joyously; "only that the merciful God has given me in addition the strength of a man in body and spirit. Oh, how blessed is that son to whom it is allowed to gladden his mother's heart with the blossoms and the fruit of his life!"

Thus he left the quiet cloister's shade, joyful in spirit and richly laden with blessings, to enter on his noble career. He was not content with going about wherever there might be a rightful cause to defend or evil to avert; the gates of the now hospitable castle stood always open also to receive and shelter every stranger; and old Rolf, who was almost grown young again at the sight of his lord's excellence, was established as seneschal. The winter of Sintram's life set in bright and glorious, and it was only at times that he would sigh within himself and say, "Ah, Montfaucon! ah, Gabrielle! if I could dare to hope that you have quite forgiven me!"

CHAPTER XXX.

The spring had come in its brightness to the northern lands, when one morning Sintram turned his horse homewards, after a successful encounter with one of the most formidable disturbers of the peace of his neighbourhood. His horsemen rode after him, singing as they went. As they drew near the castle, they heard the sound of joyous notes wound on the horn. "Some welcome visitor must have arrived," said the knight; and he spurred his horse to a quicker pace over the dewy meadow. While still at some distance, they descried old Rolf, busily engaged in preparing a table for the morning-meal, under the trees in front of the castle-gates. From all the turrets and battlements floated banners and flags in the fresh morning breeze: esquires were running to and fro in their gayest apparel. As soon as the good Rolf saw his master, he clapped his hands joyfully over his grey head, and hastened into the castle. Immediately the wide gates were thrown open; and Sintram, as he entered, was met by Rolf, whose eyes were filled with tears of joy while he pointed towards three noble forms that were following him.

Two men of high stature—one in extreme old age, the other grey-headed, and both remarkably alike—were leading between them a fair young boy, in a page's dress of blue velvet, richly embroidered with gold. The two old men wore the dark velvet dress of German burghers, and had massive gold chains and large shining medals hanging round their necks.

Sintram had never before seen his honoured guests, and yet he felt as if they were well known and valued friends. The very aged man reminded him of his dying father's words about the snow-covered mountains lighted up by the evening sun; and then he remembered, he could scarcely tell how, that he had heard Folko say that one of the highest mountains of that sort in his southern land was called the St. Gotthard. And at the same time, he knew that the old but yet vigorous man on the other side was named Rudlieb. But the boy who stood between them; ah! Sintram's humility dared scarcely form a hope as to who he might be, however much his features, so noble and soft, called up two highly honoured images before his mind.

Then the aged Gotthard Lenz, the king of old men, advanced with a solemn step, and said—"This is the noble boy Engeltram of Montfaucon, the only son of the great baron; and his father and mother send him to you, Sir Sintram, knowing well your holy and glorious knightly career, that you may bring him up to all the honourable and valiant deeds of this northern land, and may make of him a Christian knight, like yourself."

Sintram threw himself from his horse. Engeltram of Montfaucon held the stirrup gracefully for him, checking the retainers, who pressed forward, with these words: "I am the noblest born esquire of this knight, and the service nearest to his person belongs to me."

Sintram knelt in silent prayer on the turf; then lifting up in his arms, towards the rising sun, the image of Folko and Gabrielle, he cried, "With the help of God, my Engeltram, thou wilt become glorious as that sun, and thy course will be like his!"

And old Rolf exclaimed, as he wept for joy, "Lord, now lettest Thou Thy servant depart in peace."

Gotthard Lenz and Rudlieb were pressed to Sintram's heart; the chaplain of Drontheim, who just then came from Verena's cloister to bring a joyful greeting to her brave son, stretched out his hands to bless them all.

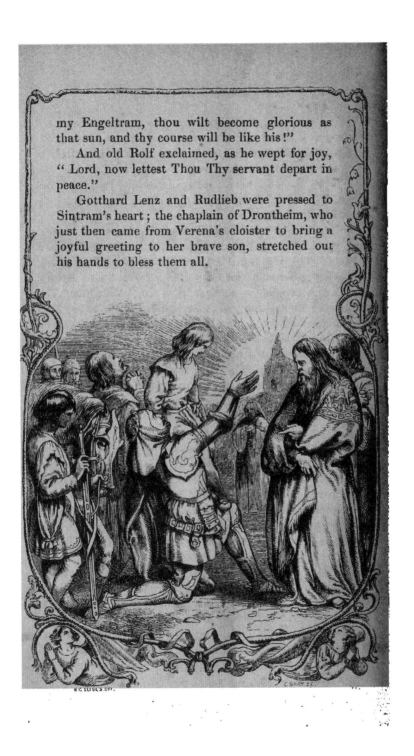

Levey, Robson, and Franklyn, Great New Street, Fetter Lane.